Places of the Soul

... one of the seminal architecture books of
recent times.

> Professor Tom Wooley,
> *Architects Journal*

The 'bible' of many architects and those
interested in architecture.

> Centre for Alternative Technology

... an inspiration to all those who care about
the influence of the environment on Man's
health and well-being.

> Barrie May,
> The Scientific and Medical Network

At last an architect has written a sensitive
and caring book on the effects of buildings
on all our lives.

> *Here's Health*

This gentle book offers a route out of the
nightmare of so much callous modern
construction. I was inspired.

> Colin Amery, *The Financial Times*

Places of the Soul

Architecture and Environmental Design as a Healing Art

Second edition

Christopher Day

AMSTERDAM · BOSTON · HEIDELBERG · LONDON · NEW YORK · OXFORD
PARIS · SAN DIEGO · SAN FRANCISCO · SINGAPORE · SYDNEY · TOKYO

Architectural Press is an imprint of Elsevier

ELSEVIER

Architectural
Press

Butterworth-Heinemann is an imprint of Elsevier
Linacre House, Jordan Hill, Oxford OX2 8DP, UK
30 Corporate Drive, Suite 400, Burlington, MA 01803, USA

First edition 2002
Reprinted 2003, 2006, 2007

Notice
No responsibility is assumed by the publisher for any injury and/or damage to persons
or property as a matter of products liability, negligence or otherwise, or from any use
or operation of any methods, products, instructions or ideas contained in the material
herein. Because of rapid advances in the medical sciences, in particular, independent
verification of diagnoses and drug dosages should be made

British Library Cataloguing in Publication Data
A catalogue record for this book is available from the British Library

Library of Congress Cataloging-in-Publication Data
A catalog record for this book is available from the Library of Congress

ISBN–13: 978-0-7506-5901-7

For information on all Butterworth-Heinemann publications
visit our website at books.elsevier.com

Printed and bound in *Great Britain*

07 08 09 10 10 9 8 7 6 5 4 3

Working together to grow
libraries in developing countries

www.elsevier.com | www.bookaid.org | www.sabre.org

ELSEVIER   BOOK AID International   Sabre Foundation

Contents

Contents

For many years now, I have sought to do what I can to encourage those involved in design and building to reflect in their work the careful balance and harmony of Nature, and to seek to restore the lost habitat of our towns and cities, of our countryside and, indeed, of our very souls – to re-integrate what has been dis-integrated and fragmented. I have also sought to emphasize the dangers of an obsession with the kind of clinical and mechanical efficiency which seems to me to remove every last drop of intuitive cultural meaning from our lives and our surroundings.

Part of the dis-integration which has been identified has laid within the larger vision – or perhaps lack of vision! – that some architects and designers have brought (and, sadly, continue to bring) to their work: the very values that inform their understanding and practice. And another part would seem to lie in the details of their designs – details of form and space, of colour, light and texture – that make up our experience of place.

In an age in which some have said that we know 'the price of everything, but the value of nothing', I wonder if architects can really only design with their heads or whether they can still bring to their work that "angelic" intellect of the heart and the soul? I wonder, too, if they can draw out for us in the present the best of our traditions, and to re-introduce those timeless qualities of harmony, human scale and character that generate a sense of belonging – enriching the soul rather than impoverishing it…

These matters have been, and remain, the concern of my Foundation for the Built Environment. My original aim in setting up my Foundation was to provide a refuge for those who, like me, were in despair at the wholesale destruction of architectural and fine art education and who wished to pass on to a new generation the knowledge of those priceless traditions that, for thousands of years, have provided a link between successive generations; and to reintroduce the vital human element into the understanding of the built environment.

It is clear to me, and to many others, that Christopher Day not only shares this concern, but is also a leading practitioner in this field, and I am pleased to note that he, too, refers to architecture and environmental design as "a healing art". For all of us must surely feel the urgent need to heal the environment that we have so brutally attacked throughout the course of the 20th Century.

Trying to break a conventional mould is a painful experience, but if we are to create sustainable and balanced communities, rather than soulless and fragmented ghettoes condemned by architecture and planning to the margins of life, try we must. I hope that this book will give those who study it the courage to do so.

Preface
New millennium: new issues

Since 1988, when I wrote *Places of the Soul* (published 1990), the world has changed. In the 1980s I had to persuade clients to include ecological features. Now, sustainability is firmly on the public agenda – indeed it's considered 'sexy'. (In the 1990s it was gender-free!) Seventy-five per cent of US designers now say their clients want sustainable design.[1] Over 50 per cent of UK architects would prioritize it over design quality[2] – though I've never seen why these should conflict! Even many high-profile architects like to do occasional sustainable buildings. (I must look up the meaning of 'intermittently sustainable'!) Rio, Kyoto, Johannesburg and their after-waves have even established it on the political agenda – anyway in words, sometimes even in action.[3]

Many trends then are now realized facts. Two-thirds of the world's population now live in cities. Cities, by their nature, depend on 'somewhere else' for food, energy and water. Sustainable cities are an ever more urgent challenge. Fortuitously, while prior to 1988 most of my work was rural, since then, most

has been urban, addressing this very issue.

Climate change is no longer just a probability. It's already here; all we don't know is how extreme it will become. This means that buildings need to be climatically robust: cooling, ventilating and warming naturally, and shedding wind. As buildings account for over two-thirds of CO_2 production[4] and air conditioning is a major user of ozone-destroying freons, this highlights environmentally responsible building issues, also the responsibility each of us has towards global climate.

Globalization brings awareness that we share – and share responsibility for – a single world. Culturally, it's enrichingly broadening, but global commerce also threatens local economy, society, culture, and even place and personal identity. *Products* travel globally, but amongst *people*, ignorance, fear and intolerance bring rifts with alarming global implications. This makes both diversity as richness and local identity as anchor increasingly important.

Sick building syndrome is now so

well recognized, it's hard to remember it used to be called malingering. Nonetheless, deep plan and high rise buildings continue to proliferate. Overglazed (so air-conditioned) and under-daylit (so fluorescent lit), full of synthetic materials and electromagnetic confusion, they're unhealthy, disconnected from life (both living nature and surrounding society) and heavily energy dependent. Awareness of how buildings can connect us with life and function in harmony with nature's forces is essential to reduce both health costs (in the US over $60 billion dollars[5]) and energy (of which buildings use half).

Building sickness isn't just about buildings, but nor is it just about bugs. Illness is statistically linked to disempowerment, so socially inclusive processes of place-design contribute to individual as well as social health. Despite increasing affluence (for most, not all!), today's world is faster, more demanding, less secure and more competitive than even a decade ago. Stress (15 per cent of all US occupational disease claims, costing $200 billion) is a major trigger factor. This brings up issues of de-stressing design – both by social arrangement and harmony-inductive environment. Places to renew the spirit and bathe the soul in peace are even more important today than in 1998.

Notes and references

1 Gould, K. L. (2002) *Teaching Green*. Metropolis, November.
2 *Ecotech*, November 2002.
3 Irksome as are empty political words and architectural bandwagoning, these actually are positive signs. The words show *intent* and the bandwagoning is usually motivated by the *conviction* of younger architects in large name-heavy practices. Both bode well for the future.
4 In the UK, 69 per cent is due to building space and water-heating. Webb, R. (2002) Insulation for a future. In *Building for a Future*, Autumn.
5 *Green Workplaces*, March 1997.

Acknowledgements

I owe deep thanks to all those who supported me in the days when this approach was unfashionable, especially Anita Midbjer, Tom Wooley, Lucia Maspero, Will Brown and Efa Wulle – who typed the manuscript. Also to my many clients, to whom values were more important than fashion, and from whom I learnt so much by working with them.

Dedication

To Heddwen, Aloma, Brynach, Dewi, Martha, Owain and Tâl.

Chapter 1

Architecture: does it matter?

Opposite: Whether you like this or not, this is not architecture. It is a photograph of a building. A semantic distinction? On the contrary. One is a static view, chosen by someone else, freezing a transient moment of light, season, weather, approach, life, etc. The other is, influences, or is an interrelating part of, our total physical surroundings: like the photograph, its effects extend beyond the physical to touch our feelings. Photographs focus our attention but let us ignore context. Architecture, however, is the frame in which we live. We don't just look at architecture, we live in it.

This book is illustrated with photographs. They are incomplete and inadequate fragments of experience, for architecture is for much more than the eyes. It is for life. And that is why it's such a powerful tool – often devastating, but potentially health-giving.

Photographs are selective. Most people's interest is in the people, whereas architects tend to concentrate on buildings – often without any hint of occupancy. While, to avoid intrusion, many of these photographs show empty rooms, try to imagine them in use for their specific functions.

Architects tend to think architecture matters. Not everyone else does. To many people buildings are expensive, but not very interesting. It's what goes on *inside* them that matters.

The argument continues that it is better to have a good teacher (or craftsman, parent, designer, manager, etc.) in an ugly shed, barrack, pre-fab, tower-block flat, etc. than a poor one in a beautiful room. But few of us are exceptionally good or exceptionally hopeless; we are middling and need support. So, how supportive is the barrack to a middling teacher? Ultimately, how good is the teaching?

How much is good design worth? Research suggests it increases land value by 15 per cent,[1] but monetary cost and soul benefit are less easily compared. When staff moved into the NMB bank headquarters by Alberts and Van Huut, however, absenteeism declined and productivity increased also around 15 per cent. A study on hospitals found improved environment reduced treatment times by 21 per cent and class A analgesic use by 59 per cent – major cost savings![2] Roger Ulrich, whose 1984

1

studies correlating patient view and recovery time pioneered this field, considers every tree leaf visible from a hospital window 'worth its weight in gold'.[3] Other projects which prioritize occupant well-being have found similar improvements. What this means for commercial buildings, where some 80 per cent of costs are staff salaries, is that a mere 6.5 per cent productivity increase would justify a building four times as expensive.[4]

Children behave differently in different environments. Even mature adults feel, think and act differently in different surroundings; though their actions may be under more conscious control, their world outlook, sensitivities and thought mobility are influenced. I sometimes wonder what sort of qualities and sensitivities my work would have if I worked in a different office – perhaps a harsh, rectangular, smooth-surfaced, evenly lit, glossy one such as many architects work in.

Many people believe that artistic ability is a matter of inborn genius, but I am convinced that the main factor is *commitment*. Likewise, aesthetics is much less a function of money than of care, but care costs time. In a world where time means money, the less care put into buildings – in design, construction and use – the cheaper they will be, but as few people want cheap-looking buildings, deceptive appearance, from brick facings and cardboard structured doors, to glossy fronts and cut-price rears, is now commonplace. So are sterile spaces which depend on cosmetic surface, mood-manipulative lighting or contents to make them habitable. Deceptive appearance inadequately screens the primacy of profit over care. Being cheated doesn't feel good – and breeds disrespect. It also does active harm, for children grow up and learn –

It is no wonder that places like this have become notorious for their crime rate. The issue is less that of easy opportunity, but of faceless, depersonalized, uncaring, insensitive harshness.

from their surroundings as well as from people – the values that will support them in later life.

A lot of people complain about modern architecture. They complain about *performance* aspects of old buildings (like dampness) but about *environmental* aspects of new ones (like anonymity). Other than architects, few people think about architecture, but many feel it. It is those who don't that I feel sad for, for their aesthetic feelings have been blunted, even obliterated – and architecture must carry much of the blame.

We all know that 'other people' tend to be negative, critical and opinionated, often identifying things unfairly and condemning them unjustly. It was an eye-opener to me to experience positive feelings from unexpected people when, about 1973, I built a house. All sorts of people, passing by, asked to look and commented in terms of real appreciation. They were farmers, carpenters, factory workers, postmen and the like – many of whom lived in, wished to live in, or built, bungalows. I realized that many people choose those sort of buildings because that's the only choice they can imagine.

These blinkers of imagination shape and are shaped by the speculative building industry and other vested-interest manipulators of wants, like fitted-kitchen manufacturers. Architectural fashion, on the other hand, is guided by what is individualistically new – a tendency intensified by architectural magazines. These focus on buildings as dramatic (and usually unpeopled) objects, though they're rarely experienced that way *by the people who use them*. Magazines foster *building* consciousness (usually with strong 'image' characteristics) – but this has nothing to do with creating *places for people*. They often have greater influence on architectural students than do their teachers, good or bad.

Small wonder that so much architecture is sick! It can make people feel ill and *be* ill. We can measure causative pathogens, but predicting consequences is less simple. Not everybody gets ill from breathing radon, formaldehyde or mould spores; there's only a tendency – and even this may not show up right away. As for aesthetic qualities, these are widely dismissed as subjective, a luxury that can be applied later after the practical problems have been solved and *if* we can afford it. I take absolutely the opposite view.

In good health, I have taken my son to hospital clinics but, after sitting for hours in rectangular grid-patterned, vinyl-smelling, fluorescent-lit, over-heated corridors, felt only half alive. The brutal vandalism of buildings unfeelingly imposed can have the same effect. In some places we feel a trapped statistic, not a valued member of society; in others, buildings tower over us as though with menace.

Quite a lot of the forms, spaces, shapes, lines, colours and relationships between elements around us don't nourish us; indeed, many are life-sapping, dead in quality. Add to this air quality, electric fields, noise, and so on. In the absence of aesthetic nourishment, the emotional part of the human being is left to seek fulfilment by indulgence in desires.

Nearly a century ago, Rudolf Steiner remarked that there is 'as much lying and crime in the world as there is lack of art'. He went on to say that if people could be surrounded by living architectural forms and spaces these tendencies would die out. When first I heard this I thought, what bourgeois nonsense! After all, the roots of crime are complex, socio-economic underprivilege playing a large part. If, however, we broaden our definition to include exploitive abuse of people and environment, and recognize that this is about *tendencies* not inevitable destinies, it's easier to see what he meant. Animals unvaryingly respond to environmental stimuli, whereas humans have the ability to transcend the situation. To rise above the level of automatic reaction requires, however, that we consciously direct our lives. None of us is perfect in this respect and that is why in any statistical sample, while some individuals don't, most people tend to react to stimuli in predictable ways.

Most people, myself included – but possibly architects excepted – don't normally look at our surroundings. We *breathe* them in. We look at picture postcards or at views from viewing platforms, and these can be interesting. However, the experience only touches our hearts when it becomes an ambience we can breathe. Most of the time we don't notice our surroundings and then they can work upon us without any conscious resistance on our part. As these surroundings are mostly *built environment*, architecture can significantly affect us.

Because we so readily take our surroundings for granted and rarely bring them to full consciousness, they can influence us powerfully. This makes architecture a potentially dangerous tool to manipulate people. This isn't just about Nazi stadiums with their theatrical mood-distortion devices. Boutiques where music, textures, colours, levels and diagonals create 'vibrant world' mood are meant to excite us; lighting and layout focus on goods we're free to touch, to sharpen our desires. Satisfaction seems linked with purchasing.

Even supermarkets, despite uninviting shed-like interiors, use lighting, sign and display colours and background music to subtly enhance the excitement of buying. Compare how many shelves of goods in your local supermarket are brightly lit with focused display lights in warm, bright, active colours or sparkling white, and how many are softly lit and in the blue range.

Is there anything wrong in this? Shopkeepers have always displayed their wares so we 'taste' or 'feel' them with our eyes. Is Soviet-era drabness more 'moral'? The threshold between something appealing – something that brightens our day, but leaves us free to choose – and something desire-manipulating – subliminally pressurizing us to make off-balance decisions – is subtle, but crucial. Mood enhancement or manipulation isn't only about making money or taking power, but about every aspect of environmental design. Whatever we do unavoidably affects the human being, the surroundings, the spirit of places and the wider world. It has human, social, biological and ecological implications. We only need to live briefly in a different environment to recognize how much our surroundings have formed us and our society in sensitivities, in values, in way of life.

Without consciously looking at them, we breathe in our surroundings with all our senses. In some places, the outer, communal, world only makes us feel exhausted and unwell. No wonder some people seek inner, private, relief by artificial stimulants.

Architecture is such a powerful agent that how it is worked with matters a great deal. A great deal indeed! How it affects people and places, how design and construction can bring health rather than illness, is the subject of this book.

Although built of matter, architecture need not be dead. It can be life-filled. Its constituent elements and relationships can sing – and the human heart resonate with them. There are many ways to go about this but to describe things I haven't personally experienced risks abstraction, wishful thinking and second-hand opinion. While I prefer therefore to describe how I myself go about doing things, I'm anxious not to preclude ways which might suit others better. Examples are, by nature, local. But the issues underlying the process by which they come into being are universal. Different people, in different locations, will need to evolve different solutions.

We each of us start life differently and live through a completely personal stream of experiences. One person's style therefore can never honestly suit another's. In this way style is very personal; while many can recognize and perhaps appreciate it as an intellectual symbol for an outlook on the world, unless that style can be transcended their feelings remain untouched.

I try not to have a style, but it's easy to lapse into one. What I hold as my inspiration is a way of looking at things to gain insight into what they really are and do, so that appropriate forms can arise. This is relevant to all people in all places. My subject is the built environment, my examples localized in time and place, but the issues are equally applicable in England or New England, in urban Tokyo or suburban Sydney, the townships of South Africa or the forests of Scandinavia. Any building, any place, in any type of land- or townscape, in any culture, climate or country has effects such as I describe. Wherever it may be located, and however differently it may outwardly appear, if architecture is to be health-giving it must work with these themes.

Notes and references

1 Report by FDP Savills Research, Davis Langton & Everest and Professor Alan Hooper for Commission on Architecture and the Built Environment, UK, *Building Design*, 24 January 2003.
2 The subjects were non-operative acute patients. Painkillers were used for 22 per cent fewer days, and 47 per cent less administered on those days. This study considered both qualitiative and social aspects, and concluded that social considerations have the major effect. It did, however, regard aesthetic issues as subjective and personal – a view I dispute. Lawson, B. (2002) Healing architecture. *Architectural Review*, May.
3 Professor Roger Ulrich, University of San Antonio, Texas, BBC interview, 2002.
4 California Office of the State Architect (1976) *Building Values: Energy Guidelines for State Buildings* (information from Tom Bender).

Chapter 2

Architecture with health-giving intent

Architecture is but a part of the built environment. Inside a building, its parts become the whole environment; from outside it's only part of our surroundings. We rarely experience larger buildings as architectural objects, but where we do, it's usually because they're forceful and dominating. Such buildings impose their presence on us and – most particularly – are imposed upon their surroundings. They're crystallized monologues – nothing about meeting the needs of people or place. Lending themselves better to photography, they're also favourite subjects for architectural magazines.

Often our experience of buildings is not as free-standing objects but of boundaries of space. The quality of this boundary is a major ingredient of the quality the place will have. Whether in country or town, boundaries made of unrelieved straight lines are harsh and lifeless. If lines, shapes, forms and spaces can be given qualities of movement, life, harmony, gesture and resolution of dynamic forces, they can bring a life-influence to the place a building bounds. These qualities, normally found in curves, can also be achieved with hand-drawn straight lines in conversation with each other. Imagine for a moment this ridge and eaves to be single dead-straight lines.

From a distance, smaller buildings are experienced as objects in relation to their surroundings. Spatial relationships between buildings give the first hint that a place – not just building objects – exists.

In the days of hand power, it was easier to go round tree roots or boulders or follow a contour than go straight through. The lines that resulted – for path, field boundary or building placement – were, for pragmatic reasons if no other, in conversation with the landscape. Powerful machinery finds it easier to disregard the irregularities of the surroundings. When you get to know old buildings and old fields you start to notice how microclimate differs when you step beyond their boundaries. This sort of sensitivity in placing doesn't occur when you design things on paper. Paper design and mechanical construction have changed the relationship of buildings to surroundings much more dramatically than first appears.

When the relationship between building and surroundings is such that the building can be seen as an object, it has a responsibility not to offend its surroundings. In an agricultural setting a balance between the two elements seems appropriate. In wilder surroundings buildings need to be more reticent.

Nowadays you can design a building in one country to be built in another, regardless of climate, culture or tradition differences. Most such 'international' buildings are made of 'international' materials, and have an artificially controlled indoor climate. They can therefore be sited anywhere in the world, but they belong nowhere. The less they fit in climatically, culturally and in material-resource terms, the greater their energy, social and monetary costs. Other than a few examples of these, the buildings I show photographs of are not transplantable.

There is considerable danger in transposing ideas from one culture, one landscape, to another. Even 'simple' concepts like freedom, rights and responsibilities vary from country to country. Buildings suitable for the Maine climate don't function well in Florida. Styles appropriate in Surrey don't fit in Midlothian. One family of materials, hence language of form, may suit buildings in Wales; elsewhere, with different materials, climate, culture and all the other contextual considerations, a quite different language of form is needed. The underlying issues of what environment does to people aren't limited to national, regional or parish boundaries but, if they're to be appropriate, the forms these give rise to will be intensely local. I find this attunement to the local situation, where all sorts of automatic assumptions have to be consciously re-examined, to be amongst the hardest aspects of design whenever I work in a new locality.

Forcing ideas on people doesn't make them healthy – it's more likely to embitter them, and make them ill.[1] Likewise, architecture won't be health-giving, if imposed.[2] Much architecture is shaped by style. This prioritizes time-bound fashion over place-appropriateness: appropriate-ness for *particular* places and the people of those places. Neo-vernacular and revivalist reactions have something hollow about them: they also seek to impose a singular idea, in this case plucked from a particular period of past history. All such approaches are more concerned with *style* than *responsiveness.*

Architecture has such profound effects on the human being, on place, on human consciousness, and ultimately on the world, it's far too important to be shaped by short-lived fashion appeal. It can have powerful negative effects, personal, social and environmental. Links with ill health, alienation, crime and climate change are now well known. But can it, if consciously worked with, have equally strong positive effects?

Anything with such powerful effects has *responsibilities* – power unchecked by responsibility is a dangerous thing! Architecture has responsibilities to minimize pollution and ecological damage, responsibilities to minimize adverse biological effects on occupants, responsibilities to be sensitive to and in harmony with surroundings, responsibilities to the human individualities who will come in contact with the building.

Ecological responsibilities involve energy conservation at all levels from strategic to detail, careful selection of building materials, with regard both to occupants' and manufacturing and building workers' health, and to their cradle-to-grave environmental impacts. Such wider criteria cast a new light on, for example, timber sources, especially tropical hardwoods; on plastics, with their huge trail of manufacturing pollution and long post-use life;[3] and on water, already the subject of international disputes.

Even aesthetic responsibilities aren't only to visual and sensory experience, but also to the intangible but perceptible 'spirit of place'. This requires putting away stylistic and individualistic preferences in favour of listening to what the place, the moment and the community ask for.

Design doesn't stop when buildings are completed. It's routinely renewed during occupation and adaption. Likewise it's normal for design refinements to continue right through construction. Hand construction may sound unrealistically out of date, but makes it easier to adapt buildings when potential benefits or shortcomings become apparent. Hand construction also gives textural scale: bricks, slates and wood are hand-scaled, mechanically erected panels crane-scaled. Where opportunities exist for the builders to become artistically involved in their work, such buildings have a distinct soul even before they're occupied. The spirit of a place can develop because of, not in spite of, the building. Hence, quite apart from its appearance, method of construction and form of contract have a bearing on the spirit of a building.

Thinking about users means thinking of buildings as spaces, their outsides as boundaries to spaces. Small rural buildings we may experience as objects *in relationship with their surroundings*, large urban ones more commonly only as *the boundaries of space*. Space is to live in. Objects are frozen thoughts. The one is life-enhancing; the other, if big enough, threatening, dominating, stealing sunlight with its huge shadows or tricking our sense of orientation with its reflections. I remember as a student how much time I wasted drawing carefully composed elevations and how little I spent on sections, internal perspectives or views of relationships with surroundings. Now it's the other way around! Now I'm less interested in objects but in *places*.

Places can't speak in human words but we can listen to what they ask for,

It is sometimes hard to imagine that a place could be as attractive and inevitable without the buildings.

what they'll accept. When I see places where the charm is in part due to the buildings, I realize this is the standard I must aim for!

Everything we build is new, and looks new till we get used to it. But after a year or two some buildings still don't belong – they look out of place. Others, bound to the fashion of the (then) moment, now look out of time. Others again, designed to look old, reveal their deceit on closer inspection. Some, however, seem neither old nor new, but eternal and inevitable. I try to design places in harmony with the stream of the past – everything that has contributed to the present – but which aren't old-fashioned or imitative; places inspired out of the future – the world of ideals, inspiration and imagination – but which still have their feet in the reality of the present moment. For the present, however future-inspired, is built upon the past. Ignoring the stream of the past is vandalistic; concentrating too strongly on it risks meaningless preservation or revivalism. Neither past nor future mean anything on their own. Future grows out of, is fed by, past; and past is always inspired by future. Development, whether buildings or any other aspect of place, if aligned with this continuum, will 'fit' timelessly in place and time. Non-aligned, imposed ones can't.

Towns without a past tend to have social problems. It can take several generations until they stabilize. Conserved historic places are little better: they can be claustrophobic to live in, and falsely cosmetic. Past and future need each other: the past informs, the future inspires. At the meeting point is the informed, inspired present – the point at which deeds are born.

To a large extent, all of this is about stopping architecture being harmful – those places which, for instance, make you cringe, feel depressed or ill in. Sometimes we blame the noise, the air-conditioning, the fluorescent lights, the crowds, the proportions, the smell – but all of it comes down to architecture, whether the circulation of people, acoustics, out-gassing toxins, colours, spatial aesthetics or construction detailing.

The trouble is we become dulled to these things. We don't notice the noise, the bad air, the harsh conflict of hard-

To be harmonious, the new needs to be an organic development of what is already there, not an imposed alien.

edged shapes and forms. We become immune to the negative forces in our environment – *and that is when they do us most harm!* Our sensitivities and our senses become dulled and our language and unconscious approach to daily life begin to reflect our surroundings. Like speech, social sensitivities can also be hardened by harshness and ugliness in the surroundings – children and adolescents are most at risk.

Architecture, at its best or worst extremes, speaks a strong language. Mass housing is quite different from homes that are individually and lovingly made in every detail – one is provided for *statistics*, the other for *individuals*. It makes a lot of difference whether things are designed *for* people or *together with* them. Architects hope their buildings will last for several generations, so however much they design with occupants in mind, they'll never meet all of them. But unless I can design something nourishing to *my* soul – nourishing, not just nice, dramatic, photogenic, novel – I can hardly expect it to be nourishing to anyone else.

We tend to think first of visual aesthetics. Concern with visual aesthetics is the major part of most architects' work, mine included. We all know that a picture is worth a thousand words, that the optic nerve is massive compared to that from other sense organs – but a smell can take us back to forgotten childhood memories, music transport us into another world.

All the senses have their parts to play – in ugliness or in beauty – but all too often each is considered in isolation. When together, giving the same message, they start to speak of the underlying essence of a place. When sensory messages conflict, environmental improvements are merely playing with cosmetics. Just as *Concorde* may look like a beautiful bird but doesn't sound like one, a beautiful well-

Light from two windows on different walls gives a life to the light which can even be seen in the frozen moment of the photograph. This life in the light is as necessary for biological as for psychological health, the pituitary gland and the soul both being nurtured by living light and both deprived by dead light. The physiological and aesthetic effects are inseparable.

landscaped architectural façade fronting a heavy main road is a nonsense. All you're aware of is the bombardment of noise. It's as hollow and meaningless as synthetic fresh bread smell outside a fast-food restaurant. The fashion for polyurethane lacquered wooden furniture comes from 'visual only' consciousness. When you touch it, the wood is hard, shiny, cold and doesn't breathe. It doesn't smell of wood and it looks glossy – a surface, not a depth of colour.

Television shows us a world in sight and sound only – a deceptive and deprived picture of reality, for we hardly notice the absence of other sensory information. The senses – all together – give a picture of a reality never adequately described by any *one* sense, a reality which we call spirit, the spirit of a person, event or place. More than just the appearance or comfort, it is this spirit which affects us deeply.

To be healing, a place must be harmonious. This means bringing change as an organic development so that new buildings seem not imposed aliens but inevitably belong where they are, responsive to their surroundings. Healing also involves invisible responsibilities like minimizing off-site pollution. But places – and buildings – must be more than that: they must be nourishing to the human being.

The concept of health presupposes sickness. We all know what it's like to feel ill, but *why* we become ill isn't so readily understood. Science has shown how illness can be triggered by material agents like viruses and bacteria – triggered, not caused. Not everyone catches an epidemic. The 'ideal' germ warfare agent – one which will infect 100 per cent of a population – has yet to be found. Tuberculosis used to be regarded as an incurable disease, but in some areas up to 50 per cent of autop-sies show its scars on lungs of people who never became ill.[4]

Some diseases show quite different symptoms in different people. Symptoms express and release what's going on within the body – a high temperature, for instance, shows the struggle between antibodies and pathogens. In the same way, illness expresses and releases inner and less visible disharmonies. To understand sickness and healing, whether medically or architecturally, we need to understand something of the different levels of the human being.

We all know the human body is a physical lump – so much flesh, bones, blood, etc. Knowledge of this physical body is essential if we want to reach shelves, sit comfortably, avoid back problems, and so on. Ergonomics and space allocation for specific positions and activities are taken for granted, and like every other architect's office I have a book of anthropometric data which shows me what space I need for a moving skeleton.

What distinguishes the human being from the corpse is the fact that it's alive. Architecture can either support or damage physical health. Most support is simple, like keeping the body within an appropriately tempered environment – neither too hot nor too cold, too bright nor too dark. But even this is subtle.

Different kinds of heating and lighting feel healthy or unhealthy, inviting or unpleasant. The light from a log fire has a similar spectrum to sunlight. Its radiant heat seems particularly warming – to soul as well as body. Open fires may be energy inefficient but they're enjoyable – and bathe you with well-being. Many people complain of dry throats, stuffy noses and lethargy with forced-air central heating; some feel claustrophobic and oppressed by it. The physical causes are negative-ion depletion (which also aggravates, and is aggravated by, any indoor air pollution), over-dry air, airborne dust (especially that 'cooked' by the heater) and undifferentiated temperature, with overheated air and under-heated radiant surface. With such different effects on our well-being, it comes as no surprise that what *feels* better *is* better.

The sparkling quiver of candlelight, however inadequate in brightness, has a life that the mechanically even vibration of electric (especially fluorescent) light can't ever achieve. So also does the daylight in a room lit by several windows, creating an interplay of lights, hues and shadows from different sky directions. Mono-directional light from a single source, be it window or window-wall, doesn't have this life.

It is no accident that such light feels 'alive', for it is life-enhancing, in a strictly biological sense: growth and other hormones are controlled by the pituitary, pineal and hypothalamus glands, and these are stimulated by light. Not any light, but gentle rhythmical living light, particularly daylight with its many moods and colours from different directions endlessly changing throughout the day. Being the archetypal light humanity has grown up in, it also nourishes the soul, while our nourished organs make us feel well. Just as smell is nature's way of telling us that things are good or bad for us, so there is a meaningful coincidence between the aesthetically satisfying and the physically healthy. What nourishes the soul nourishes the body.

The science of building biology is still in its infancy and many of its assertions are challenged, particularly by industries whose products are threatened. But even without scientific data we can, to some extent, *sense* when a place is healthy and physiologically life-supporting and when

it isn't. We share this realm of life and biological effect with everything that lives – but we are more than that. However insensitive we may be, environment affects our *feeling* life. Tourism (and the picture postcard business) depends upon places that people choose to visit, if only to look at them.

Some sorts of places, like widenings in a corridor with a window seat, induce casual social meetings; others, like lifts, stifle such interplay. Similarly, some shapes, like round tables, bring people into community, and others, like uninterrupted corridors or long rooms, don't. A narrow, low, not quite straight, invitingly textured and lit passage for unhurried uses, like those of a monastery cloister, can be a real delight; a smoothly surfaced, evenly lit, straight corridor for large numbers of people in a hurry is quite the opposite, and it makes even the most well-meaning building into an institution.

Architectural psychology studies the environmental requirements of places in which we can feel good, private, sociable, and so on. On the whole, however, we don't need to look at a book to know what effect design decisions will have – but rather we can refer to our own experience, using ourselves as instruments of assessment. Of course, everybody has different preferences and associations, so we need to distinguish between what are individual or cultural and what are universal responses. Black, for instance, we associate with death – but in the East they use white! Colours, however, have physical characteristics and physiological effects from which no one, whatever their personal likes and dislikes, is immune. Geometry has similar universal effects, as has proportion, founded as it is upon the measurements of the human body; so do scale and speed.

If you want to institutionalize a building, you need corridors. But to raise movement from A to B so it becomes a renewing, preparatory experience, cloisters work better. Cloisters are semi-outside spaces, around a garden; if glazed, they cease to be cloisters. Nonetheless, we can build some of their quality into passageways so that future destination can take second place to the experience of where you are now. How else can eternity live in every moment?

Once we recognize that many qualitative aspects of environment have universal effects in addition to personal and cultural ones, we must recognize that the human being – each of us – is potentially an *objective instrument of assessment*. That which many dismiss as 'subjective' can in fact be assessed objectively: entirely new distinctions between objective and subjective can thus arise based upon these new criteria.

What makes the human being really *human*, however, is the ability to distinguish what would be the right or wrong way to act. Unlike animals we can transcend instinct, habit or behaviour-conditioned learning by using our thinking and moral and aesthetic sensitivities to consciously choose our actions. In our surroundings we also make distinctions as to what we like or dislike. We can be nourished by artistic qualities which go beyond mere psychological technique. To uplift the spirit, places must, in some way, be artistic.

With this approach we can develop a qualitative vocabulary to nourish the human soul, but to be healing we must go further. If we picture the human as a being of four levels – body, life, feelings and moral individuality – as I've described, we can see disharmony at the most inward level expressed in progressively greater substance as it's transformed through each level until it becomes a physical aberration, like a tumour, which can even remain on a dead corpse. Treatment, by surgical, chemical or other means, can destroy physical and psychological ailments at those (outer) levels, but unless the deep-seated disharmonies are addressed, new ailments have the habit of emerging. Healing means transformation at the inmost level – something individuals can only do for themselves. How then can this be accomplished? What has it got to do with architecture?

Once we recognize that every situation is unique, and once builders work not as mechanical executors of others' orders but as artistic individuals, even every door handle will be subtly different from each other.

Different activities, hence different rooms, induce different moods. Every time we go through a door, we have to realign to a different inner state. The more deliberate our physical journey, the easier our soul one. Doorway gestures shaped to suit us, doors of weight, latches that we feel, move and hear aid such inner transitions.

The sequence of preparatory experiences we pass through to approach,
enter and use a building do more than affect our experience of it. They
change our inner state, which can both enhance our receptiveness to
health-giving qualities in our surroundings and trigger transformative
processes in our inmost being. All healing is founded on such inner
transformations, albeit initiated by outer agents. Threshold, sequence
and 'oasis' have, therefore, important health-giving functions.

It is hard even to recognize the need for such inner transformations, and harder still to start them. Something from outside, like counselling, homeo-pathic medicine or some other agent, is needed to initiate and support the process. Environment is one such agent: it can provide nourishment, support and balance for the human spirit as much as it can starve, oppress and pervert it. The more it works with universal rather than personal qualities, the more it can trans-form feeling responses from personally indulgent desires to artistic experiences.

But environment – even static, mineral, architectural environment – does more than this. Our environment is part of our biography. It is part of the

The experience of walking along this path
is woven of alternating obstructed and
expansive views, steps and turns and,
especially, the textures of light and shade.
It gives a particular sense of coming down
to the lower town or up to the town
centre. Like the surrounding architecture
the path is pleasant though unexceptional,
but the journey is a delight.

stream of events and surroundings that help make us what we are. As Churchill observed: 'We shape our surroundings and our surroundings shape us.' If, for a brief tolerant moment, you entertain the possibility of reincarnation and destiny, you're faced with the question: why have we chosen one particular life path, one progression of environments, and not another?

There are punitive and positive theories of reincarnation. The latter suggests that, in our path of personal development, we need to meet and resolve those things previously unresolved or sidestepped. Throughout each life we draw to us opportunities, often in the outward form of obstacles, that we need. This is not to say that our surroundings should necessarily provide a wide range of obstacles; rather, if they provide qualities which have been meaningful in earlier lives, the resolve to transform obstacles into opportunities in *this* life can be strengthened.

Timeless qualities have a profundity that can bring us to a threshold experience of inner change, change that sets in motion healing transformation of the inner self. Entering into the experience of a work of art brings us to such an inner threshold, and this is the foundation of art therapy.

Our surroundings are potentially the most powerful art form we experience in our lives. Whether they will bring illness or healing depends upon all of us whose decisions and actions shape human environment.

Notes and references

1 Studies correlate disempowerment and illness. See: Lindholm, R. In *New Design Parameters for Healthy Places* (*Places*, Vol. 2, No. 4, USA); and Day, C. (2002) *Spirit & Place*. Architectural Press.

2 This also brings up design-participation issues. See: Day, C. (2002) *Consensus Design*. Architectural Press.

3 Plastics commonly require some 15 or so synthesis operations, each around 50 per cent efficient, so only some 0.002 per cent of the original material is final product. König, H. (1989) *Wege zum Gesunden Bauen*, p. 33. Ökobuch Verlag, Freiburg. For economic, inconvenience and sorting-complexity reasons, most plastic *isn't* recycled.

4 Spock, B. (1975) *Baby and Child Care*. New English Library.

Chapter 3

Architecture as art

When you try to observe what the innate essences of things are and how and why such things affect us, it is easy to see that there are rules underlying all universal, and therefore profound, experiences. To be healing, however, we have to transcend these; move from rules to art. But what is art?

I have heard poetry described as that which makes your skin prickle when you read it. That is close to my definition of art – the experience of something which leaves you never the same again. It has brought an inner step forward. Medical, psychological and spiritual healing involve processes by which something outer is brought to patients so that they can make an inner step. Just as healing is quite distinct from medical, psychiatric or ideological 'treatment', this is a process of enabling, not of manipulating.

The arts – whether painting, architecture, even cooking or gardening – are involved with raising material *matter*. In this sense art is the imbuing of matter with spirit, and it is this spirit that the user unconsciously experiences and that

has a healing influence. But how to make this step from rules to art?

Unfortunately, it's not enough just to have good intentions or theoretical understanding. Good intention remains abstract until worked out in deeds and products. Graceless actions bring a disharmony which easily negates those good intentions, whereas artistic work roots them more fittingly in matter. When I left architecture school, I saw many of my fellow students whose ideals I admired abandon them as untenable in the 'real world'. What needless tragedy, for, if true, good ideals – however unfashionable – are essentially practical, craving to be worked out practically, artistically, in the world.

We've become used to the idea that money may be spent to beautify places for recreation and leisure, but that places of work or for practical activity should be shaped first and foremost by utilitarian considerations. The implication is that if half our working life is spent as efficiently but inartistically as possible, the other half is free to be artistic and inefficient. The assumption that practicality and aesthetics are mutually contradictory only holds good when the definitions are narrowed: practical to the monetary, aesthetic to indulgent self-expression. Yet when we realize the relationship that exists between aesthetics and health, this severance of utility and beauty can be seen to be as unhealthy as it is philistinic.

It is necessary to *cultivate* a sense for beauty, for the artistic. 'Necessary' because our culture tends to suppress this sense, and 'cultivate' because everyone has it latent within them. It used to be so strong that pre-industrial common people could not make a spoon, a cart, a boat, even a house look ugly. To do so would have been like a crime against themselves. Everything, from reaping corn to blessing a meal or carving a chair, was an action giving thanks for God's creation, an artistically satisfying activity. All they made and did was essentially functional: there was no time, energy or space to make anything without a practical purpose; beauty and utility were inseparable.

Today it's the reverse. Beauty and utility are widely regarded as completely separate streams. We all need utility, but beauty? Isn't it an indulgence, peripheral to our main concerns in life? We have the means now to produce quantity – unnecessary quantity. Quality is a secondary consideration. In the eighteenth century audiences used to weep during concerts; today not uncommonly the emotions are compelled by decibel power.

We can never return to pre-industrial values, for these were quite unconscious and habitual. Their forms were dominated by stereotypes, their inner and outer horizons confined. Today, thank goodness, if we choose to consider beauty and utility as inseparable we do so in full, committed consciousness. We can consciously choose to direct our

artistic work towards that *appropriate to the needs of circumstance* rather than the personally indulgent. But what do we need from the *architectural* environment?

All of us from time to time experience boredom, insecurity, loneliness or stress – states of mind which need something outside ourselves to provide a balance. Where our environment can offer intriguing interest and activity, timeless durability and a sense of roots, connection with the natural world and its renewing rhythms, sociable and relaxing places, and harmony, tranquillity and quiet soothing spaciousness, it can provide soul support – the first step to recovery. Where these soul needs aren't met, dependence is common. Dependence on prescribed or narcotic drugs, alcohol, television, consumerism. We can find endless 'soul needs' to suit our ever-changing moods, but if our surroundings are to be supportive, there's a more limited range that *must* be found. How many homes have the social – and physical – warmth focus of a hearth? How many people have access to the freshness of happily singing water?

When, to attunement to the *needs of the soul*, is added an understanding of the *universal characteristics* of our artistic vocabulary and a sense for *beauty*, the results are both artistic and appropriate. Spiritual functionalism we could call it. Colour, for instance, can be used functionally – a Steiner kindergarten room should support imitative physical and imaginative mental activity within a warm, supportively secure, almost dreamy environment. The appropriate colour lies in the warm pink range. On the other hand, a classroom for older children needs an environment which helps the teenagers bring the outer activity of earlier childhood more into

The classic example of the underlying archetypal idea responding to the locally individual influences of environment, active through both place and time. Architecture works with the same polarities.

themselves inwardly. In contrast to their earlier education, this encourages the intellect to be more active. The appropriate colour lies in the cool blue range – but *very* delicate. But *how* the rooms are coloured, the exact hues, shades and variations, depends upon a dialogue between colour, natural light and space. A kindergarten in Oslo or Milan would be quite different, even if the practical needs of colour are more or less identical.

This conversation between the universal and the particular, the inspiration and the local circumstances – the moment – is the same as between the archetypal oak tree principle and the battering winds focused by topography. The results are both individual and universal in the same moment. It is the same as between the principles of cosmic geometry and the demands of climate and site surroundings, or between pure idea and the requirements of building materials and construction – like gravitational principles in a stone arch or tensile ones in a tent.

Conventionally there are two streams of architecture – high and low. One concerns itself with cosmic rules – proportion, geometry and classically-differentiated elements representing universal principles: relation to the earth, to the vault of the heavens, to the vertical boundaries of free-stretching space, as experienced in the human limbs, head and torso; also to the finely tuned shape of space, form, and so on. Like classical music it must work within but rise above these rules to become art, something to elevate the human spirit. This is the stream of great architecture – temples, cathedrals, sometimes palaces and civic buildings. In scale and commitment to a singular idea, such buildings often dominate the surroundings.

The other stream is the vernacular. Its keynote is response to climate, materials, social form and tradition. It's much concerned with textures, meetings of materials, and tends to be rich for the senses. Almost without fail, the resulting landscape and townscape forms warm the soul. Internally, however, the stereotyped idea of how people should live from generation to generation can be oppressive.

The high architecture stream is inspired by cosmic ideas, the vernacular stream rooted in daily reality. One is learnt by prolonged esoteric study, the other by making, doing and building; by mud, dirt and wood shavings. Both are artistic but neither is complete or balanced without the other: they need to be brought into conversation.

Real conversation is never a compromise. Something dies in a compromise, but in a conversation something new is born. It is in this something, this 'spirit of conversation', that the universal and the uniquely particular are fused into a work of art. As with design conversations with clients, what arises is better and *more appropriate* than either of us could have done on our own. Appropriate is a key word. Things are only appropriate if they meet the needs of the circumstance – and there are many needs: as well as those of the building users, the surroundings, the wider community, the health of the earth, all have needs.

Very few of these needs can be voiced in words. We have to listen to the unspoken, listen with all our senses. It is this listening as an exercise that develops our sense of what is *right* – our sense of beauty. If we look at the world around us, the places most rich in life are meeting places – and not only cafés and city squares. In nature, life is at its most vigorous where the elements meet –

warm sun-drenched marshes, humid jungle. When we seek rejuvenation in natural surroundings we're drawn to those places where the spirit of place is strongest – where there are meetings between elements – places which emphasize the meeting of, for instance, earth and sky or water and rock.

If we sit and watch these meetings – how at the rock the water swirls, eddies, splashes, gurgles, sings, smells wet and cool – we realize that what is happening is too rich and mobile to be depicted or described. But if we immerse ourselves in the mood of what is going on, we can become in a way attuned to 'rock-water-iness', to the spirit of what is happening.

To cultivate abilities to work with the *appropriate* and the *beautiful*, we need to do exercises like this. Exercises like looking every day at the dawn – it's different each day and changes every moment, yet at every moment has something eternal, as do the endless but ever-changing waves of the sea.

There are many such exercises – but what they all have in common is that they're *listening* exercises. Listening to what is already there is the first step in any meaningful architecture just as it is the first step in any therapy. The physician 'listens' to the patient – to what he says, how he speaks, his appearance, face, and so on. Listening is the fundamental requirement for any conversation – or indeed for any healthy social process! We only go forward by recognizing that which the process enables to come into being that wasn't there before. Success depends upon putting personal preferences aside and *listening* without any judgement (except as to truth) – even listening to the unpalatable. In architecture this means listening to the needs of people – which few can voice properly – to the needs of the place, to those concealed opportunities which unfold as design, then construction, then use, progresses. There are techniques to aid this,[1] but the vital element is the cultivation of the ability to listen.

Architectural demands so often lead in different, potentially conflicting directions – like energy conservation versus occupant health, cosmic geometry versus organic response to environmental circumstance, straight or curved – that the results will be one-sided and disastrous unless they can be brought into a conversational balance. Similarly, architectural elements need to be brought into conversation or they fight against each other.

This isn't about what is nice or not but about what is *nourishing for the human spirit*. To be nourishing, things must match what we need, just as a stoker and a meditating hermit need different diets. Our surroundings therefore must satisfy necessary material functions, provide the right biological climate, and support for our life of mood and feeling. But to carry architecture beyond the threshold of the materially useful, the biologically supportive or the emotionally satisfying, we must cultivate and bring together both the inspiration which gives moral force to our ideas and the sense of listening to environment which makes those ideas appropriate. This interweaving conversation between idea and material can only exist in the artistic sphere.

Reference

1 These are described in detail in: Day, C. (2002) *Consensus Design*. Architectural Press.

Chapter 4
Building for planetary health

It is easy to see how much harm human activities do to the world. We read daily of poisoned groundwater, radioactive waste, food and health scares, dying forests, dead seas and collapsing ecology in whole regions – all caused by industry, corporations, financiers, governments, etc. But this isn't just what *other* people do. It is product and by-product of the way we build and live – of *our* choices. This sort of pollution hardly existed before the industrial revolution and much of the worst of it has only been invented in the last few decades. It isn't the only way to live and to build, but it's the normal way these days. Normal but not necessary.

We can view almost every product as bought at the price of environmental or human damage. Out of this attitude, rising to (albeit limited) popular consciousness around 1970, grew the 'restricted damage' approach to building. Zero-energy, ecologically autonomous houses and self-sufficient farming became a select fashion. Three decades later it's easier to take a wider overview and see that architecture, like any other art form, can bring spiritual benefits to humanity and to the earth, outweighing the material damage it causes. The world would be a poorer place without Chartres Cathedral, but it took a lot of stone quarrying. We *can* build wholly biodegradable buildings from earth, straw and small branches, but *all* buildings which satisfy the performance criteria we expect in the developed world cause ecological damage to some extent. Even buildings that generate more energy than they consume do so by their building. Building materials are almost entirely mined from our surroundings – even modern forestry is mining. Manufacture and transport add further pollution and energy costs. Nonetheless it isn't hard to reduce environmental costs to but a fraction of today's norm.

Buildings modify climate to keep us warm or cool. But they do this at the expense of global climate. Half the CO_2 and freons we produce – the major drivers of climate change – is due to buildings: what they're built of, and – particularly – how we heat, cool, light and use them.[1]

Add in all the things we put and use in, and near, buildings – nearly everything we buy – and travel between them, and the figures go up. Some of these things, some of this travel, is unavoidable, but some is a result of how buildings are *designed*. Rooms we can't live in without personalizing and softening by furnishing, ornaments and artwork; places we can't work in; places we can't wait to get away from. There are also places so bland, or ephemerally styled, we need to revamp them every few years. Zero-energy design doesn't necessarily mean zero-energy lifestyle. Unless places also feed the soul, they'll feed travel and product – hence energy – demand.

With most energy being fossil fuel generated, greenhouse-effect global warming is a direct consequence of profligate energy consumption. Though still cheap in monetary terms, energy has a huge price in terms of ecological damage, a price we've already started (but only started) to pay in floods, storms, forest fires and famines. Though of a totally different order, even renewable energy has an environmental price. Hydroelectricity, though infinitely less dangerous than nuclear power, displaces people, kills fish, and disrupts river and watershed ecology.

Buildings are the single biggest energy users. They use twice as much as transport, three times industrial process heat. We all live in buildings so this is something easy to do something about. As buildings consume five times as much energy over their lifetime than they do to build, this is both about how they're designed and how we live in them. Soberingly, as rising expectations of comfort have paralleled improved thermal insulation, this proportion has barely changed over three decades.

In design, it makes energy sense to take account of local climate. Where I

Shape affects size of the shadow cast. Shadow may benefit car parks, but not gardens, parks and pavements. Fewer plants grow in shadow and they grow less well. In areas of permanent shadow very little grows at all – beneath the lank vegetation is bare mud, poor to play on. The consequent low level of soil life is slower to break down organic refuse like bird droppings, dog mess and old leaves. Less plant growth means less air cleansing. In cool climates, shadows bring gloom and poor health to cities – they are a product of size, orientation and shape of buildings.

Left: High thermal capacity to even out daytime and night-time, and even seasonal temperature variations.

Right: Cooling airflow induced by building shape.

Left: Wet, heavy snow slides off.

Right: Light, dry snow stays on the roof for insulation effect.

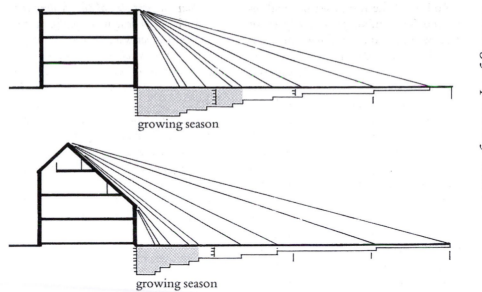

growing season

growing season

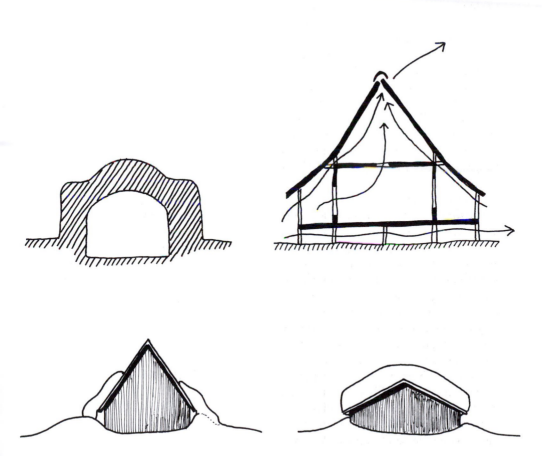

live, wind cools more than low temperatures. Ground-hugging buildings do well here. Heating buildings means heating space, so the smaller and more compact the heated volume the less energy needed – a point even the energy-conscious easily forget! To minimize energy use – and other effects like shadow size – the first step is to think small. Compact spatial arrangement doesn't necessarily mean cramped environment. As I will discuss, other qualities can have a greater effect than dimensions.

Different climates require different building forms. Hot climates need shaded, airy spaces, like verandahs; also plenty of air-space – especially height – indoors. Different humidity, temperature and night/day variations have led to different traditional cooling layouts, giving rise to vernacular forms ranging from large ventilated roof-spaces (often doubling as crop-drying lofts) to high thermal capacity mud-brick buildings.

Like globalism, virtually every magazine style is independent of locality and climate. By contrast, vernacular buildings were adapted to local materials, climate, way-of-life, culture and values – the body, life, soul and spirit of places. They *meant* something. Today, with few of these links-to-meaning intact, copying old forms is just plagiarism. Nonetheless, before departing too radically from them, we should think carefully about what previous generations took for granted. If we don't, our buildings will depend upon large energy inputs for heating or cooling.

Solar collectors need not be added-on boxes, but can be integral with roof design.

We can laugh at British colonial administrative buildings standardized in design with corrugated iron roofs and fireplaces even in the tropics (I'm told that the fireplace was cool enough to stand in, elsewhere was like an oven). On the other hand, we take it for granted that office blocks are mechanically cooled and ventilated. Yet every building that requires energy inputs to provide a habitable environment achievable by design means is responsible for completely needless pollution.

Many people think first in terms of alternative energy gadgetry. I think of these last. It's always cheaper to conserve than to produce energy. Nonetheless some alternative energy is simple to produce. The economics depend on your accountancy assumptions: solar hot water can be proved to be a money-saver *or* never to pay for itself. As hot water accounts for 16 per cent of the CO_2 due to UK buildings, this is about more than saving money.[2]

There's nothing complicated about solar water heating. I normally use the most basic system – hence there's the least to go wrong. In this, the heat exchange fluid thermosyphons to a pre-heating cylinder. It therefore works whenever the sunlight – or summer cloudlight – is warmer than cold water. The problem with solar heating is of architectural integration: avoiding nailed on appendages! I mostly therefore use aluminium fins clipped to copper piping to allow any shape and dimension. The size and shape versatility makes it easy to incorporate within almost any roof, outweighing its low efficiency. Visually sensitive buildings can use piping beneath roof tiles or ground-level collector panels. My own house utilizes a

Solar design doesn't necessarily require parallel rows of buildings.

seasonally integrated system of solar power, back-boiler in a cooking-heating stove and small-scale hydroelectric power, any surplus not being used by appliances going into water or space heating. Few people are lucky enough to have their own electricity from wind or water, but terraced houses with 'neighbour insulation' easily save the 1.3 kW that my generator provides.

Our world is solar powered. All life depends on the sun. It powers the water cycle and, together with the earth's rotation, drives the wind. Only small parts of the world are consistently comfortable for human life. Most are too hot, too cold or alternate between extremes, so to survive we need heating or cooling. But we won't survive for long unless we can do this sustainably – which means using sun power in one form or another.

Even in cloudy Britain, the average house gets 14 per cent of its heat from the sun. By crude mathematics, south windows three times bigger bring this to

Although the need for space heating is greatest when sunlight hours are shortest, the sun can make a significant contribution even where it must be supplemented by other forms of heating. This system (near Stuttgart) utilizes air circulation to heat radiant walls and floors.

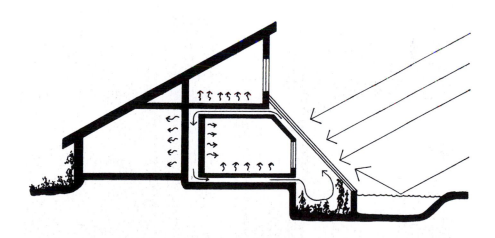

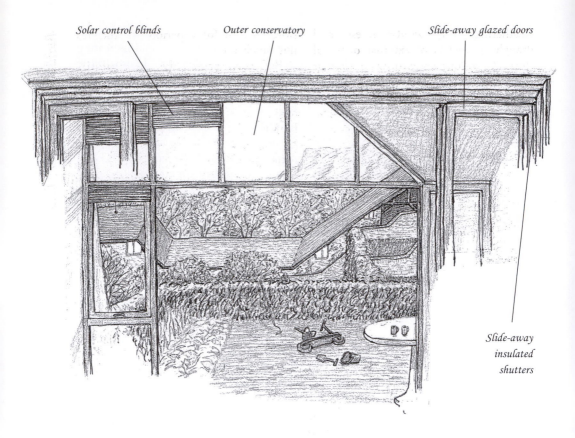

*Slide-away
insulated
shutters*

half. If only life was so simple! Even the best insulating glass loses more heat than a well-insulated wall. But this isn't just a matter of balancing (say) six hours sunshine (three hours either side of noon) against eighteen of heat loss. Multi-layer curtains or insulated shutters can bring window insulation to wall standards for the two-thirds of the winter day that is night. This of course depends on someone – or automated motors – being at home to open and close them. Internal shutters avoid the

Layers of insulation.

weathering, rot, wind-firmness and draught problems of external ones; all they take is floor space to swing, slide or fold into (but beware of trapping the cat!).[3] All in all, south windows equalling 30 per cent of floor area is the solar heating optimum in Britain – namely, three times the average size!

Even in cold climates, solar heat isn't always welcome. Winter sun, doubled by snow reflection, can be hot – but only in the sun. Also sunlight fluctuates: one cloud and it's shut off! Unless we can buffer these extremes, solar heating is an inconvenience. And unless we can store its heat for a period of time, it's not much use.

Buffering spaces, like conservatories and glazed passages, dampen down the fluctuating extremes reaching rooms. So does thermal storage. The greater a building's capacity to absorb heat, store it and release it slowly, the more comfortable – and energy saving – it is. Heavy materials store heat best: clay, brick, stone, concrete, even plaster. They're most effective if dark-toned and in full sun – otherwise they won't get warmer than room air, so while they may buffer against overheating, they

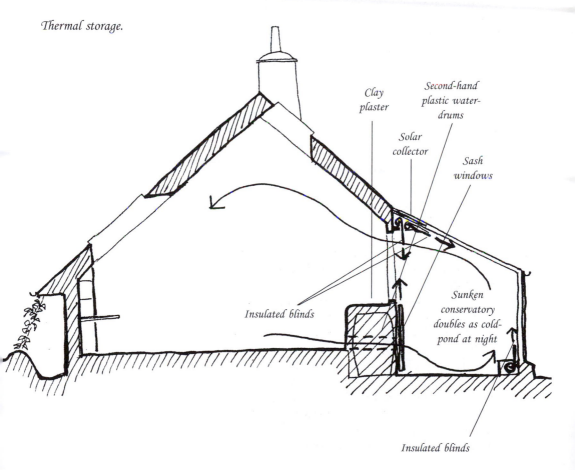

Thermal storage.

Clay plaster

Second-hand plastic water-drums

Solar collector

Sash windows

Insulated blinds

Sunken conservatory doubles as cold-pond at night

Insulated blinds

Building around a heat source: this stove chimney heats downstairs and upstairs rooms, reducing heating needs to a third of the average. Such planning is complicated by another requirement of minimum energy design: the need for compact space. Spatial economy requires central circulation spaces with rooms around them, whereas heat economy requires central chimneys!

Solar buffer zone: resilience by adaptive opportunties.

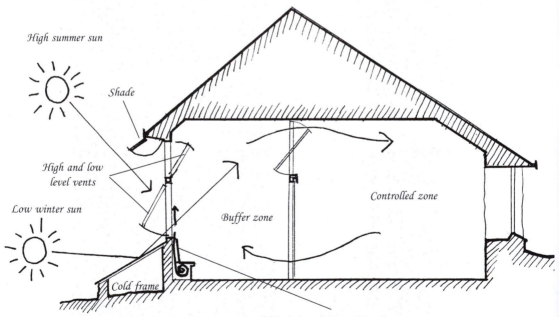

High summer sun

Shade

High and low level vents

Low winter sun

Buffer zone

Controlled zone

Cold frame

Insulated blinds from below. This allows:
* non-horizontal window head
* high-level light so maximum illumination for minimum heat loss
* cold air to pool behind shutter not circulate into room
* blind to act as shade while top vent open

hardly give off warmth when it's needed. The first two to four inches (50–100 mm) are enough to store a day's heat for the night – or a night's coolness for a day – but unless weather is predictable, it's nice to have a longer-span heat store. Inter-seasonal heat storage would be ideal, but 30 years of experiments haven't yet found a cheap and reliable way to do this. Because cooling creates convection currents, water is the best (simple) heat store, as heat can be retrieved from its whole volume. Plastic drums (steel rusts!) on the living-room floor aren't everyone's aesthetic preference. They're more acceptable – though less efficient – plastered to make a bench or wall. Heat and 'coolth' can also be stored in latent form at low temperature, by melting or condensing substances like Glauber's salt or styrene wax. Such low-temperature storage means less heat lost and easy charging at lower temperatures. Access for replacement is a wise precaution.

Neither weather nor the way we live in buildings are predictable. Nor do we really understand airflow, heat flow and building performance. Hence, while it's wise to engineer solar design, it's even wiser not to rely on this. Plenty of 'adaptive opportunities',[4] especially ventilation options for different wind, rain and warmth conditions, make systems resilient and adjustable.

Six basic principles for solar heating are:

- Excellent insulation.
- Large south windows.
- Movable insulation for night-time.
- High thermal mass, well placed.
- Buffering spaces.
- Overheating prevention: movable or seasonal shading, particularly in the afternoon, and generous ventilation.

Utilizing solar energy: hierarchies of efficiency

(simplest is cheapest, most reliable, resilient to misuse, easiest to use and maintain – hence best value)

solar space passive
↓
solar hot water
↓
} or (depending on climate and location) bio-fuel

wind
↓
photovoltaics[5]

Where cooling is an issue, water often is as well. Roofs and roads multiply the amount of rainwater available to collect – or cause flooding, if not intercepted or delayed!. This Californian urban project collects up to five times the scanty rainfall per planted area. We led all rainwater in shallow open channels to dished depressions around trees; these overflow to gullies and oil interceptors, thence to storage cisterns.

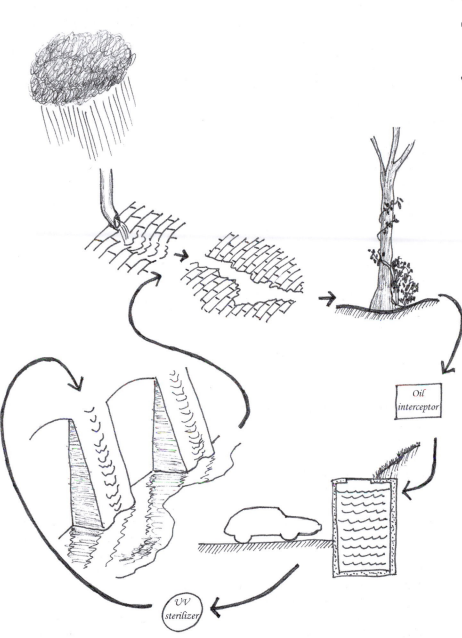

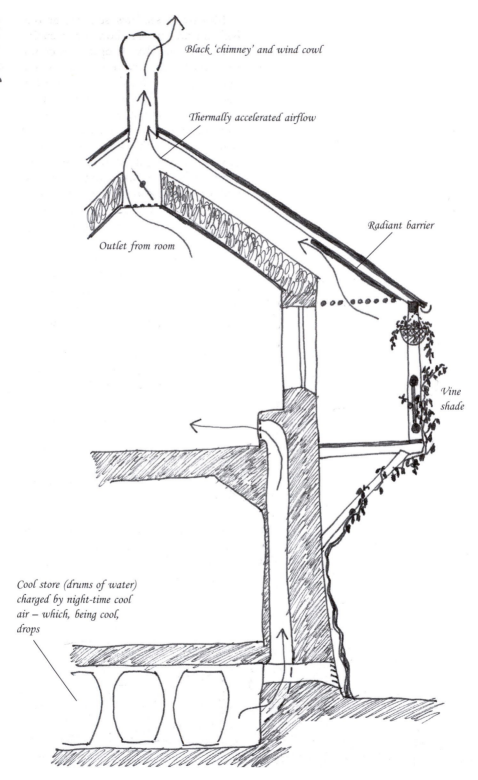

Black 'chimney' and wind cowl

Thermally accelerated airflow

Radiant barrier

Outlet from room

Vine shade

Cool store (drums of water) charged by night-time cool air – which, being cool, drops

It's easy to see how sunlight or bio-fuel can heat us, but how can it cool?

Nature does this. It optimizes conditions for life by passive means. Snow is lightweight, air-filled – an excellent insulator. In Northern winters, there isn't much sun, but plenty of dark sky to which white snow radiates less heat than would dark earth. Damp, cool ground is dark; it soaks up sun. But sunlight bleaches dry ground so, like white roofs, it reflects more heat than it absorbs. From wet ground, heat draws forth leaves. Transpiration from foliage cools air by about 4°C (8°F). Shading is also worth some 15°C (30°F).[6] Moreover, leaf season, like heat, isn't symmetrical about midsummer solstice but later,[7] so shading is season-matched. Leaves also clean air – reducing particulates to one-tenth[8] – and absorb and mask noise. Leaf cleaning is significant. In the Chinese 'war on flies', all vegetation was cleared from Beijing. The result: dust-storms and respiratory problems – a greater health threat than ever flies posed.

Warm air rises, so sun can induce air movement. Solar chimneys, dark roofs – especially photovoltaic ones which produce warmth as a by-product – 'lift' air. Even more so if space between hot roof and insulation tapers as it rises, so accelerating airflow. This drives the outlet side of solar cooling.

Iranian wind-catching towers channel breezes down between water-evaporating porous pots, and thence to rooms. Some have pools or deep water-cisterns at their bases. Arizona-developed 'cool towers' are a modern version of these. Fountains, water-sluiced walls, misters, spray-cooled pavements, and cascades and rills alongside streets also cool by evaporation.

Flowforms, fountains or other water-features in the shady side of a courtyard

Solar-driven cooling.

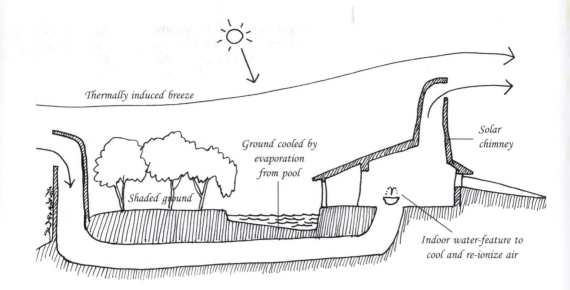

Thermally induced breeze

Shaded ground

Ground cooled by
evaporation
from pool

Solar
chimney

Indoor water-feature to
cool and re-ionize air

maximize temperature difference to sun-heated wall and roof surfaces opposite, so inducing cooling breezes. Dark, tall, solar chimneys with draught-accelerating venturi outlets further improve on this ancient Tadjik technique.

Beyond these technical functions, both leaf and water, dappled shade and dancing light can be orchestrated for delight. All these cooling – and delight – systems are driven by the power of the sun.

Buildings shaped by solar cooling look quite different from the so called 'energy-conservative' office blocks of the 1970s and 1980s – glass, but deep-plan, so effectively windowless for people working within them. Prone to overheating and dependent on air-conditioning, these weren't in fact energy-conservative at all, but energy-expensive sickness incubators. Unfortunately, overglazed, sealed-skin, deep-plan buildings are still with us, however 'artistically' styled and claiming eco-friendliness. Such buildings aren't habitable without air-conditioning. And

Solar-driven cooling: modern hybrid adaptation of traditional wind-catching towers, earth cooling and evaporative cooling.

air-conditioning is expensive: expensive to maintain and run, and typically 40 per cent of building cost to install. Moreover, it needs major replacements every 15 years.[9]

Air-conditioned buildings aren't good to live or work in. They may be cool, but fans are often audible, sometimes reverberent, contributing to background stress. The air is usually too dry, ion-dead, and often recirculated-pathogen rich. Its even temperature, humidity and air-change rate don't stimulate our senses. These need constant subtle variations in stimulus to stay alert. There's no innate reason why machinery should invigorate air. No surprise such air feels 'dead'.

Natural air, by contrast, carries scents and sounds of season, weather, time of day and activities going on. Moreover, natural ventilation is free. All it needs is narrower buildings. This means more daylight and views – a gain, not a cost! Being propelled by the forces of air

Indoor air is renewed by outdoor air. This in turn is renewed by air inflowing from countryside or sea. No city makes clean air, though vegetation can alleviate pollution.

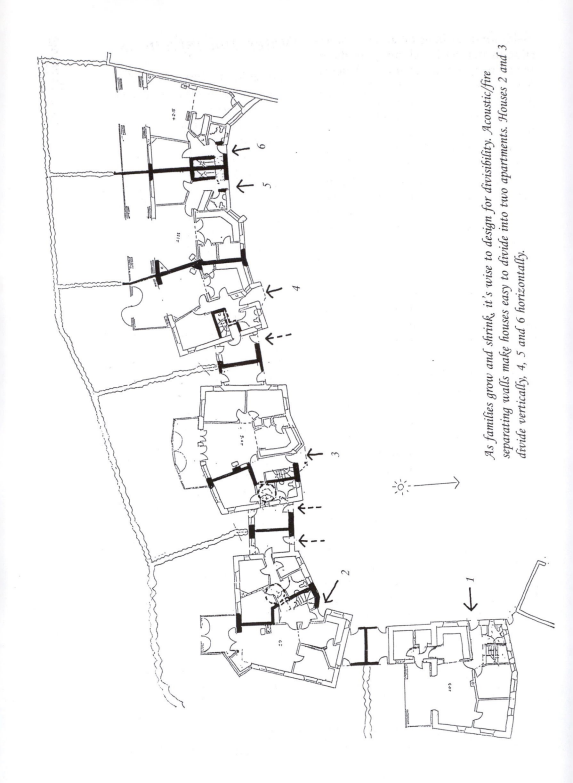

As families grow and shrink, it's wise to design for divisibility. Acoustic/fire separating walls make houses easy to divide into two apartments. Houses 2 and 3 divide vertically, 4, 5 and 6 horizontally.

itself, wind-catching or airflow-accelerating shapes, vertical chimneys or differential temperature increase efficiency. Air quality is renewed by living processes, photosynthesis in particular. It is driven by, given quality by, life. Indeed it is *all about* life.

This is the *soul* side of microclimatic design, building biology and ecological architecture. It's not just that 50 per cent of energy, materials, waste, CFCs and HCFCs is a criminal price to pay for buildings. It is about how sustainable design can *sustain us*.

But does architecture for the soul have any place in our eco-crisis times? Not only need there be no conflict between ecology and soul nourishment, these naturally tend to converge. Sustainable architecture has moved from austere pioneering fringe to prime market appeal. No surprise, for forms that condense from local materials, climate, way-of-life, culture and values have archetypal roots. However new the forms, by being respectful of circumstance, they'll naturally tend to blend seamlessly into the continuum of the old, to fulfil soul-archetype needs.

Soul-sustaining environment isn't just eco-by-product. It's vital for sustainability. Places of beauty, especially those we've taken part in making, we value. What we value, we maintain and protect. Value is the root of longevity. Building and place longevity give durable roots to our surroundings. These give society a stable framework. This fosters social stability – another factor in building longevity. All this makes for healthy society, beautiful places and low environmental costs. Without these, however eco-technically accomplished we are, nothing we do can be sustainable.

Notes and references

1 Edwards, B. (1996) *Towards Sustainable Architecture.* Butterworth Architecture.
2 Robert and Brenda Vale, *Green Buildings.*
3 Attention must, however, be paid to condensation risk by, for instance, minimizing trapped-air volume and maximizing humidity-buffering surfaces (like clay plaster or unsealed softwood). Narrow air-spaces overcome trapped-cat risk. Automated systems need safety cut-outs.
4 A term coined by Michael Humphries (2000) Paper at TIA, *Teaching Sustainability Conference,* Oxford.
5 Bio-fuel is carbon neutral. Wind power produces 'free' electricity at the price of the engineered equipment. Photovoltaics are so low efficiency that it would take 25 years for 80 m^2 (800 sq. ft) to save as much CO_2 as a log house locks up. Liddle, H. and Grant, N. (2002/3) *Eco-minimalism, Getting the Priorities Right.* Building for a Future, Winter 2002/3, AECB.
6 Temperature difference between sun and shade is very variable; sun strength, surface colour and air-cooling rate affect it.
7 In Britain, this time lag is around six weeks or 40 days. Celtic festivals are 40 days after solstices and equinoxes.
8 London Ecology Unit *Building Green.*
9 Ford, B. (1998) *Sustainable Urban Development through Design.* RIBA CPD Lecture at Cambridge University, 12 February.

Chapter 5

Building for human health

Vital as saving energy is for planetary health, for *human* health, our approach needs another dimension. Concentrating on sunlight as energy makes it easy to overlook its disinfecting, health-giving and mood-elevating effects. Just as grievances between people often result less from *what* was said than *how* it was said, *quality* can be more important than material description.

Heating is a prime example. We gain and lose heat by radiation as well as convection, so can feel comfortable in cool air when warmed by radiation from sun, stove or warm walls – or feel cool in warm air, by radiating body heat to night sky or cold walls. Nonetheless, it's easier to *think about* heating in terms of air temperature. But heated air doesn't feel so healthy – indeed it *isn't*. Convected, it carries dust – which we breathe.[1] Heater surfaces over 45°C carbonize this. Fan-forced air carries even more dust. Moreover, ducts are good pathogen breeders. Also, friction and magnetism (most ducts are steel) can eliminate negative ions.[2] Static electricity from synthetic materials has similar effects.

Scientists dispute whether this affects health, but less negative ions mean more micro-dust in the air, so it's less fresh. Ions also affect blood serotonin content.[3] Most people feel healthier and more fully alive in ion-rich air with a 60:40 negative to positive ratio.[4] With low negative ions, many experience headaches and lethargy.

Electronic devices can make air 'fresh as a mountain stream' but at the price of noise and electromagnetism. More like 'a mountain stream', flowing water also ionizes air. Fountains can freshen exhaust-polluted city squares. Flowforms have been developed to enhance this through particular water movements.[5] This same effect works indoors: as well as masking office noise and de-stressing us, water-features freshen air.[6]

Fluorescent lights save energy – doubly important in air-conditioned buildings as incandescent bulb heat would increase cooling load. But they save energy at a health price. Normal fluorescents, with their sub-visible mechanical flicker, flat, even light and restricted colour spectrum, can cause

headaches and eye strain.[7] They also increase levels of cortisol (a stress hormone) and ACTH (a growth hormone and source of adrenaline), exacerbating stress and, for children, distorting development. In schools, they account for much moodiness, hyperactivity, attention deficiency and fatigue,[8] and a third of all absenteeism.[9] Additionally, their 120 flashes per second can induce hyperactivity and trigger epileptic seizures.[10]

Natural daylight is broad spectrum, with invisible as well as visible components, all vital for health. Experiments with plants and laboratory animals show that restricted-spectrum lighting causes serious ill-health.[11] Coloured solar-control glass isn't just gloomy, but physiologically harmful. Even normal glass obstructs most ultraviolet – good for sensitive skin and fabric longevity, but not good if you can't get out to open air, so long-stay hospitals and retirement homes need special glass.

Undue concentration on one-dimensional themes, like warmth, light, acoustic absorbency or ease of cleaning risks ignoring what effects things have on the human body – not to mention the soul. We all know that poorly ventilated buildings fill up with old breath and body odours, but a Danish study of 15 offices *without* health complaints showed this accounted for only 12 per cent of total indoor pollution.[12] Even today, knowing what we now do about sick buildings, many places are much worse.

Sick building syndrome is expensive: in the US it costs over $60 billion a year.[13] As mechanical ventilation is a major cause, add in costs for this. Over a building life of, say, 80 years, plant renewal costs alone are more than double building cost. Sick building doesn't just cause absenteeism, but also serious illnesses. These, however, are less

Flowforms are specially proportioned vessels which induce rhythmic oscillations in streaming water so left- and right-handed vortices combine in figure-of-eight movements. They enhance the constantly spiralling movements natural to flowing water, which help keep it fresh and invigorating. This flowform cascade is incorporated in a handrail.

economically visible – until they become litigation issues! This isn't just about ventilation. Sick building has microbiological, particulate, chemical, thermal and electrobiological dimensions. This may sound complicated, but it's easily avoided by simple common sense measures.[14]

Up until the last war, buildings were normally constructed of natural or simply processed materials: 30–40 per cent organic, 60–70 per cent inorganic (like bricks and lime). Nowadays 90–100 per cent synthetic-material buildings are common.[15] Synthetic materials are often the cheapest, most convenient to use or have the best material performance – but they're not good to live with: harmful to breathe, electrostatic, lifeless. In fires many, especially plastics, become killers. Until a few decades ago, firemen competed as 'fire-eaters'. Nowadays, in many building fires, smoke kills in seconds.

All synthetic materials emit traces of synthetic chemical vapours, some inconsequential, some highly toxic. Modern building materials include some 70 000 chemical combinations,[16] releasing perhaps 1000 chemicals to the indoor air.[17] These 'cocktail' and have synergistic effects with, for instance, temperature, electricity and air ionization. Formaldehyde, being highly reactive with body chemistry and carcinogenic, is of particular concern. A common source is urea-formaldehyde in insulation and glued products like fitted carpets, chipboard and plywood – namely lots of veneered furniture.[18] Urea-formaldehyde is water soluble – that's why chipboard doesn't last outdoors – so humid atmospheres, especially if warm, increase formaldehyde release. Phenol-formaldehyde is insoluble, so used in exterior-grade ply and strand-board. Safer indoors, but safest is no such glue!

Sick building symptoms include headaches, irritability, hyperkinesis, learning disability, fatigue, dermatitis, asthma, rhinitis, 'flu mimic conditions, and irritations of the bronchia, mucous membranes, throat and eyes – all easily mistaken for 'normal' ill-health.[19] Some view these as nuisance irritations, others as early warning signs of more serious illness in the longer term.[20] As cancers generally only appear many years after exposure to carcinogens – and many products haven't been in existence that long – caution seems wise.

How do we know what's safe? Some things are written about.[21] Most aren't. The first question is: is something natural? Have people – or animals – lived with it before? After that, we must resort to intuition. Intuition, the zone beyond the frontier of personal knowledge, isn't reliable but can be refined to make it more so. How do we feel near it? How does it smell, feel or taste? If you've ever sawn, chiselled or nailed arsenic-impregnated wood (e.g. CCA, 'tanalized' or 'celcured') you'll know how dead it feels, sounds and smells to work. This sort of sensitivity we can develop.

I don't wish to imply too materialistic a picture of simple and inevitable cause and effect. We are after all beings of spirit, not merely responders to physical laws. Toxic environment is no more certain to cause disease than pathogenic bacteria. Even with *Bacillus legionellus*, only 1–7 per cent of those who breathe it become ill.[22] Illness doesn't just have physical causes, but also emotional and spirit-outlook ones.

For humans as for planet, immune defence systems are weakening. Allergic reaction is now the greatest source of illness in Western society, affecting one-third of us.[23] Hay fever has doubled in a decade.[24] A growing speciality in medicine relates allergies to environmental causes. One American doctor even wears a gas mask to interview patients in case they're wearing perfumes he's allergic to![25] Allergies involve many factors including pollutant synergies. Research in Sweden – with disproportionate allergy growth in the north where air is cleaner but houses super-insulated – strongly implicates buildings, even when pollen is the trigger agent.[26] When a police station had to be closed because policemen were suffering from skin rashes, building sickness could no longer be dismissed as hysterical oversensitivity.[27]

All buildings modify human environment from what has been 'natural' over millennia to that which is a recent biological experience. It isn't only that we live in buildings. How these are designed, what they're built of, how they're maintained, furnished, cleaned, and heated and ventilated are significant. These involve owners, builders and users as well as manufacturers and architects.

We nowadays spend 90 per cent of our lives in buildings or vehicles. Moreover, modern buildings are quite different from those of even only a generation ago. Health problems from dampness, cold, draughts, lack of sunlight and overcrowding have almost disappeared.[28] Toxic vapours, radiation and electricity are to a large extent entirely new problems. New materials, new construction and new standards have brought new and hitherto unanticipated problems – so much so that when in 1971 the state laboratory for foodstuff inspection in Geneva moved into a new building, suddenly all foods examined had unacceptably high levels of toxicity. Gases from paints, plastics, chipboard, etc. were sufficient to contaminate even the food samples.[29]

Not only vapour emissions have biological effects: the way inert materials

are put together also do. Rats, according to experiments, decline in fertility after three generations in a Faraday cage, likened by some to a reinforced concrete building.[30] When, in wartime Burma, the rumour got around that anti-malaria tablets caused impotence, troops refused to take them. Tower blocks have got off more lightly! In multi-storey buildings, biological effects from the earth's geomagnetic grid and terrestrial radiations filtered through underground (or piped) water currents are progressively amplified by each reinforced concrete storey until some consider it unsafe to live above the eighth floor.[31]

All materials shield against cosmic and terrestrial radiations to some extent, but some, notably plastics and metals, do so more than others. Does this matter? What are cosmic radiations, and how do they affect us? Sunlight is obvious.[32] So is the moon's effect on tides, animal and human behaviour and plant development. But what about all those other radiations that we can't feel or see? After millennia of life in natural surroundings we're not adjusted to cosmically isolated environments. Moreover, all life lives at the meeting of cosmos and matter, and more than a few miles from this meeting, nothing lives. Humans, unlike birds or earthworms, live at exactly that meeting point, with our feet on earth, our waking heads in the air. Reduce these influences and we reduce the life-renewing, fertilizing power and health-giving balance of the marriage of earth and cosmos.

Terrestrial radiation, distorted and concentrated by passing through water running in friction, is widely thought harmful. Effects range from insomnia to rheumatism and cancer. As with electricity, we're only just discovering how much we *don't* know about water; how it retains physical, chemical, electromagnetic and vibrational imprints.[33] Scientifically, how these affect us for good or ill, we also don't know much about. Intuitively, however, traditional folk-cultures did. Underground currents and waterways can be located by dowsing, which it seems our ancestors did before building. The meandering lines of medieval streets weren't random. An infrared study of Regensburg showed that streets followed the lines of subterranean water courses, thereby ensuring that houses avoided them.[34]

Many modern building interiors are some 25 times more radioactive than the external environment. Of documented nations, Sweden suffered amongst the most heavily from Chernobyl, yet on average people receive ten times more radioactivity from their own houses. Average radiation[35] in an insulation-block detached house is 200 Bq/m^3 of indoor air. But some kinds of lightweight concrete produce 800 Bq/m^3, *without any ground radon contribution.* Sixty years in such a building makes lung cancer 80 times more likely than death in a fire.[36]

Most of this comes from radon gas – a decay product of uranium. Traces of uranium are everywhere, but most is in materials of deep-earth origin like granite or volcanic rocks. Most radon comes from ground overlaying such geology. It degrades to products which can attach themselves to house dust. These we breathe and so keep some time in the lungs. Radon is trapped in houses – especially draught-sealed or underground ones. 'Radon wells', beneath new buildings or alongside old ones, can suck it out of the ground then disperse it to open air. Vapour-sealing solid floors from the ground (in so far as possible), underfloor ventilation or under-slab airways with ventilation stack are minimum precautions. Radon has always been around, but indoor living and draught-proofing make it a modern problem.

Radon also comes from building materials. Being incombustible, uranium is concentrated by burning. Consequently, insulation blocks of pumice, blast-furnace slag or pulverized fuel ash can be up to 20 times as radioactive as bricks or limestone concrete blocks,[37] and phosphogypsum plasterboard – from desulphurization filters on factory chimneys – 100 times more than gypsum plasterboard.[38] Recycled furnace-product materials, though appealing, aren't always healthiest.

'Electrical diseases' are an unfamiliar concept, but bodily processes are electrochemical and we're nowadays exposed to electromagnetic radiation some 15 000 million times as strong as that reaching us from the sun, and over a 50 Hz to 7 000 000 000 GHz waveband. Upsetting the body's electromagnetic balances and vibrational patterns can induce headaches, weakness, disturbed sleep, nausea and loss of potency.[39] Longer term, there can be more serious consequences, including miscarriages, metabolic misfunctions and cancers. Some people are so electricity allergic that normal life is impossible.[40] Studies have linked 15 per cent of childhood cancers to electromagnetic fields.[41] The links between unguarded VDUs and miscarriage and foetal abnormalities,[42] and mobile phones and brain cancer are now well known.

Rubbing on synthetic carpets, wallpaper, paints or handrails can charge us with static electricity, up to 15 000 volts.[43] The drier the air, the worse this is. Apart from shocks – painful, but not dangerous – a negative charge attracts dust to the skin, causing rashes and eye irritations. Static electricity also 'ages' air, contributing to under-oxygenated blood ailments like depression and lethargy.[44]

If synthetic clothing can produce sufficient electrostatic charge to detonate explosives,[45] think how it is to paint a house with synthetic paint and fill it with synthetic furnishing, foams, carpets, bedclothes, veneers and electronic gadgetry from TVs to microwave ovens. Offices also have computers, fluorescent lights and multi-storey networks of complex underfloor cable.

We can't do much about electromagnetic proliferation but we can locate buildings, particularly housing, well away from transformers, telecommunication masts and power lines (including railways), or the zones between them and large bodies of water. Within buildings, we can route cable in metal conduited spur layouts in less occupied areas. As we regenerate cells during sleep, and hence are at our most sensitive, this should be at least 1.2 m (4 ft) from beds, also preferably from sitting and working positions.[46] Dimmers, night-storage heaters, electric blankets, televisions and mains electric clocks aren't a good idea close to beds! 'Demand switch' circuit-breakers can cut off all power to bedroom zones whenever appliances are off. Instead of bedside lights, I use pull-switches to ceiling lights.[47]

Except for interference with electronic equipment and major hazards like power lines, mobile phones and microwave transmitters, electrical health issues get little attention. The military, however, take these things seriously: electromagnetism, light and sound have weapons potential, allegedly already developed and in use.[48]

In many people's eyes a modern house is more healthy than a damp, mould-growing, draughty old one. (Though new construction isn't immune from such problems: concrete takes three to five years to dry out!) The real difference is that health hazards in modern buildings are much less visible. Old buildings were draughty. Lots of air meant that dampness, even radon, had little effect. Draughts are uncomfortable. This isn't just about leaky windows, but also hidden construction joints. Draught-proofing makes good energy, comfort and money sense. It's indispensable to cold-climate low-energy buildings. But less draughts mustn't mean too little ventilation, or there'll be condensation. Condensation brings mould – on impervious surfaces, visible, smelly and unhealthy to breathe. Rot within the building fabric threatens the building itself. Vapour barriers solve this problem.[49] Consequently, most modern timber-frame buildings have an indoor environment wrapped in a plastic bag. Modern masonry techniques with foam-filled cavities (warning: formaldehyde!), impervious paints or vinyl wallpapers (warning: vinyl chloride and fungicide in wallpaper paste!) do the same.

It's bad enough to wear plastic clothes, but living in a plastic bag means we breathe lots of undesirable stuff: outbreathed air, tobacco smoke, gas cooker or heater fumes, dust, mineral fibres, and toxic vapours from building materials, fittings, furnishings and motor-heated equipment (like computers). Consequently, indoor pollution – and moisture – is usually many times outdoor levels. Healthy (natural) materials, extract fans, cooker hoods, smoking bans and equipment-fume extracts at source mitigate, but can't eliminate, this. A lot of fresh air could solve these problems but this means either foregoing comfort or excessive heating bills. The other way is to eliminate the plastic bag – to build buildings that *breathe*.

Buildings can be seen as the third human skin (skin is the first, clothing the second). Skin performs many functions: it breathes, absorbs, evaporates and regulates, as well as enclosing and protecting. A building which through its fabric is in a *constant state of moderated exchange* between inside and outside feels – and is – a healthy place to be in. It has a quality of life. A sealed-fabric building is full of dead air.

Traditional buildings were made of earth and plant materials. Some rocks have infinitesimal vapour permeability. Build them into a house with strong cement mortar and you have, effectively, concrete. Lime-based mortar, on the other hand, has a greater permeability and capacity to absorb vapour. If you demolish old granite and lime-mortar farmhouse walls, the moisture content of the core of the wall differs little from winter to summer. Such walls have a very high moisture moderating capacity. All conventional materials like brick, plaster and wood do this to some extent, so masonry buildings buffer humidity extremes, albeit too slowly for comfort. But they can't do this at all if sealed – so any paint should be water-based, non-acrylic. Humidity doesn't just mean steamy torpor, condensation, mould, water-soluble chemicals or thermally transmissive air, but also favourable dust mite environment, hence increased asthma.[50]

Clay, with its curious colloidal properties, is the mineral nearest to life. It can quickly absorb and dissipate water – clay models dry before our eyes! Humidity indoors isn't constant; it tends to come in shock loads from cooking, bathing or clothes drying. Clay can absorb this, releasing it slowly to be ventilated away. As absorption speed is crucial, the first 10 mm (half inch) does all the work, so the larger the exposed surface area the better. This has led to the development of clay plasters and ceiling-board and a resurgence of clay-building techniques like cob, pisé, leichtlehm and adobe.[51] Drier indoor air makes earthen buildings feel warmer than thermometers say they are.

Lime was once shellfish,[52] timber once trees, bricks once clay. Plastic and steel are long removed from any history of life, and buildings of these materials have no moderating, breathing, living effect on the internal environment. Trees, on the other hand, had to moderate extremes of weather to stay alive. Consequently, timber moderates humidity, temperature and airborne toxins with its extensive internal air spaces.[53] If not sealed (by synthetic or oil-based paint or varnish) or wood-preservative poisoned, it's one of the healthiest materials to live within. But only if it's not in a plastic bag!

Are there ways to dispense with vapour barriers? To avoid interstitial condensation, vapour permeability of each layer of construction must increase progressively, with the outermost one at least five times as permeable as the innermost. One technique reverses common brickwork-clad wood-frame construction by using a slow-permeable masonry or earthen wall inside insulation and rear-ventilated timber, slate or tile cladding. This also puts thermal mass in the right place for a stable environment – *inside* the insulation. As weather and building use defy prediction, moisture will, at times, condense within the insulation. Mineral insulation can't absorb this, so droplets run together into hidden puddles, with potentially major health and building-decay consequences. Organic materials, like sheepswool, cork, cellulose and cotton fibre, being hydroscopic, can absorb this moisture before it becomes free water, then diffuse it when conditions change. Rapid diffusion is crucial. Straw absorbs water rapidly, but dries faster than it soaks, so thatch, though biodegradable, has roofed and insulated buildings over thousands of years.[54]

If buildings can breathe in more than out, heat trying to leave them warms air filtering in – hence the term 'dynamic insulation'.[55] This also minimizes interstitial condensation risk, and because pollutant molecules tend to be larger, and so 'get stuck' in the building fabric, the air is naturally filtered. Dynamic insulation depends on vapour-permeable walls or ventilated ceilings (better, because heat collects there) and some kind of air extract, from 'stack effect' chimney to powered fan, to ensure negative air pressure indoors. Draught-proofing is therefore vital to avoid 'short-cut' ventilation. Ever-changing conditions of weather and occupancy make this sort of construction complicated to calculate, whereas conventional vapour-sealed construction is simple. Simple because it's unidimensional, lifeless.

This issue of life-full or life-less is at the heart of architecture. Much construction is designed to protect buildings, not their inhabitants or living surroundings. When a building has woodworm or rot, is it acceptable to preserve it, but poison its occupants? Of course, buildings are cleared before spraying, but working on ones treated some months previously, I've felt the effects. Future occupants will breathe impregnated dust and have skin contact for many years to come. Fortunately, there are biologically safer alternatives: wood heat-treated at 50–60°C becomes indigestible to woodworm. Chemicals based on borax or pyrethrum have low mammalian toxicity.[56] The UK Building Research Establishment regards poisoning dry rot (serpula lacrymans) as merely a secondary treatment – more essential is the elimination of conditions.[57] The poison, however, comes with a 30-year guarantee: more responsible methods depend on the architect's insurance!

Ordinary wood-preservatives come at high environmental price. If I use them, I must accept joint responsibility for manufacture, spillage and disposal pollution. And afterwards, what about the timber offcuts or the building itself, when eventually demolished? If burnt, they produce dioxin- or arsenic-laden smoke. Chemical preservation – and, indeed, most chemical solutions to physical problems – are typical of mono-track 'efficiency' thinking: one function improved, but at the expense of everything else. Advertisements for uPVC windows claim: 'Save a Tree, Use uPVC.' But how many trees died from the chemical factory fumes? Like the effects of buildings, our responsibilities extend well beyond the boundaries of the site.

Ecological consequences involve a whole world of *relationships*, biological, social and atmospheric. Even a single building affects microclimate, flora and fauna. For rodent control, barns used to have entrances for barn owls. This sort of symbiotic consideration has almost disappeared. When we cover an area with buildings and paving what does this do for winter floods, summer temperatures or air quality? In cities, the air quality differences between parks and paved areas are striking. Just to replace the oxygen breathed by one person needs 1 sq. m (10 sq. ft) of grass or a 5 m (15 ft) diameter tree crown.[58] And people breathing is the smallest part of urban air problems – nothing compared with traffic! The more vegetation buildings support, the better the air quality, the more rain take-up and less stuffy are hot summers. Local, minimally processed, materials reduce transport and manufacturing pollution, and the more locally appropriate and approachable will such buildings look. In cities, as in countryside, the more harmoniously balanced the ecology, the more artistic the effect.

The built environment is shaped by the decisions of many 'responsible' professionals: politicians, developers, planners, architects, surveyors, engineers

and endless others. Yet the results rarely show it! Too often our surroundings make us feel less well, less at peace within ourselves and less able to cope with biographical crises, eroding our strength to resolve them as inner turning points.

To what gods are these decision-makers responsible? In the choice between building profitability or occupants' health, economic factors are weighed against life in the same way that governments balance health service expenditure against taxation. (Needless, because more humanly nourishing buildings are proven to be profitable, just as healthy people contribute more to the economy than sick ones.) For all their faults, governments at least *have* to think about this choice. Most of us, however, never bring this issue to consciousness.

In many city streets, the pedestrian zone is the most polluted. It is here that we need pollution absorption and redress by plants and active water. These we need also for health of spirit.

Flowform in a pedestrianized city centre.

But whatever our role – architect, builder, building owner or user – we are all co-shapers of our environment. And this won't support life unless we consciously choose that as a priority – whatever the price.

Notes and references

1 Sammaljärvi, E. (1987) In *Det Sunda Huset*, p. 120. Byggforskningrådet.
2 Mechanically handled air has typically about 5 per cent of the ion content of fresh air: 50 ions per cc compared with 1000, and mostly positive.
3 Planverkets rapport 77, *Sunda och Sjuka Hus*, p. 111. Stockholm, 1987.
4 Seventy per cent of us respond this way. (Research by Sulman, Hebrew University, Jerusalem.)
5 Flowforms were originally developed by John Wilkes, Flow Design Research Group, Emerson College, Sussex, UK.
6 As low-level legionella contamination is possible, in places for the immuno-deficient, great care is needed that droplets aren't breathable.
7 Eble, J. (1986) Lecture at *The Living Language of Architecture Conference*, Järna, Sweden; *Environment Digest*, No. 9, February 1988; Weatherall, D. (1987) New light on light. *Management Services*, September, p. 30.
8 The non-visible spectrum components of full-spectrum electric lights tend to have a short life. This makes electricity

a weak subsititute for daylight. Even this is spectrum limited through most glass. No wonder humans were designed for outdoor life!

9 *Health News*, Higher Nature, Summer 2001.

10 Bruzelius, B. (1988) Dold olf bo i sjuk-hus. *Byggforskning*, No. 3, p. 17. Stockholm, April.

11 John Ott's experiments with plants and mice in restricted-spectrum light show how unhealthy this is to live in.

12 Bruzelius, B. (see note 10).

13 For sick leave; also $1 billion for medical care: *Green Workplaces*, March 1997.

14 These I describe in detail in *Spirit & Place* (2002). Architectural Press.

15 Schimmelschmidt, M. (1989) Unpublished paper.

16 Hejdenberg, K. and Sävenstrand, I. (1987) Allergiutredningen i Sverige. In *Det Sunda Huset* (Dawidowicz, Lindvall and Sundal, eds), op. cit., p. 34.

17 Fredholm, K. (1988) *Sjuk av Huset*, p. 14. Brevskolan, Stockholm; Jaakola and Heinonen, p. 50; Sammaljärvi (1987), pp. 120, 132. In *Det Sunda Huset*, op. cit., p. 89.

18 Bruzelius, B. (see note 10).

19 Levy, F. (1987) Sykdommer assosiert med bygninger. In *Det Sunda Huset*, op. cit., p. 89.

20 Högberg, J. (1987) Kroppens varnings-signalar på toxiska effekter av kemiska ämnen. In *Sunda och Sjuka Hus*, op. cit., p. 140.

21 See, in particular: Curwell, S., March, C. and Venables, R. (eds) (1990) *Buildings and Health*. RIBA Publications, London; Mason-Hunter, L. (1989) *The Healthy Home*. Pocket Books.

22 Dr de Nutte (1989) Indoor air quality. Paper at *Sick Buildings and Healthy Houses Seminar*, London, 22/23 April.

23 Fredholm, K. (1988) *Sjuk av Huset*, p. 51. Brevskolan, Stockholm.

24 *Sunda och Sjuka Hus* (1987) Op. cit., p. 197.

25 Pfeifer, G. and Nikel, C. (eds) (1980) *The Household Environment and Chronic Illness*. Thomas Books, Illinois.

26 Sammaljärvi, E. (1987) How to build a healthy house. In *Det Sunda Huset*, op. cit., p. 119.

27 A new police station in the city of Umeå. Fredholm, K. (1988) *Sjuk av Huset*, op. cit.

28 But not in the developing world! Smoke haze now covers almost all Asia.

29 Vassella (1984) Third skin. *Permaculture Journal*, 14, 23.

30 Vassella (1984) Ibid.

31 Eble, J. (1981) Unpublished lecture.

32 Its gross effects are obvious. Subtler aspects, like solar rhythms and sun-spots, we don't yet know much about.

33 See, for instance: Hall, A. (1997) *Water, Electricity and Health*. Hawthorn Press; and Hagender, F. (2000) *The Spirit of Trees*. Floris Books.

34 Eble, J. (1981) Unpublished lecture, Järna, Sweden.

35 Eastern bloc nations weren't documented. *Belarus and much of Ukraine suffered appallingly.*

36 Swedish figures, *Radon i bostäder*, Social-styrelsen, Statens Planverk, Statens Strålskyddinstitut, Sweden, 1988, p. 3.

37 German figures from König, H. (1989) *Wege zum Gesunden Bauen*. Ökobuch, Freiburg.

38 Curwell, S., March, C. and Venables, R. (eds) (1990) *Buildings and Health: The Rosehaugh Guide*. RIBA Publications.

39 Hawkins, L. (1989) Health problems arising from geopathic

stress and electro-stress. Paper given at *Sick Buildings and Healthy Houses Seminar*, London, 22/23 April.

40 *Dagens Nyheter*, Stockholm, 5 November 1987.

41 *Environment Digest*, August 1987, p. 6. The increase in computer games where children sit right in front of the screen can only make this worse. Roger Coghill attributes 90 per cent of cot deaths to electromagnetic fields: Power frequency hazards. Lecture at *Sick Buildings and Healthy Houses Seminar*.

42 Risks increase by 53–80 per cent. *Environment Digest*, 14, July 1988, p. 6; and Hawkins, L. (see note 38).

43 Sjöblom, L. (1988) In *Byggforskning 3*, p. 28. Stockholm, April. Sammaljärvi (1987) Op. cit.

44 Sammaljärvii (1987) Op. cit.

45 British Army allegations that this causes premature detonation of IRA explosives must, however, be regarded with considerable suspicion.

46 To avoid induced current, distance from water piping is also wise. Pipes should be earthed as near their entry to buildings as practical.

47 I list EMF precautions in greater detail in *Spirit & Place* (2002). Architectural Press.

48 Besly, K. (1986) Electronic warfare. *Peace News*, 7, March.

49 Usually in fact 'vapour checks', because they're imperfect barriers. For brevity I use 'vapour barrier' to include both 'barrier' and 'check'.

50 25°C (77°F) at 83 per cent relative humidity is dust mite heaven (or 70 per cent according to Wright State University, USA). Howieson, S. (2003) Centre for Environmental Design and Research, University of Strathclyde, Scotland; letter in *Building Design*, 17 January 2003.

51 Leichtlehm is a straw-rich clay mixture. European pisé is clay mix including small stones. American pisé includes 10 per cent cement. As 10 per cent is as much cement as in a concrete block, in a 2 ft wall it's a lot! I do *not* recommend this. For further details on earth building, see: Minke, G. (2000) *Earth Construction Handbook*. WIT Press; and Houben, H. and Guillard, H. (1994) *Earth Construction*. Intermediate Technology Publications.

52 Much of it certainly was; there is some dispute as to whether all of it was.

53 Vassella (see note 29); Busch, H. (1989) Biologically safe building fabrics and the indoor climate. Lecture at *Sick Buildings and Healthy Houses Seminar*.

54 Indeed, Norfolk reed thatch can outlast fibre-cement roofing!

55 A system pioneered by Gaia Lista (originally Cobolt) Arkitekter in Norway.

56 Synthetic pyrethrum-based Permethrin has low mammalian toxicity to protect bats, whereas Lindane remains toxic for 30 years. Borax-based sap diffusion (e.g. 'Timbor') impregnated timber is insect and rot protected, but effectively non-toxic. Borax, however, is water soluble, so unsuitable for wet locations. Best of all is to use a wood that doesn't easily rot, and design construction that drains and ventilates dry.

57 'Moisture reservoirs' and existing fungus must both be removed. Dry rot: its recognition and control, *Building Research Establishment Digest*, 299, July 1985.

58 Engelhard, A. (1990) Solararchitectur im Industrie- und Verwaltungsbau. In *Gesundes Bauen und Wohnen 1/90*, March, No. 38, p. 38.

Chapter 6
Qualities and quantities

One definition of architecture is 'the design of buildings'. One definition of buildings is 'durable enclosures of controlled environment' – the creation of environment appropriate for certain (usually human) functions.

Out of this approach has grown specialized areas of study. Environmental science is concerned, on the whole, with quantitative descriptions of environment suiting for our physical needs. There are lists of the temperatures and lighting level we need for various activities, like sitting or exerting ourselves, and reading or kitchen work. These sound definitive, but rarely distinguish between radiant or body-contact heating – which need balancing by cooler air – or convection; nor whether light is from sun, incandescent bulbs or fluorescent lights. Moreover, not everyone enjoys the same temperature – indeed there are over 100 thermal comfort indices[1] – nor even the same light. Nonetheless, these standard lists describe what's appropriate to whatever *physical* situation.

These quantities, however, tell us nothing of what is a *nice* atmosphere to read or cook in, even though this nice atmosphere is made up of the right warmth, right light and so on. It is this *atmosphere* that gives meaning to the quantitative physical descriptions. To create nice and, more importantly, meaningful, *appropriate*, atmospheres we need to focus not on the quantities but on the qualities.

There are instruments to measure quantities – for instance, how loud something is and of what frequencies the sound is made up. Also tables to evaluate these quantities: noise over so many decibels disturbs sleep, intrudes upon conversation, tenses heart muscles and so on. Instruments give objective information, but they're selective. A wind-rose from anemometer readings can tell us where best to site a windmill (though it doesn't tell where to avoid destructive gales). For siting buildings, however, we need to know the temperatures, humidities and seasons of the constituent winds – which ones really matter and which don't. Several instruments, a computer and the patience to wait several years can tell us this, or we can ask some of the older neighbours. Instruments unquestionably bring an objectivity beyond that we can discipline ourselves to, but their selectivity can mean that their answers often don't correspond to our questions. What is so often dismissed as human subjectivity is the unconscious ability to synthesize many factors; however, because it's unconscious many personal preferences get muddled in.

How can we find a similarly objective basis to evaluate qualities? It is possible to quantify human responses by averaging answers to questionnaires or recording how laboratory rats behave. It may be that there are meaningful ways of doing this, but I myself have been put off on the one hand by the oversimplicity and obviousness of conclusions which we all know anyway, and on the other by the fact that I'm trying to be human and not a rat-like responder to behaviourist stimuli. In buildings or places where we feel good (or bad), it's likely that our feelings are also shared by others. I don't mean ones which we *think* something about, but those where, before we start to think, we *feel* something.

From the evidence of sick buildings it becomes clear that qualities widely liked or disliked, whether heat, light, sound or whatever, probably *are* beneficial or harmful. For some scientific measurements, the human being is in fact the best instrument. In developing the Olf and Decipol system of measuring indoor air pollution, Professor Fanger found human assessment to be more sensitive, accurate and meaningful than any chemical analysis.[2]

Subjective preference can be a good guide as to whether places are good or bad for us. But it's notoriously unreliable. The problem is that there are *personal, cultural* and *universal* layers of response. Normally, these are all muddled up together; we just respond. We don't think why. For our individual selves, we don't

need to – but to design for others, we need to distinguish these layers. With disciplined exercises in dispassionate objectivity, we can see past the personal. The better we can do this, the more accurately can we use our *own selves* as *objective instruments* to evaluate qualities of environment.

The amount of space we need between ourselves and strangers to feel at ease in varies from culture to culture.[3] Quantitative space requirements are predominantly cultural – to Europeans, for example, the scale of American houses, cars and cities is striking. We also have personal spatial preferences: some like the cozy, some the grand. In absolute terms, however, distance affects how we need to speak, move or focus our eyes. It therefore has bodily effects which, regardless of our expectations and preferences, influence social relationships.

Colour is highly personal. Each of us has colours we prefer to wear or can't abide. But there are also fashion colour currents which flow through society around rocks of established convention. There are also *universal* aspects of colour: red speeds the metabolism, blue slows it down. This is a physiological fact – everyone responds this way. Different colours stimulate different glands: for instance, yellow – thyroid; blue – pituitary; red – male sexual; violet – female sexual glands.[4] Knowledge of this kind can be used to manipulate people and can also be used therapeutically. A home for maladjusted children in England had a swimming pool illuminated underwater making the children's splashing bodies appear coloured: red helps activate autistic children, encouraging them out of themselves into activity; blue calms down hyperactive ones, bringing them more into themselves.

All colours have universal effects. Not little blobs of colour, but whole *experiences* of it – coloured light, walls and ceilings of colour, totally coloured environments. Heavy, strong colours are often too forceful to live comfortably with; their use requires great skill and sensitivity. Traditionally they're applied in a variety of hues and shades utilizing harmony and counterpoint. Strong colours can easily be manipulative – they dominate the furniture and other oddments and also *us*. They *force* their mood upon a room.

Where colour works as a delicate breath, however, is in the light. Coloured light has a different effect from pigment – with light you can feel raised up into a mood, but with pigment pressed down into it. Imagine (if you can't arrange to experience it) the room you're in bathed in yellow light or painted yellow – or blue or red.[5]

Except for special rooms for special uses, coloured glass often feels out of place, especially as most windows are for looking out of. Other ways of influencing light-mood include translucent curtain-veils, also 'Lazure' painting. This technique washes transparent veils of pigment – so thin as to be barely visible – over a textured white ground. Unlike the static surface-impenetrability of opaque paint, the delicate breath of light reflecting through these colour layers has a living quality.

Green is a colour of balance; it has a peaceful, calming, soothing effect. (In Steiner schools, it's the balance colour for classrooms at the mid-point of childhood.) Yet it requires considerable skill to paint a room in opaque green without it becoming heavy and dead, for green is such a lifeless colour to paint with. Worse than that, there's the risk that reflected light will green people's faces creating, by association, a disquieting mood. By contrast, light shining in through foliage can be both life-filled and peace-bringing.

Whether light, material or pigment, the colours I use aren't random, nor just heart-warmers or attractive, but are specific for their function. What colour, for instance, could help transform a cafeteria from utility-food canteen to centre of sociability? What colour would best prepare us for entry to a church? This is no matter of rules, but of *cultivating awareness* of how colours speak. The next step is to bring colour into conversation with the light – unique to every room – and then work with these ingredients artistically.

To work with the qualitative vocabulary of architecture we need to cultivate this *awareness* in all spheres – not just think about it from outside. We need to experience more consciously that which it's all too easy just to float along through. We need to wake up our senses, the gateway between external reality and our inner feelings. Our senses tell us about what is important in our surroundings. Mostly, we experience things through the outer senses: sight, smell, taste, sound, warmth, touch. Architecture, in the sense of environmental design, is the art of nourishing these.

This starts with making places *look* good. Even if nobody looks *at* them, everybody responds to background visual impressions. We see this visual 'mood', can talk about it afterwards, remember it for years – but when asked to draw any of it, have hardly any idea how it actually looked! Much of this visual mood is made up of colour, visual texture, scale and the quality of how things meet. Much of our response is due to the quality of light.

It doesn't matter how nice a place looks if it smells of bad drains. The aroma of fresh bread or coffee can be a shop's best advertisement – better than any visual display. Salesmen sometimes look oddly at me when I ask: will your product (say carpet) smell? And even more oddly when I sniff their samples! It's no good designing a place that looks nice but smells horrible, especially as that smell means something about the air we breathe.

Adults don't go around biting their surroundings – but babies do. When one sinks its teeth into a plastic or wooden toy it gets quite different tastes. When we taste copper or lead in drinking water, we may well wonder if the pipes are poisoning us. In acidic water areas I therefore prefer stainless-steel piping to drinking taps.

Warmth can have such different qualities: radiant heat from a blacksmith's forge can be bearable even in summer, but warm-air heating is never pleasant, even in cold winter. The focal radiant warmth of a stove or fireplace, reinforced by the sound, smell and sight of the fire, gives a spirit to a home. We call this part of a building the hearth – its heart. Anyone who enjoys a hot-water bottle or lying on sun-warmed rocks can imagine the luxury of Russian stoves built to sleep on. What a difference between conducted heat and air-conditioning!

Most of us don't go around deliberately touching buildings, yet without thinking about it, we touch them all the time. The textures we walk on or feel with our hands (or eyes) make all the difference between places which are approachable and which aren't: few people prefer a concrete bench or steel table to a wooden one. Few of my clients ask for any particular materials in their buildings, yet a lot of them ask for wooden floors.

Part of the individuality of countries, towns and places depends on their unique soundscapes. How rooms sound – whether they echo, resonate or absorb – makes all the difference to their mood. A church, living-room or restaurant should *sound* different. We don't feel homely in hard echoing rooms. Dead acoustic spaces aren't good to sing in. Noisy clatter turns restaurants into canteens. This is a matter of design and materials.

These are the outer senses. They are our contact with outer reality, what in the East is called *Maya* – illusion – although through them we can see beyond it. We also have finer senses with which we can perceive the invisible reality that lies behind this. This spiritual essence is *very* real. One example is how a shop feels where the only object is to maximize profit, compared with one motivated to provide a socially beneficial service. Profit and service aren't incompatible – it's where the balance lies that colours a place's spirit.

We can cultivate our sense of what a place *says*. We can begin to sense the unspoken values that lie behind the outer phenomena. These are manifest in the way it has been planned, the way it has been built, the way it has evolved, is cared for and used.

This sharpens our sense of the individuality of places – not just the outer differences but the differences of spirit between places. Part of this is the extent to which different sensory experiences reinforce or contradict each other. But to design with these surface phenomena alone is merely playing with cosmetics. Places really speak through their spirit of place. The phenomena accessible to the outer senses are just manifestations of that spirit. Mass housing, system designed, system built, imposed upon town or landscape, isn't going to feel a great deal better if painted attractive colours, or with road-noise screens. It still remains containers for statistics, not homes for individuals.

We also have senses which tell us about our own state: our physical balance and movement. Least conscious of all, we have a sense of health. It is exceptional to consciously *feel* healthy, but when we're *not* healthy, feel ill, thirsty or tired, we do feel this. This sense is relevant to architecture because in many buildings we feel less than well; some actually make us ill. Often the effects are only vague, like bad sleep, tension or exhaustion, so we don't recognize the causal link.

On the whole, however, our senses give us good guidance as to whether places are harmful or nourishing to both body and spirit. Unfortunately the senses are so undermined these days that unless we cultivate them, they may speak too weakly for us to understand their message.

Physiologically – let alone psychologically – working all day in artificial light doesn't do us any good, can even do harm. Inadequate light – limited brightness, duration, spectrum – can cause Seasonal Affective Disorder (SAD), associated with depression, lethargy and suicides. There are electrical devices to counter SAD: super-bright lights, full-spectrum bulbs, 'light-cabinets' and gadgets to constantly vary light for sense stimulation – also, in northern countries, chemical ones like coffee and alcohol! But there's no substitute for daylight. The light of spring can bring such joy to the heart, it can get invalids out of bed!

Several smaller windows are better than one large one, not only because, from the energy-saving point of view, for the same heat loss there's a better distribution of light, avoiding gloom–glare extremes, but also for quality. In addition to their life-filled and health-giving light, windows on two sides give two view directions instead of one, so it's easier to orientate yourself: windows on three sides show the sun's rotation, so orient us in time as well as space. Even for occupations which theoretically don't need natural light, windows connect the artificially-controlled indoor world to the life of activity, weather and season outside – the lifeless, unvarying with the life-renewing, ever-changing. When you don't know which way round you are or what time of day it is, you easily feel victim to the building. Whatever its function, it becomes an institution. More windows mean more views for more people. Gazing through windows reduces stress and helps clarify overview thinking. In hospitals, window views are calculated to save $500 000 per bed-space![6]

Nasty smells warn us that something is bad for us. Smell is how we sense minute quantities of matter. Minute doesn't mean harmless. The lungs have a huge surface area – we breathe several thousand gallons of air per day. So even small amounts of airborne toxin can have very significant effects. Anything that smells is giving off vapour. Plastics (anyway as rubbish) seem to last 'forever', but they smell. They aren't in fact absolutely stable; that's why they embrittle. They give off vapours of plasticizers, stabilizers, pigments and unattached monomers.[7] It is these we smell.

Generally things only affect us in subtle ways. We have to cultivate the ability of our senses to recognize what's good or bad for us. The messages are also subtle: only when we *touch* polyurethane-coated wood do we know there's something wrong. It feels hard, smooth, cold; it doesn't breathe and the finger's sweat condenses on its unyielding surface. It *looks* like wood but our other senses say this is a lie. It's hardly the best food for our spirit to be surrounded with lies. Nor will it help to bring children up to be honest. Nor does the paucity of sensory experience nourish the soul.

To nourish the soul means finding qualities in our environment that provide the right balance to the imbalance of the moment. Of course, there are lots of imbalances and lots of soul needs, but only a few are major. Sometimes we lack society, stimulation and challenge. Sometimes we have too much and feel stressed. Sometimes we need to withdraw to a secure private domain like fireside, inner garden or personal retreat. Can we find fulfilment of such needs in our daily surroundings?

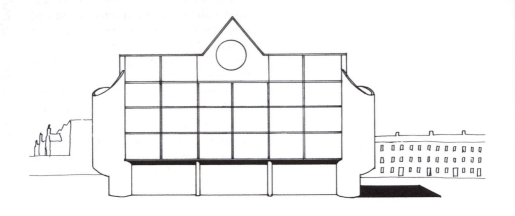

The harder and more lifeless our surroundings, the more tired, tense and sapped of life we tend to be. Likewise, the softer and more alive they are, the more renewed, relaxed, even healed we become. Soft lively air rather than rough funnelled draughts,[8] absorbed sounds rather than hard echo, moderated enlivened light dancing off water or through leaves, or even just the ever-changing interplay of subtly different light and shadow from different windows.

Vegetation brings softness, life and seasonal rhythm. Because of upward sap-flow and transpiration, plants negatively ionize air. So strong is this that 30 metre (100 ft) trees frequently release 'point discharges' of 600 V or more, even in good weather.[9] Ferns, being damp-condition plants, are particularly good ionizers. Plants buffer humidity, temperature, trap dust, absorb pollution, and dampen and mask noise as well as oxygenating air. Indoor plants not only soften architectural hardness but freshen and renew air. Outdoors they so effectively moderate microclimate, I always design planting for this function.

Human activity – especially industry, traffic and heating – pollutes the air we breathe. How do we manage to get fresh air? Cities, roads and buildings don't make it. Only plants – from marine plankton to terrestrial trees – do. This is why wooded 'lungs' are often incorporated into urban regional planning, and cities without them suffer smogs and high rates of respiratory illness.[10] Central Europeans wonder how British industrial cities survive without trees, but these just rely upon island sea breezes, generally from the west, to blow pollution across their eastern parts and the underprivileged who live there.

Vital as they are for air quality, we enjoy trees and other plants for their

As well as improving air quality by oxygenation, humidity regulation, ion breeding, dust absorption and smell masking, plants soften the impact of hard materials and shapes, harsh light and hard acoustics. Their transformative effect far outweighs their cost.

restful appearance, life-filled shade, leaf sounds and scents. They're breath for the soul as well as the lungs. Climbing plants, as well as absorbing street noise and dust, soften hard corners, make unyielding textures approachable, enrich walls (and deter graffiti) and can clamber or cascade over roofs or around archways. Vandalism, security, wind damage and maintenance can be overcome with protection, low-branch pruning, species selection and after-care. Some vegetation, like moss and lichen, requires no maintenance. Spraying buildings with cow manure encourages these – but not everyone takes this suggestion seriously!

There are people who dislike trees. To them they're just slippery leaves on the pavement, sticky secretions or bird-droppings on cars, or robbers of window light. But such objections are out of proportion to the benefits vegetation can bring. There are also problems with the wrong plants in the wrong places. It's much easier to buy cultivated than wild varieties. Many have been bred for one-sided development like coloured leaves or extended flower season, so may look all right in garden centres but feel quite out of place when planted. To really benefit wildlife, not to mention maximize survival prospects, the right plant needs to be in the right place – the microclimate, soil and 'abuse' conditions (like being walked on) that it would grow wild in.

It's also possible – though rare – to have too much vegetation. Much as I like them for aesthetic, landscape-harmony and ecological reasons and have often been asked for them, only five or six times have I had the right projects for turf roofs. As these clean air, slow rainwater run-off, replace the earth's living skin, absorb noise and offer visually soft skylines, they're often more important in cities than countryside. They come, however,

at a price: the waterproof membrane and its industrial biography. A simple alternative is to train climbers over roofs. This doesn't help with flood control, but gives foliage without pollution.

We can have too much of something or too little – after all, all life on earth lives in a very narrow band between earth and cosmos, between absolute matter and the heat of the sun. Healthy life is always a delicate balance between extremes. Healthy society depends on the right balance between initiative freedom and regulatory safeguards – imbalance means merciless free-for-all or stultifying bureaucracy. Likewise, soul-nourishing architecture is also a narrow band. Underdo it and we don't support soul moods. Overdo it and we become manipulators.

All activities demand different states of being. If we're in the wrong state for the job, we feel stressed. Our environment can provide the soul mood appropriate to the situation. When work makes us tense and claustrophobic, we need spacious, peaceful views to induce mental space and peace in ourselves. Practically, these can't always be distant views over calm water, or even wind-stirred treetops; sometimes they'll be no more than focus on changing clouds. Or the place itself can be relaxing and calming just to be in, perhaps bathed in rose, greenish or bluish light, filtered through leaves, flowers or coloured glass, or reflected from walls lightly veiled with transparent colour. Or perhaps we need coziness, warmth, enclosure and focus, as when we sit around a fireplace – not the place for windows unless they have interior wooden shutters to close out the wintry outside. Or we may need exciting, socially stimulating places where we can feel a part of human vitality – particularly important for young people as part of the process of stretching their social horizons.

While roofs shelter building occupants, they rarely have a beneficial effect on local outdoor climate. Vegetated roofs, however, can absorb airborne toxins, redress oxygen, ion and humidity balances. Even more importantly, they reduce flood risk by spreading rainwater discharge over a day instead of minutes.

Choosing what is *appropriate* isn't about manipulating people or paternalistically determining what they 'ought' to want. It's about *offering* an environment supportive to balance. Inner freedom depends upon this balance. Different environments are appropriate to different social groups. It's not just a matter of cultural responses – intolerable overcrowding in Montana is spacious in Bombay; wild landscape in the Netherlands is practically metropolis in Lapland. There are also the classic differences between what sort of home appeals to those who work in urban environments, alienated and stressed by crowds of strangers; or by those with weather-battered outdoor jobs like farmers and trawlermen. One group needs space, peace, light, air, long views and *private* green realms – hence suburbia. The other needs coziness, enclosure, protection. Traditionally, their houses were solid with small windows; they slept in snug cabin-like cupboards or high-sided drawer-beds.

I know old Welsh farms 'improved' with spacious kitchen extensions – the kitchen being the room everyone lives in – but in 'modern', sterile style. But the modernized house now seems empty, unfriendly; despite central heating, the family complain that it feels cold. The lack of warmth isn't due to low temperature. Nor because the walls are too cool a white, though this is part of it. It's because the house has lost its heart. It has lost its soul warmth.

Even though instruments may say otherwise, this failure to nourish the *soul* is experienced also as failure to provide the right *physical* environment. Qualities are more important than their quantity.

Notes and references

1 Humphries, M. (2000) Paper at TIA *Teaching Sustainability Conference*, Oxford.
2 *Byggforskning*, No. 3, April 1988, pp. 17–19.
3 See, for instance: Hall, E. (1966) *The Hidden Dimension*. Doubleday Anchor.
4 Bayes, K. (1970) *The Therapeutic Effect of Environment on Emotionally Disturbed and Mentally Subnormal Children*, p. 31. Gresham Press.
5 Experiments on physiological and psychological reaction to colour are, in fact, more often carried out with light than pigment. See: Bayes, K. (note 4), p. 30.
6 Savings calculated over a ten-year period. McKahan, D. C. (1994) *Ensouling Healthcare Facilities*. Lennon Associates, Del Mar, CA. See also: Wyon, D. (1987) Buildings fit for people to live and work in. In *Det Sunda Huset*, p. 196 (Dawidowicz, Lindvall and Sundal, eds), Byggforskningrådet. See also Roger Ulrich's work at San Antonio University, Texas.
7 Katalyse Umweltgruppe und Gruppe für ökologische Bau- und Umwelt Planung (1985) *Das ökologische Heimwerkerbuch*, p. 197. Rowohlt, Hamburg. Phthalate plasticizers are of particular health concern. See also: Curwell, S., March, C. and Venables, R. (eds) (1990) *Buildings and Health*. RIBA Publications.
8 Gusts caused by high buildings kill some 200 people each year in Britain.
9 These are invisible to the naked eye. Hagender, F. (2000) *The Spirit of Trees: Science, Symbiosis and Inspiration*. Floris Books.
10 See, for instance: McHarg, I. (1971) *Design with Nature*. Doubleday/Natural History Press.

Chapter 7

Conversation or conflict?

However appropriately we match sensory qualities to the needs of a place and its users, these can't be considered in isolation. Most, although they work upon us anyway, we *consciously* notice only by contrast. We notice warmth when we come into a warm room from the cold, move closer to a fire or step into sunlight. We notice the smell of a city, industry or house when we first arrive there; the next day we don't. If sensory qualities, however appropriate, are to bring joy and refreshment to the soul, we need variety – not endlessly the exact correct temperature, lighting level, the same view, the same sort of shapes, space, or movement through space.

Without constant stimulus our senses wither. Inadequate stimulation makes life boring, joyless and uninspiring – but too much can be alarmingly over-stimulating! For a stress-free life, we need sameness, predictability; but to feel alive, our senses need contrast, stimulus. Psychologists call this 'difference within sameness'.[1] Dancing leaf-shade patterns, lapping wavelets, gurgling streams, endlessly re-forming clouds, combine calming tempo with the security of a reliably constant world, but one constantly stimulating our senses to life and delight. In such settings, we feel at ease. This also explains the appeal of variety-within-unity in vernacular settlements, mature cities and mixed woodland. Uncontrolled variety is discordant. Unified variety gives delight.

With variety, one experience is set against another. We become aware of *meetings* – particularly visible ones. Most of these are meeting edges, for while the *being* of something may live in its centre – say a field of colour – the meetings occur where it meets another colour. This edge between them can be hard, or so subtle you can only say where the centre of each colour is; the rest is just 'somewhere in between'. *How* they meet makes all the difference!

In every aspect of life there are two extreme ways of meeting: conversation or confrontation. In one you are open to what the other brings, in the other you seek to impose your own pre-formed viewpoint. Whether in relationships between individuals, groups within society, nations or power blocks, confrontation leads to polarized positions and seeks to resolve matters with force. Regardless of who wins or loses, it's a destructive process. The loser is oppressed, the winner demeaned.

Conversation is the process by which two or more individuals come together to create a whole *more than the sum of their parts*. They must listen to each other and to what comes into form through – and only through – the conversation. The individuals need to be able to adapt their plans according to the needs of each other but *without compromising their essential nature*. The natural – given – world is based on conversation. Water is much more than oxygen and hydrogen, rich coastal ecology more than land and water. Few man-made things converse, however. Most confront. We tend to be better asserters than listeners.

Listening is much harder than it sounds, because we need to put our own thoughts aside for a while. But adapting without compromising is easier than it sounds, because uncompromisable principles, if *honestly* and *morally* founded, will not be incompatible with each other. This conversational ideal can be a light to guide human relationships and daily life. It is the essential foundation for harmony. Neither socially nor in any art can you build living harmonious relationships out of rules. They depend upon listening responsiveness. For harmonious surroundings in which we can feel alive, at ease and peaceful enough to feel ourselves, architecture needs to be based on this conversational principle.

A lot of time in architectural design is given to creating *shapes*. Elevations are drawings of shapes – many of which, being unrepresentative planar views, don't exist. There are also many other shapes which, though existing as drawn, we don't see because we can't stand back

and see everything all at once. What we *do* see a lot of is *edges*: outlines, corners, openings through solid walls, meetings between planes.

Shape, whether we consciously look at it or not, affects us. So also does how it is edged. A table with hard rectangular edges is sharper, more aggressive, than one with them rounded. Rounded-off corners ease the movement of eye (and hand) from one line to another – and 'attack' us less when bumped into. Such subtle shape modifications make a tremendous difference to how we respond to things.

Such effects are about more than just niceness. Imagine a small white room, almost square, one high-level window only, no view – a monk's cell. Softly undulating plaster, a subtle curve on the ceiling and above the window; a clay-tiled floor in not quite straight lines; the sunlight enlivened on the uneven surfaces of wall and floor.

Imagine it again, the edges knife-edged, the walls shiny smooth; ceiling, walls, floor meeting each other in hard, precise lines; the sunlight a sharp rectangle.

The first is a room for prayer, a place of tranquillity set aside from the hubbub of the world. The second is somewhere you can't wait to get out of – it's more a prison cell.

For practical reasons, especially construction and storage, we need straight lines and their products – rectangular forms. But these aren't forms found anywhere in the human body, in human movement, human activity, nor anywhere in nature. Rectangular forms are forms that suit machines and mechanistic thinking. An excavator has difficulty digging a curved trench.

I can draw the same curve with a computer or a pencil. But the nature of the two curves couldn't be more different. The drawn curve has bodily movement

Built in the 1950s, this room was a severe and sterile rectanguloid. Minor ceiling shaping, hand-finished texture on the walls and the interplay of light from different windows make all the difference. These minimal edge-softenings make the room habitable. Light quality, colour and reflected colour-light create its mood. Space, shape, light and colour all weave in conversation with each other to create one atmospheric whole.

built into it; the most alive and firmest curves are drawn from the toes, not just with the fingertips. The computer can only reduce my uninterrupted, flowing, evolving, living gesture into a lifeless binary code.

Nothing alive ever fits exactly in any hard-edged category, as I'm reminded each time I fill in a questionnaire. Design by placing coordinates on a grid may make things easy to measure, but it

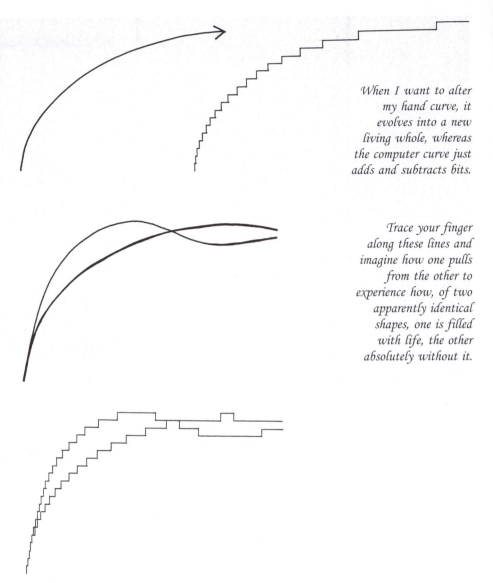

When I want to alter my hand curve, it evolves into a new living whole, whereas the computer curve just adds and subtracts bits.

Trace your finger along these lines and imagine how one pulls from the other to experience how, of two apparently identical shapes, one is filled with life, the other absolutely without it.

However striking, sculptural or imposing, architecture like this is the product of the rational but arid intellect, not the heart, for it seeks powerful images at the price of more delicate feelings. Such buildings do not create places to feel good in, nor indeed, with hand, eye or heart, to feel at all. Nothing can live in a hard, rectangular, mineral world without artificial support – without vehicles, lifts, air-conditioning, prestige flattery or consumerist entertainment they would be uninhabitable. It is no coincidence that New York City uses as much electrical energy as the whole continent of Africa. Places resulting from this approach to architecture are for machines, not for the human soul. Cruelly, these matter-bound values made this building such a symbol of Mammon that heartless minds could ignore the humanity of its occupants.

describes the world in the same unequivocal way as the computer's yes–no code. It's no accident that a world made up only of rectangles is death to the soul. Hard mineral matter, hard lines, hard corners, repetitive unambiguous form. We can't live in such places without something else to sustain us. This abstraction and artificiality feeds alienation. Add other 'shut-off' factors and it becomes easy to walk with open eyes blank past an accident, past a cry for help.

The straight line is – as we know – the shortest route between two points. In other words it has only *one* concern – not the most gentle, most lively, but the *shortest* route. Machines make *dead straight* lines. The feeling hand – unless trying to imitate machine standards – makes *nearly* straight lines. Dead straight and nearly straight are as different as the movements of the clock and the movements of the universe: one dead, one alive.

When you plane a plank corner, the edge you get results from the geometry of the tool. The plane imposes straightness upon the material. When, on the other hand, you shave it with a knife or chisel, the tool responds to the grain and knots. (This needs great subtlety or things can look a bit 'ye olde'.) The difference may seem infinitesimal, but rooms made up of sharp-planed edges are harsh, those of responsive knife-shaved edges much more life-filled and welcoming.

When the Bauhaus movement so enshrined the geometric solids cube and cylinder, it was also choosing the most economical forms for the machine age. Bauhaus derivative buildings that followed were increasingly shaped by monetary criteria – so machine-extruded forms were highly suitable.

We experience life in reference to three axes – in front–behind, above–below, side-to-side. We orientate ourselves (and our spatial thinking) in

Conflicting lines, planes and shapes can be brought into conversation, even song, with each other. Try not to see the picture but to imagine the experience of going up these stairs, turning, and passing into the room beyond. Now try to imagine it with every meeting right-angled, every corner unsoftened, every line dead straight.

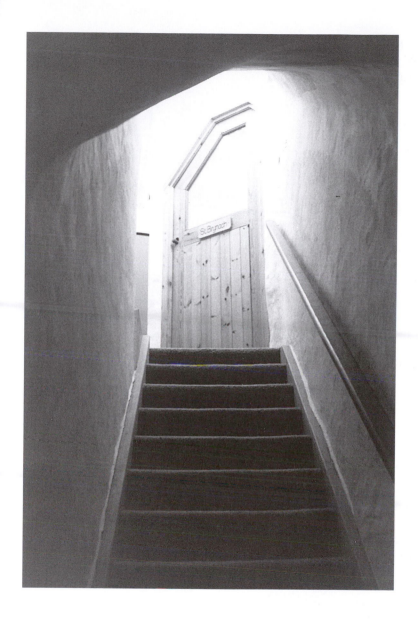

three great planes – forward, vertical and horizontal – the product of these axes. These axes have completely different characteristics: one is the axis of time (past and future), one of surroundings, and one of oneself, standing in tension between cosmos and earth. Horizontal and vertical couldn't be more opposite in structural principle. Dead-front to side couldn't be more opposite in terms of human movement in, or around, a building. When these planes meet at right angles, their different characteristics at the maximum, their meeting is without give-and-take or metamorphosis. It is forceful but dead.

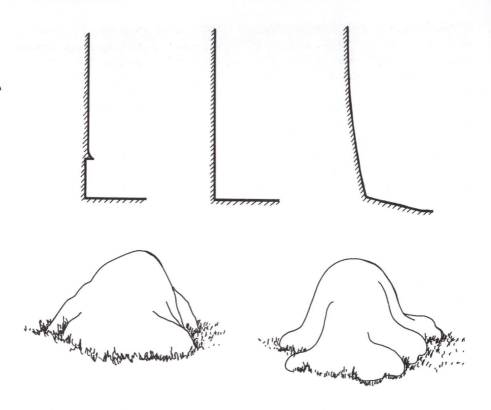

Traditionally the corners of stone buildings
have a two-angle flare. In the first 70 cm
(2 ft 6 in) of height, wall thickness reduces
perhaps 15–20 cm (6–8 in) then again
another 15 cm (6 in) reduction in the next
2–3 m (6–10 ft). Easy to describe but less
easy to do exactly right! It needs feeling
hands to create the quality of a rock
bursting through the ground rather than a
drooping lump of jelly.

Traditionally, buildings tended to be
rootingly anchored to the ground.

Another aspect of right angles is that, structurally, straight lines are lines of tension, tension between points. This therefore can give firmness to forms, but the line ends – the *points* – are strong. If line meets line at right angles, this point – the corner – becomes doubly strong.

While acute angles are uncomfortably compressing and obtuse angles invitingly embracing, right angles have stable balance. We can benefit from their organizing characteristics, but unless we bring life to this balance, its mechanical, lifeless qualities will dominate. Without softening textures or furnishings, rectangular rooms with rectangular doors and windows and hard smooth surfaces aren't places for living occupants, only for mechanical bodies. Such rooms can easily feel like boxes: uncomfortable, claustrophobic and life-suppressing.

Just as words are as suited to poetry as to the parade ground, meetings between planes can be *mediated*, bringing their different characteristics into poetic relationship. Textural softening or breaking up of the lines and planes helps. Converting old buildings, I'm often stuck with vertical walls, horizontal ceilings and rectangular rooms. Undulating plaster and exposed beams transform such rooms from boxes to attractive places.

How buildings meet the ground makes all the difference to whether they belong in this particular place or have merely been parked there.

There is a lot of difference between a straight line which suddenly swings into a curve and one in which the curve is implied in the straight and the firmness of the straight in the curve. If your eye journeys with the lines, the quality of one is of unrelated steps; the other weaves both past and future qualities and has a dynamic life in the straight, an organizing firmness in the curved.

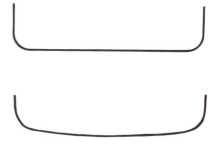

Classical architecture always grew from bases. Vernacular walls invariably widened at the foot, usually with a two-angle flare. Such walls are more solid, rooted in the earth, more timeless, quiet, reassuring and restful than those exactly vertical. Only in modern times have we become used to vertical walls rising straight out of the ground without base or interceding element. I don't use a uniform taper but increase or swell it at the base to obtain firm, strong forms, varying the angles and gesture to suit the circumstance. I also like to have a little of this quality internally. These buildings *belong* on the earth, whereas others which meet it vertically are only *parked* here.

Of all meetings, how a building meets the ground is perhaps the most important and yet the least commonly considered. A vertical, right-angled meeting (or worse, a concrete pillar) takes no account of any rooting meeting between ground and building. One or both needs to be shaped to the other.

The claustrophobically entrapping quality of a harsh meeting between ceiling and wall can be transformed into one of welcoming enclosure if the ceiling can rise a little. Shape matters even more in a building's 'eyes', those frames through which our view or we ourselves pass in and out – windows and doors. Even the slightest curve in the top of a window makes the frame softer; it's also a structural shape – in brickwork, an arch; in timber beams, where the stress-line passes from cantilever to span.

I use a similar approach to meetings of planes in plan – where rectangular meetings are unavoidable, corner furniture can intercede between two walls. Our ancestors did this all the time – corner cupboards between walls, skirting boards and mouldings at floor–wall and ceiling–wall junctions. To soften a harsh meeting often needs only very subtle treatment. Triangular corner blocks in the tops of rectangular windows only 1 cm × 3 cm (½ in × 1½ in) or a plastered edge finished by hand instead of straight-edge can make all the difference. Even the most subtle shape modification starts to imply a gesture. A horizontally proportioned corner block at the window head feels quite different from a vertical one. Similarly, should a ceiling arch only gently or reach down to the wall?

Three straight lines together can imply a curve – even more so if the corners are rounded and those lines are soft, perhaps even gently curved. The straight and the curved have markedly different effects. One gives firmness, orientation; the other life, fluidity.

An example of life-filled, life-enhancing curves is the movement of water in a mountain stream. Here all the lines and movements are alive, ever-changing – but not random. Water swings from side to side, accelerates, decelerates, rushes down, eddies upstream, slides and pulses; its swirls expand and contract in a breathing rhythm. This living complexity results from the interaction of forces – gravity, momentum and friction, also finer ones like thermal variation and lunar influence. In this way, it manifests the interweaving relationships between the different elements of water, air and earth. Likewise, the ever-changing pictures we see in the sky display different elemental combinations: air, water, warmth and condensation-nucleus particles. These are life-structured curves. There are also curves not generated by such enlivening conversations or formative forces. A squiggly line, although the product of human fingers, has no other inner formative principles.

All these curves have a certain dream-like characteristic: we can sit and watch a stream for hours. We can't watch squiggly lines for hours but, remote from any

How different would be this street and corridor if dead straight?

Unlike the curves of nature, a totally free line has no inner formative structure. (It's hard to draw one, however, as the movement limitations of shoulder, arm, wrist and fingers tend to control the curves, so impart an underlying 'living geometry'.)

practicality, they're good lines to doodle with. Free curves, in other words, are mood-enlivening and life-enhancing but can lull us into a dreamy state, forgetting the practicalities of the real world. In contrast, straight lines are 'businesslike'. Easy to understand, they help us think clearly. This makes them lines of organization, often of power. But they're life-sapping. A balanced, healthy human life lies somewhere between these two extremes.

Sometimes we need more firmness from our environment, sometimes more fluidity; sometimes more thought, sometimes more feeling; sometimes more organization, sometimes more life – but never one extreme entirely without the other. Not compartments all straight or all curved, but both sewn together. We need therefore to impart life to the firm geometric – especially rectilinear elements. We also need to give firmness to the non-straight – especially fluid forms. The former we can do by moderating the *meetings* and the *planes*, the latter by bringing structure-giving principles into otherwise amorphous forms, making forms, for instance, which are visibly bound by the principles of gravity or accelerating–decelerating curves. These have a strength and vigour which arcs of a circle don't.

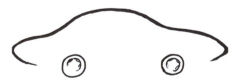

The environment provided for us is dominated by straight lines, whereas objects that we choose frequently utilize curves to enhance appeal.

Part of the charm of traditional places is that even though made up of rectangular elements, the lines are not dead straight.

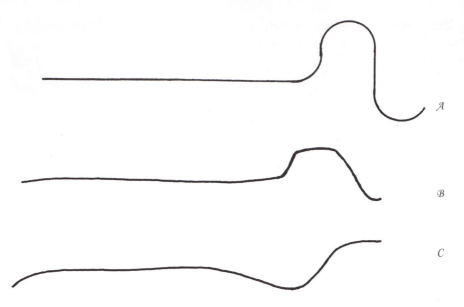

A

B

C

Both curves and straight lines are one-sided. They need each other, need to be able to weave their positive aspects together. Not just added to each other (A) but rather, the straight (firmness and organization) in the curved and the curved (life enhancement) in the straight (B and C).

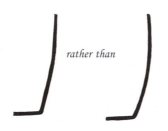

rather than

As a general rule, it's easier to make a firm curve out of straight lines, and a life-filled straight line out of curves (that is, curves drawn by the hand and arm which tend to radial movements).

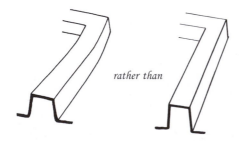

rather than

The balance between organizing principles and fluid life-forms isn't about just weighing one quality against another, but at every moment weaving these dynamic polarities into a single whole. A patchwork of dead and amorphous pieces, like alternate functionalist and organic buildings along a street, is no conversation.

Most buildings are predominantly rectangular. They're practical, and largely already *provided* for us. Most artifacts (and especially cars) that we *choose* amongst have curvilinear forms. This maximizes consumer appeal and increases scope for individual personality expression. The harder the one, the more reactively fluid-formed the other. This schism of practical and feeling, of sterile rectanguloids and persuasive curves, undermines the whole-ness of the human being. Like all polariza-tion this makes moderating harmony increasingly hard. As with all reactions we

Different planes and angles can be brought into relationships where they converse together as one single whole.

The simplest conversation between windows and ceiling shape is when they reflect each other's shape. We can go on to develop one as a metamorphosis of the other so that a single organizing principle gives a different form in every new situation or material, much as the forms of landscape, cloudscape and current patterns on water can be metamorphoses of each other. Different elements can start to sing together as in multi-part harmony.

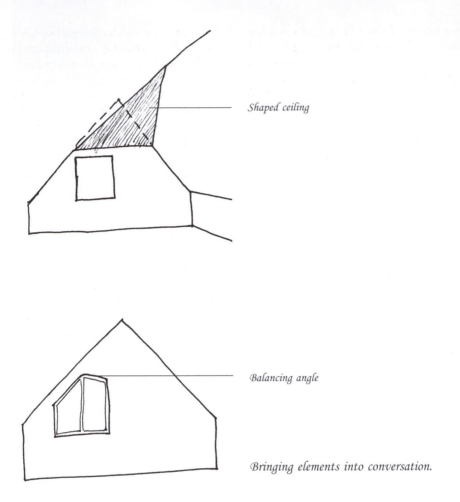

Shaped ceiling

Balancing angle

Bringing elements into conversation.

become less and less free, for our actions result not from our own conscious choosing but from whatever we're reacting against. The better we can meaningfully integrate the essence of the straight and the curved, the more we can support wholeness, freedom and health.

Conversation is the art of raising disparate elements into one whole, raising each above the level it was previously trapped in. This applies to every sort of architectural relationship: spaces, forms and all adjacent visible elements.

Also to those sequences of experience where form seen from outside metamorphoses into indoor space. It makes whole the relationship between user, architect and builder, raising it above individualistic narrowness.

To meet, elements often need their forms modified to respond to each other. A square window can look out of place against a sloping ceiling. One or other (or both) needs to acknowledge, respect and make shape concessions to the other. Similarly, the change of mood you experience moving from one space to another needs to be brought into meaningful relationship – the space needs to metamorphose to reflect and reinforce the mood metamorphosis. An arched corridor metamorphosing into a shaped-ceiling room does this. So does a doorway metamorphosing into room gesture.

This conversation principle can be brought into every form of meeting so that elements don't just collide with each other but *speak* to each other – indeed, so that they sing together.

Harmony in our surroundings is no mere luxury. Our surroundings are the framework which subtly confines, organizes and colours our daily lives. Harmonious surroundings provide a support for outer social and inner personal harmony. Harmony can be achieved by rules – but rules lack life. Or it can arise as an inevitable but life-filled consequence of listening conversation. So central is this inspiration to my approach to architecture that I couldn't imagine working without it. But, like all principles, this can manifest in many different ways. Even between the same group of people, different times and places trigger different conversations – even more so when the people are different. This one principle can give rise to many forms – not just the way I do it!

Reference

1 A term coined by Fiske and Maddi (1961) *Functions of Varied Experience*, quoted in: Rui Olds, A. (2001) *Child Care Design Guide*. McGraw-Hill.

Chapter 8

Space for living in

We have looked at how things meet, but what about the things themselves and the space between them? What about the effects of different shapes of forms and spaces?

If you make forms in clay, pour plaster over them and scrape out the clay, you get spaces exactly the same as the original forms. It is possible, therefore, to define space as 'negative form'. But the spaces don't have the same effect as the forms had. In fact, the experience of space is quite different from the experience of form. So what is form? What is space? What is the essence of their different characteristics?

If, in an empty landscape, there's an object – especially a man-made object – our eyes are drawn to it. Even something we would choose *not* to look at does this. Statistically, a factory chimney may be an infinitesimal part of our field of view, but its presence colours a vast landscape. In the same landscape, a mere hint of enclosure, especially where different elements – like earth and water or woodland and clearing – meet, makes an inviting place to sit and eat a sandwich. Objects have presence; space invites life.

'Form' is the property of objects. Objects are, in a way, beings. They may be dead in themselves but their presence radiates influence all around them, some more so than others, like a formica table in an otherwise homely room. 'Space' is the space in which things can happen, in which living things can be. Buildings are objects from the outside, space within. Their presence is made even stronger by what goes on within them. Sometimes their form, uniformity or lack of fenestration conceals what goes on inside. Big buildings like this are like lifeless giants.

All over the world the era of well-intentioned urban renewal created threatening, lifeless monsters standing in expansive seas of no-space. They haven't proved popular. Indeed, the idea that entirely new spaces, forms, scale, social and proximity arrangements and construction materials will automatically be appreciated is open to question. Up till the mid twentieth century, such things mostly evolved. Then, for 50 years, newness – even social experiment – was paramount.

Nowadays buildings are more varied in form, but there's still a tendency to think

The circle is the shape for meditative or social forms. To enliven the static geometry in this circular chapel, a subtle axis was introduced by this window grouping. The rock wasn't planned; it appeared during excavation. We considered dynamiting it, but would the violence of an explosion be the right spiritual foundation for a sacred use?

that interesting individual buildings improve the environment, that novelty will have enduring appeal. Architects think of buildings, look at buildings, react to buildings. For other people, however, buildings are part of the landscape; and parts of buildings – their façades – part of the townscape.

Things which happen inside and near buildings interest us; the buildings themselves merely set the mood. This is so even for great architecture. People didn't go to the medieval cathedrals to look at the architecture but to take part in religious sacraments. It's similar for the buildings of Renaissance or modern times.

Yet, to go to the opera in an unadorned prefabricated shed – however good the acoustics – would, to most people, be an inadequate experience. Architecture, in other words, *sets the mood*. It also provides space or boundaries to outdoor space in which things happen. It influences both the physical mechanics and the mood – the soul relationships. The mechanics of how we come into contact with people influence the quality of our relationships. However attractive the surroundings, cross-flow in a busy railway station aggravates travel stresses. In one restaurant project, my client wanted the sink facing the customers, so the washer-up was part of the community, not an excluded menial servant.

Shape affects relationships. A circular table can bring people who hardly know each other into group discussion, whereas a rectangular one with over six seats usually produces separate conversations. A circle has a single focus. You can build a brick dome by tying your bricklaying hand to a peg in the centre. When you sit with your back to the wall in a circular room, you're as bound to the centre as was the radial string which marked the room out. A circle is centre-focused, communal, egalitarian – a good shape for village community dance, consensus discussion, or a meditation chapel – but it's inflexible.

The Sioux Indians lived in circular family teepees arranged in a tribal circle, in a world which was conceived as a circle – a unity of spiritual forces. But the focus of the teepee – the fireplace – was not dead centre, nor is the plan of a teepee exactly circular. The circle of the world was intersected by a cross – the directions of the active beings of north, south, east and west. This set alive the circle's rigid geometry. Cross and circle make the archetypal mandala – also children's first drawings. When government soldiers rehoused the Indians, first in square forts, then in rectangular houses on reservations, they severed them from a spiritual relationship to the world around them, manifest in their built social forms, and destroyed the roots of their culture.[1]

If you walk around a square you experience abrupt and regular changes in direction. Orientated on polar axes, this is a good shape to reorientate yourself if you've lost your inner bearings. It's firm, balanced, but differentiated by the light. This is the shape for curative eurythmy rooms.[2] If unrelieved and too exact, square rooms risk the deadness of symmetry and repeated measurement. Flat ceilings turn them into boxes. Shaped ceilings set them into life.

From the purely functional point of view, right-angular forms have little reference to the forms, movements, mood-of-enclosure requirements and mobile thinking of the human being. This isn't to condemn the rectangle, but to try to experience its *being*. Of the many rectangles around us, few have been consciously chosen as the most appropriate shapes, forms and spaces; most are just to simplify design and adapt construction to industrially-processed materials and prefabricated systems.

Simple geometry emphasizes the effects of proportion. In a rectangular room proportions are obvious; not so in a cave. There's nothing inaccessibly mystical about proportion. The classical architectural proportions are found in the human body, in nature, mathematics and the physical wavelengths of music. It's not surprising that these proportions feel harmonious. They are, in a sense, 'natural'. If we think of a building as an outer body, it has a naturalness if organized in a similar harmonious manner to the human body. But what *is* proportion?

Proportions describe different states of

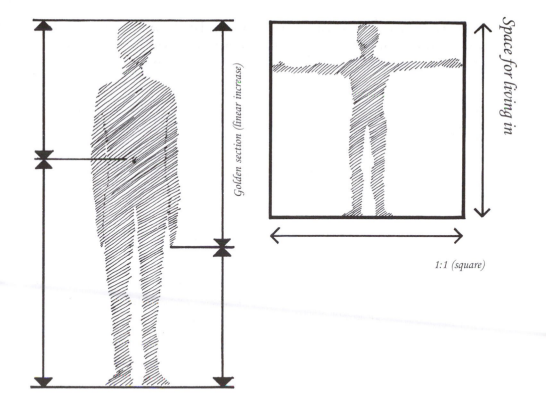

1:1 (square)

Space for living in

Some proportions are found in the human body as vertical dimensional relationships. Some are between standing height and reach. These proportions all, therefore, mean something.

being. At right angles to each other, they relate to different states of balance. Balance is something dynamically alive: it brings movement to rest, rather than freezing it. Proportions in sequence relate parts to whole or show progressive development.

Even without understanding their bodily origin, cosmic foundation or spiritual significance, different proportions have a different feel to them. With buildings made of rectilinear elements, it isn't difficult to work with proportion. Non-rectangular ones are. For these, we need to cultivate a *sense* of proportion, a sense we can use even when elements, like curves or sloping lines, can't be defined dimensionally or are unclear – as with windows, where, depending on the light, we sometimes read the size of the opening, sometimes only the glass size.

Some rooms are definitely too low – coziness exaggerated becomes oppression. Some are too high – unsettlingly vertical; some too broad – too open a view can make spaces too outward-oriented, unprotected, for their function. Everything has its right measure of size and proportion. If I shorten the handle of a spoon by 5 mm ([1/4] in), broaden a window by 5 cm (2 in), or raise eaves by 15 cm (6 in), the qualities change noticeably. If I concentrate on the soul moods a place needs, the proportional relationships suggest themselves. They are definitely right (or wrong) for the spiritual function: normally only afterwards do I check them mathematically.

Sacred architecture as the measure of God's kingdom on earth is an architecture of proportion. Its degraded form, given a different impetus by mechanical-geometric thinking and industrial component manufacture, is the rectangular architecture of today. While the legacy of cosmic architecture could have taken a variety of forms (as in Islamic designs), the main direction has been towards rectangularity. In view of the materialist shift of philosophy and everyday thought from the Romans on, this is no accident.

A rectangular grid can order the chaotic. With vertical dividers to shelves we can bring calm order to previously confused clutter. The divine order of ancient architecture required such an uncompromising geometry to give it earthly expression. The Romans, increasingly concerned with order in the material world, used rectilinear grid planning for this order-giving purpose. Government-organized colonization of North America likewise used rectangular grids to apportion administrative districts, private landholdings and, in due course, roads. Although arbitrary interaction of plan pattern with topography can be

Sometimes building plans convey the impression that the architect's concern was the storage of people.

From the outside also, buildings designed this way are, in many people's eyes, stacks of people-storage boxes.

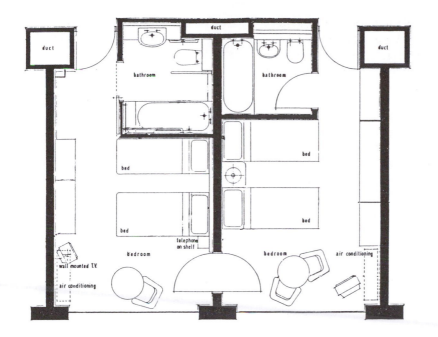

dramatic, such layouts have tended to foster similarly box-styled buildings set as regular blocks. Life-filled, stimulating, varied and harmonious forms are lacking. It is no coincidence that the USA (especially in the 1960s, the heyday of the rectangle) led the world in exotically curvilinear automobiles and hallucinatory drugs.

Throughout the 'developed', material possession-rich world, the predominant house form is rectangular. Thatching reed grows straight; so, theoretically, do trees – though rarely in practice. But old buildings weren't slaves to straightnesss or rectangle. The dominance of their precision has paralleled a growing mechanistic world conception. Indeed, throughout history it is countries with rectangle-based built environment that have led technological development – the applied science of the materially practical. Rectangular spaces may not be life enhancing but they are, after all, the best shapes to store objects in. Organic filing cabinets aren't very practical.

These days most rooms are rectangular with hard smooth finishes. Few even have the distraction of ornament or patterned surfaces, nor fireplace breasts, shelf recesses, diagonally-set doorways, bay windows and elaborate mouldings which the Victorians used to moderate their boxiness. Some rooms are indeed designed as boxes for storing people: you can read this thought in the designer's mind as you look at the plan or step into the room.

Such rooms are made occupiable by their furniture, house plants, decorative objects and other things to divert attention. You need quite a lot of things to achieve this. Minimally furnished, they're not calm, holy, sacred places but empty, sterile boxes. Some rooms have loaded shelves on every wall. Like shop windows, these displays give interest. Others need

plenty of nice – and usually expensive – things to make their barrenness welcoming. Many rooms and gardens need ornaments with no practical purpose other than to make them habitable.

It's not just that rectangular rooms are convenient to put things in; they *need* a lot of *things* to make them rooms we can live in. They are both product of and *fuel for* a materialist culture.

I must stress that it's not the *rectangle* which is the problem, but its *life-sapping characteristics*. Fortunately, materials, textures, colours, light, living line and human activity can reinvest such forms and spaces with life. Nonetheless, non-rectangular, or shape-moderated, spaces are much easier to make humane.

For all their sterile and materialist associations, rectangular buildings have been the mainstay of European architecture for a thousand years. They're materially practical and culturally normal. These used, however, to be imprecise in plan, and their forms greatly softened by roof shapes. In modern times, rectangles have become more geometrically pure and their surfaces and roof-lines harder. Most importantly, the spaces that rectangular buildings bounded were rarely exactly rectangular – and often further enlivened by sloping ground, subtle variations in buildings and asymmetrical trees and features. A typical town square was more likely to be squarish than square. The spaces – namely *the places where human life takes place* – were alive, not rigidly bound by a dead geometry.

Although straight lines – and other geometrical principles – underlie the forms found in living nature, living forms don't show them. Forms made up of straight lines meeting at right angles could not be more opposite to the forms of the natural world; they are solely man-made forms. Their use in ancient sacred architecture is a language of human

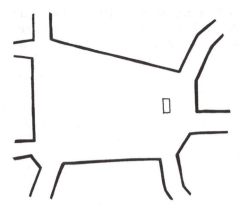

relationship not to outer surrounding nature, but to the cosmic world, the world of geometrical principles.

They're also lines of power. At Versailles all avenues radiate from the palace at the centre, the seat of 'Sun King' Louis XIV, so concentrating power, control and magnificence. Long, boring vistas appeal to dictators, right or left – Hitler, Mussolini, Stalin and Ceaucescu all built them. They're good for parades, neo-Roman symbols of fascist power and, for Napoleon, clear cannon shot to control the populace.

In due course straight-line forms became forms of status; a rich man's house or a craftsman's planed surface was set apart from a peasant's by precision and geometry. In our time, straight-line forms and computer-calculable geometry are the forms best suited to machine production. Without the elements of cosmic principle and careful craftsmanship, these are forms which lack life. Wholly organic forms which nature surrounds us with, on the other hand, lack any imprint of human consciousness. Life-filled forms for human environment must lie between these two extremes, as does the human state.

Before the era of consciously-designed town planning, a typical town 'square' was rarely geometrically square.

Places we live in and use are at least a step away from nature. Indeed, most buildings, even old ones with earth floors, are entered by a deliberate step. Steps don't suit wheelchairs. Thresholds, therefore, need other markers, like changes in flooring, light, acoustics and mood; also approach markers like paths, arches, gates and hollow-sounding bridges. Changes of level make so much difference to how one place is distinguished in mood and use from another. A large living-room with kitchen and bedrooms opening off it can be a traffic crossroads or a place of peace. As well as locating doorways so through-flow doesn't compromise places to stop, sit and *be* in, level changes, like steps *up* to light and elevated view and *down* to enclosure, make all the difference. Where the floor levels can't be stepped, differences in ceiling heights, lighting level and relationship to outside ground level are almost as effective.

How we enter spaces has a great bearing on our first impressions. Even rectangular spaces; non-rectangular ones, even more so. The pentagram is known variously as a holy space and the devil's form, depending upon which way up, or round, it is. I could never understand why until I tried to live into the experience of how we meet the shape. Enter in the middle of a side and we see an inviting-angled enclosure. Enter from one corner, and we're symmetrically confronted, trapped, our individual freedom crushed. Subtle perhaps? But if I wanted to make a fascist architectural experience, say for a courtroom, I would enhance the pentagram as shown below. Try to imagine it. The experience is so powerful, so unfree, that I wonder that it has not been used.

Geometric forms and spaces can be dangerous to play with. The great pyramids were forms of embalmment. At the focus not only were stray mice

Even a small window makes a closed door less excluding.

Stepped levels can keep a four-doored room an oasis of calm, not a crossroads.

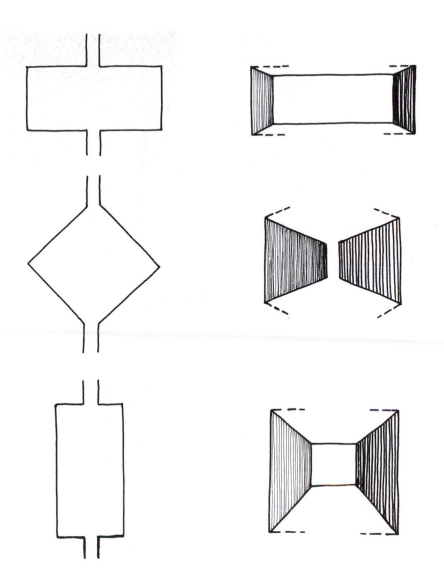

*How we enter a rectangular space has a
great bearing on our impression of it.*

The pentagram: holy space or devil's form?

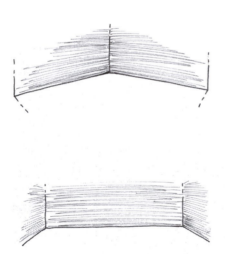

When we enter a pentagram from the middle of a side, the enclosure is inviting (top); from one corner, however, the rear wall confronts us.

The devil's pentagram can be developed into a powerful fascist space.

The power of geometry to oppress (KGB Training Academy, Moscow).

Welcome involves scale, materials, informality and, especially, gesture.

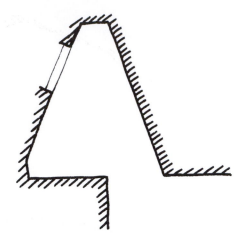

embalmed, but the Pharaoh could, as part of initiation, experience death. Pyramids also allegedly sharpen razor blades. Building them to 'recharge' yourself is strong stuff unless you know what you're doing!

The right angle and pentagram are about *corners*. What about the quality of these corners? A corner can be at any angle, any curve. It can be welcoming and enclosing or excluding, disquieting. Like arm gestures, open or pistol-pointing, the more generous the internal angle, the more inviting the corner, whereas narrow angles are uncomfortable and confining. Obtuse external corners are gentle to go round; acute ones arrow aggressively at us.

A very uncomfortable plan shape to be in can be made pleasant if the acute angles are blocked off to become obtuse. Now the room is a private enclosure, especially if we add an asymmetrically placed window.

Angles wider than the right angle are more welcoming. They tend, however, not to be very firm; as they bring little emphasis, they're difficult to bring into balance. If all the lines are the same length, things are a bit dull. If one is too long, the shape easily goes out of balance.

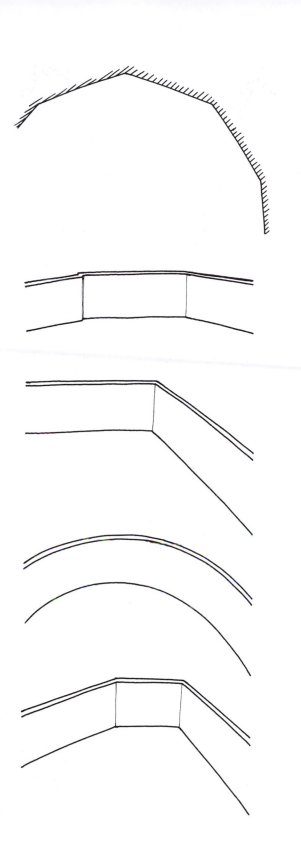

121

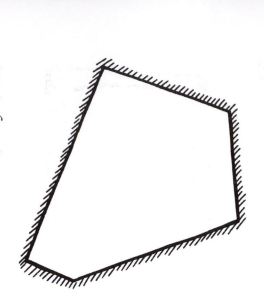

To give firmness, such spaces often need one or two right angles as 'anchors'. This is not a rule, just something I often do without thinking about it.

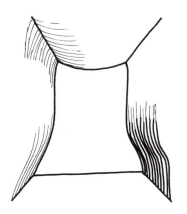

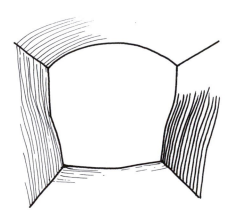

This is not a secure space. The ceiling weighs heavily – it sags. The walls droop. Not so bad in canvas perhaps – but terrible in concrete.

This, on the other hand, we experience as stable, enclosing, secure.

These are spaces in plan. We experience shapes quite differently in section. What we need here are walls which bear on the earth, ceilings which enclose. Moreover, different materials suggest different forms to achieve this: tents are naturally concave, but sagging concrete looks alarmingly near collapse.

Such shape gestures *imply* enclosing curves, yet only some are made up of curves. Others are made of straight lines, though preferably not 'dead straight'.

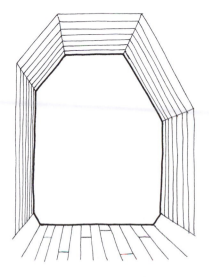

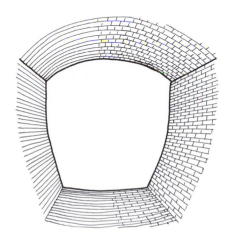

Two shapes for timber, one for brick.

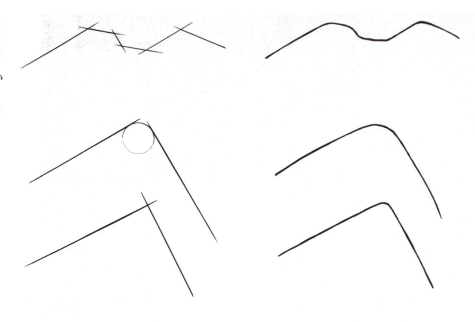

These lines emphasize the line and its straightness; the meeting is incidental. I was taught that architects should draw like this.

These lines feel the turn; the lines are only supportive to the qualitative key point. As you draw it you can feel the shape and how it turns with your whole body.

We think in terms of lines but we never actually *see* them. We see *edges* where one colour or tone meets another. Drawing by making lines around things is merely a code for what we see. Outlines blind our perception by replacing it with frozen concepts, yet architecture depends upon them. Design needs drawings and drawings need lines. Only the sort of sculptural forms that must be modelled can do without lines. Lines make architecture – but what sort of lines? Some are complete abstractions produced by the edge of a straight instrument, some are lines that enliven the boundary they describe. Whether an architect draws a line with feeling or disinterest, it'll still get built – built as drawn!

Even organically formed buildings find it almost impossible to avoid at least some more or less straight lines. Where appropriate for firmness, I choose them instead of curves. But I want life and gentleness in these lines. Colour, texture, shape modifi-

*Curves are both restful to the eye and
gently unobtrusive in natural surroundings.*

Sewage water has its life-bearing characteristics enhanced by flowing in rhythmically oscillating, three-dimensional curves. It progresses through a series of 'flowforms' and open, vegetated ponds. Conventionally, sewage's excessively one-sided biological load kills water. Here, movement-nurtured biological processes transform it into life-filled water.

cation, interceding elements, cut-off corners and elusively-formed surfaces can bring gentleness, harmony and life – the quality of curves – to the straight.

Whereas straight lines bring relationships of tension between clearly defined hard objects, curves sing. They bring life and freedom – the mountain stream is full of life, markedly cleansing itself from biological pollution in a few miles. So life-enhancing is the three-dimensionally curvilinear, rhythmically oscillating movement typical of natural water flow, that flowforms have been developed for river revitalization. Water flowing in straight lines in spillways, canals or drinking-water pipes has a reduced ability to

We can look at the Chinese tradition of Feng Shui as conversation between matter and cosmos: planetary qualities given earthly embodiment and in appropriate relationships to each other were considered to be health giving. Curvilinear lines bring where they come from, where they go to and what they pass through into receptive conversation with each other. Straight lines, with their insensitive, imposed and alien nature, obstruct and destroy this harmonious, life-giving force.

sustain life. In some reservoir outlet channels and smooth-bore pipes, so straight is the flow nothing can live.

Traditionally, in China, locations with harmonious combinations of qualities were identified as the well-spring of a health-giving force. This force was led across the landscape by systems of curvilinear lines both natural, like rivers, and man-made, like roads. Straight lines impede this flow of health, making some places unhealthy to live in. These were the sites to be sold cheaply to the Western colonialists.

Mobility of shape encourages inner mobility. Harsh, colliding, hard-edged rectangular forms, uninviting textures, unresponsive ground surfaces, conflicting sensory information and the like have a hardening, distorting, stultifying influence.

But if all the shapes around us are too soft, it's hard to remember our tasks in the world. Travellers' 'benders' are round sagging tents of willow twig and canvas. Wonderfully enclosing, womb-like places to *be* in, but not places to want to work or concentrate or *do* anything in. To orientate our lives, give daily life a framework, we need firmness (but not to be dominated by it) – enough strong lines or their strength in strong curves, organizing geometry or structural principles.

What do I mean by 'strong' curves? If you draw an arc of a circle, it has a constant quality. But an uncontrolled wiggly line has no form, other than that imprinted by your bodily movement. If, however, you breathe with this line – breathing out, breathing in, accelerating, decelerating – the curves have quite a different quality.

This is the basis of Celtic 'knot work' design – bringing breathing life into line. By controlling the visual 'breath' they could touch upon the same archetypal focus that the actual breath does in speech. For the sounds of speech aren't random;

An ellipse is anchored by an additive formula (a + b = c) to two points. To make one you need a bit of string with a nail at each end; keeping the string taut, move the pencil around the nails.

they're related both orally and physiologically to how we use our breath to create mood and meaning without words. In this sense, we can interpret Gothic architecture with its distinctively active curves as speech without words, as spirit-meaning written into architecture. This is only one aspect, of course. It took most of a lifetime of occult study to master these secrets in Gothic times. Nowadays we have lost all connection with that secret wisdom. To understand how shapes affect us, we must try to be conscious of what we actually *experience* in differently shaped spaces: which spaces welcome, exclude, are tense, relaxing, dominating, or allow us to feel ourselves free individuals.

We can also understand curves through mathematics and science. Like a circle, an ellipse is formed with a fixed length of string, but it has two foci. It is therefore a form which has both one-ness and two-ness in it. This makes a good

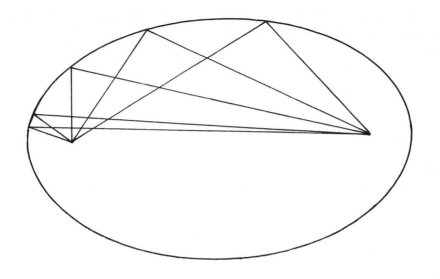

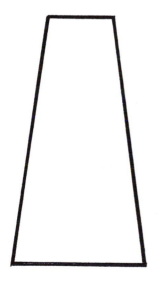

The hierarchy-stressing shape of the trapezium.

shape for a hierarchical room with democratic pretensions – conference tables are often this shape. If democracy isn't important, they can be trapezium shaped – both power-concentrating and practical: everyone can see and is focused towards the principal character. Auditoriums are often variations on this shape, in section as well as plan. These are shapes for hierarchical relationships. If we wish to be more egalitarian, for instance to turn a 'lecture' into a discussion, we pull our chairs into a circle.

Scientific observations throw another light upon straight lines and curves. 'Desire lines' – straight lines to destinations – are an abstraction. Animals walk in curves. So do people. We don't change direction in exact abrupt steps as does the computer screen, but all in the fluid process of walking.[3] Studies of moving fluids show that they always seek curvilinear forms. No river is straight unless confined by uncom-

The slower a river flows, the more
pronounced is its meandering form.

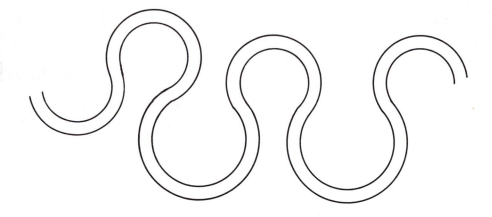

Meanders are not made up of regular
circles.

Arcs of circles without relationship to
other forms.

While curves often have a welcome softening, harmonious effect on buildings, alien added curves jar more than any straight lines.

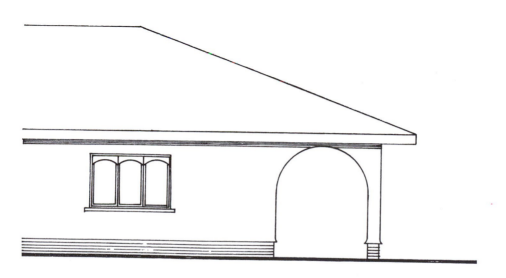

promising geology or canalization. The slower a river flows, the more pronounced its meandering form.

Meanders aren't made up of bits of circles, but a live relationship between that which is accelerating into curve and that which is decelerating into straightness and eventually into a curve the other way. Accelerating–decelerating curves are always therefore in a tension between straightness and curve. Segments of a circle are, by contrast, static.

From time to time builders ask me the radius of a particular window head curve. I never used to know. I just draw the shape that feels right to me. Now I realize that these curves aren't arcs of circles, but intuitive structural catenaries.[4] Curves are now back in fashion but many are arcs of circles without relationship to any other forms. Curves that *grow out of* the energy latent in the lines at either end belong there; curve and (almost) straight feed each other. Arcs nailed onto straight lines just fight them.

If you make (or even just trace your pencil over) an accelerating curve, you can feel the latent strength that this line accumulates. Once you've developed this feeling for *living* curves, you can imply curves and activate movement with just three or four flat planes of, say, plasterboard.

This is all about *spaces*, but forms can also have powerful effects. Not only in Moscow do rows of rectangular giants chillingly oppress the freedom of the individual. In the Soviet Union, as indeed all over the world, the intention was to give people homes. Khrushchev started a 'million homes' programme. Bureaucracies, however, tend to treat people as numerical statistics, but a short step from treating them as material objects. They readily assume – and create – a dependent relationship between individuals and accommodation-providing institutions.

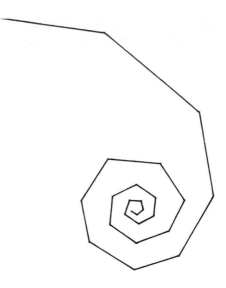

Accelerating curve built out of straight lines.

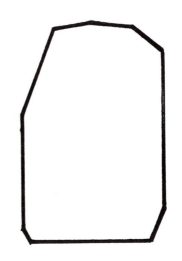

Curved enclosure made of straight-line material such as planes of plasterboard.

Repetition without metamorphosis.

The tower blocks that resulted were appropriate forms for such a philosophy. They were of course a quite unconscious choice of form – and because it was unconscious, the results were inevitable.

It isn't just the boxes, their huge size and the absence of distinction of individual homes that are oppressive, but also their repetition. An abstract idea can be repeated endlessly until it comes into relation with reality, then it has to be modified. In every seed there is, more or less, a pure plant, an archetype. As the plant grows, the individuality of its surroundings – soil, climate and so on – causes it to modify this archetype. If you look closely, two adjacent clumps of grass are different. Trees can be so different that we recognize them as individualities. Even development in time is a metamorphic process: young and mature and early and late leaves have different shapes.

When we build objects that don't evolve, we deny this life process and this response to surroundings. We impose dead ideas, often ideas which aren't even modified by materials (in the way that clouds often form the shape of a landscape, itself made up of a metamorphic series of forms).

Commonly, built forms are repeated. When you repeat things and the spaces between them, you start to make a rhythm. If neither the spaces nor the objects change, the rhythm becomes boring, dead but compelling. To leave the listener or observer free, both objects and spaces need to evolve, to respond to one another. This lets us participate in the rhythms of life: growth, decline, substantiation, enrichment, inversion and so on. Interwoven with the rhythmic metre of the body – heart and breath – this living evolution is one essential that distinguishes music as art from music as manipulator. Beat without metamorphosis, merely reflecting bodily rhythms, floods the soul with bodily desire emotions, overriding individual judgement. It is no empty coincidence that armies march to the drum.

Like strong colours, repetition leaves us unfree. It's hard not to give ourselves over to repetitive music. Rhythm brings the first transformative influence of life; metamorphosis carries it further.

If, without variation, we repeat a window shape, we take no account of its different relationship and functions outside or inside the building. The vertebrae of the spine each carry a slightly different load and accept a slightly different movement. They're not identical. Each window likewise has an individual set of requirements to fulfil – unless we're just providing containers for people, albeit elaborate ones. It may be ridiculous to make every window different just for the sake of being different, but it's even more ridiculous to make every one the same just for the sake of being the same, or to shape them just to impose an elevational pattern.

Repetition is the basis of rhythm. It can bring an anchoring structure, but organization by repetition is organization by the imposition of lifeless systems; think of an avenue with identically pruned trees. Organization by metamorphosis arises out of living processes; life brings the disparate into unity.

It's not difficult to design powerful forms – especially if they're large. What is difficult is to bring life to them, to make them inviting neighbours to live with. Dynamic shapes can be unsettling, especially two-dimensional simplification emphasized by rectangular plans. These are the product of *shape* rather than *form* consciousness.

If you make sculpture you can approach the form from the outside, imposing shape-sections upon it, or you can work like Giacometti, with the energy bursting from the centre out. You can also push things around so that one form changes into another. You can design buildings in these three ways: you can impose shapes from the outside creating three-dimensional shapes but never forms, or allow non-rectangular plans and sections (which describe spatial experience) to create non-rectangular forms. You can try out variations with a clay model, easy to push around.

As you can make anything in clay, buildable or unbuildable, it's often necessary to follow this up with a constructional model. There's also a risk of thinking about a project more in terms of forms than of spaces, so I like to keep both clay model and sectional room- and place-sketches going at the same time. By working from the inside out, even simple plans, simply roofed, can produce a variety of forms depending on where the ridge is, whether eaves or ridge are horizontal and roof pitch constant or not.

Even a simply roofed plan can give rise to a variety of forms.

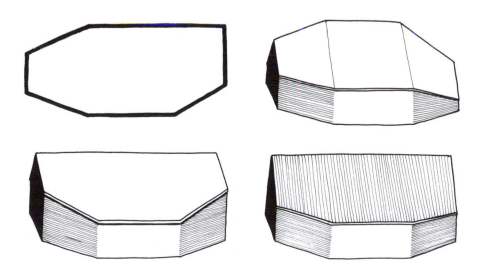

135

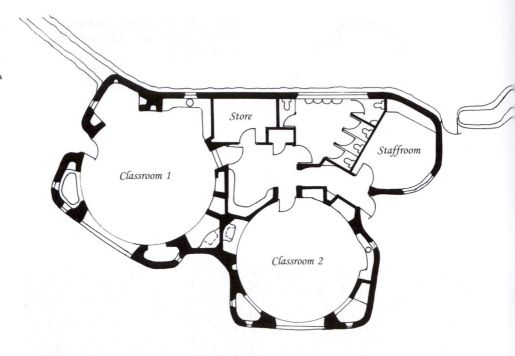

Plan of the Steiner kindergarten.

There's even more richness from simple geometry with conic sections. In a Steiner kindergarten, two cones rise off square(ish) plans, but the planar sides aren't at right angles, so are different sizes. Also, a simple roof unifies the two principal units, bringing them into conversation with one another.

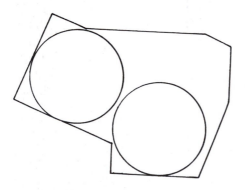

The kindergarten is made up of social (circular) and individual-play (corner) shapes on plan, making, in form, cones on square bases.

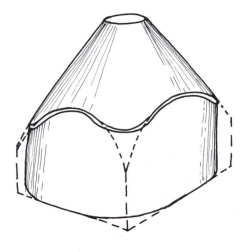

The interaction between cone and (rounded) square gives the roof eaves this undulating curve.

These curves can become gestures of entry and outlook.

The outsides of circular space – circular forms – are difficult to bring together to make places with; much harder than with straight-line forms.

Convex forms are more self-contained than simple rectanguloids. Being stronger as *objects*, they're harder to make into satisfactory *boundaries of space*. The most difficult objects of all are spheres. Spherical buildings around a space don't make it into a *place*. However personally freeing their interior spaces, egg-shaped 'living-pods' or geodesic domes clustered together can achieve no better than suburban spatial relationships – objects with leftover space between them.

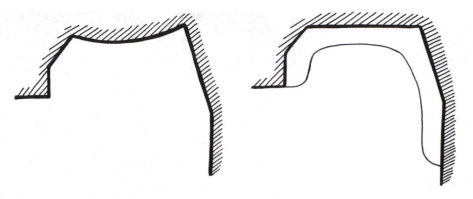

The same problem can occur inside buildings when backs of space-enclosing forms intrude upon other spaces. In this project the plan of the structural walls (left) needed to be transformed from a repelling to a welcoming gesture (right).

Non-rectangular forms are less harsh and oppressive than rectangular ones – just imagine the experience of walking around a right-angle-cornered building or one at 105°.

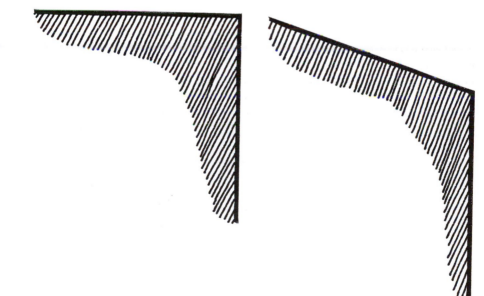

Indoors and out, non-rectangular, especially curved, spaces are life-enhancing, but concave rooms make convex buildings – poor place enclosers. Planar, especially rectangular, spaces enclose place better, but easily deaden rooms. The issue is not between rectangles and non-rectangles: why do something differently from the normal way unless there's good reason? It's between *living* and *lifeless* forms and spaces, life-renewing and life-sapping environments. Cutting off corners, non-rectangularizing or curvilinearizing shapes won't do more than make buildings look curious unless we work seriously with the question: what shape language is appropriate for human – and therefore spiritual – needs?

Notes and references

1 See, in particular: Nicholas Black Elk and John G. Neihardt (2003) *Black Elk Speaks*. University of Nebraska Press.

2 Eurythmy seeks to translate that which underlies music and speech into bodily movement. This can be strengthened in a space which makes visible the planes to which we unconsciously relate our experience of the world. Eurythmy can be developed in experiential or therapeutic directions or for artistic performance. Different emphases modify the basic requirement of a balanced, organizing, measured, upright space in one or other direction.

3 See studies by: Grillo, P. J. (1975) *Form, Function and Design*. Dover Publications.

4 Hang a chain from two points and the curve it makes aligns every link for tension. This is a catenary curve. Invert this curve and build it as a brick arch, and every brick is in compression.

Chapter 9

Design as a listening process: creating places with users and builders

We have considered space – how to make its proportions and qualities appropriate to use. The right spaces, however, are only a beginning. Unless we're architects, we don't pass from one space to another; we go from *place* to place. But how do places come into being?

Traditionally places grew slowly, each additional building, each reinforcement to, and evolution of, the sense of place meeting a need. First perhaps there was a ford across a river, a crossroads, perhaps a few houses, then a bridge was built. Then came the tavern, blacksmith, village square, a little way away a sawmill, more houses squeezed between hillside and river, then a fountain-trough for horses to drink, a chapel and so on. Different political, geographical, economic and cultural situations influenced growth patterns and sequences, producing widely varied village forms. Despite the unique individuality of every place, its physical form always grew out of *activities*, out of the meeting of users and environment.[1] The growth was organic.

It doesn't usually happen like that these days.

The process of design and building is now much more rapid. There's little room for evolution, little room to correct things even if they become obvious before buildings are finished. Buildings are shaped by their owners' needs – but these may have nothing to do with the place's needs. Buildings and the spaces between them often are little more than enclosers of quantitative space – so many cubic metres for this or that activity.

When someone engages a professional to undertake a project, a relationship of specialist and client is established. Normally the client states specific functional objectives and the specialist is free to find the most appropriate form to satisfy these. In architecture this freedom can be interpreted as the opportunity for individualistic expression. A relationship of delegation, where the architect's job is isolated from the project initiator, just to 'get on with it', encourages this designer-ego-trip approach.

I can't work this way: my work *depends absolutely* on my clients and users. I don't feel I have the right to assume they'll like my decisions, and even less right to indulge my own whims. After all, it is clients who will bear the huge expense of building, and users who will live, work or do things in them. For many smaller projects, clients and users are one and the same person. Their needs, however, are frequently obscured by rigid ideas about what they want built.

The process of designing a small project, like a one-family house, usually goes like this: the owner-users and I sit down together for a mutual design session that *I* know – though they don't usually believe me – will last five, possibly eight, hours. We have a lot of semi-transparent paper and a scale drawing of the site or building to be converted, and we've already walked around, discussed and observed possibilities and limitations on site. Invariably they know what they want. They want things they've seen elsewhere (usually in magazines) to be put together and that is my job. Is it? Are these frozen concepts what they need, even what they really *want*?

I try to open up the implications of what they ask for; identify the conflicting requirements, the priorities. We work towards the qualities they're looking for, qualities that had become frozen in their minds into objects, adjectives into nouns. Now, with these qualities, we get close to what they really want.

I describe this with words, but actually most of it is done with a pencil. All the time I'm trying to describe the *limitations* of every suggestion and its *possibilities*. The drawing process, therefore, alternates continually between plan laid over plan which show how things are arranged, sections which show the space in which we live, the views, light, etc. and sketches – mostly interiors of rooms or of external spaces, of how it will *appear*.

From time to time we need to chalk out spaces on the floor. Are they big enough? Too big? We measure familiar spaces, move furniture around to show the size rooms will be, and so on. If we're near the site we can put sticks in the ground to show where the buildings will be, what view there will be past or over them, how they enclose outdoor space, articulate pathways. In existing buildings, we can chalk window shapes on the walls, lay out planks for walls, or try to imagine the view through a wall that one day won't be there.

It's difficult to project the imagination beyond what we can see. There comes a time when we need the abstraction of paper to think beyond the confines of the present. Barriers to sight, particularly floors, don't let us see how buildings are organized. Only paper can tell us. We can also check things quickly: we may need to cut out shapes of special pieces of furniture – grandfather's table perhaps – will it fit? Will it go up the stairs?

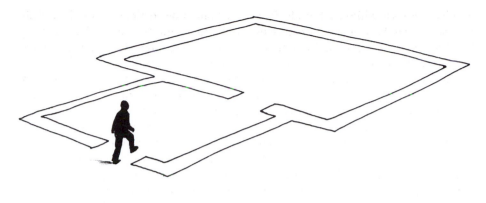

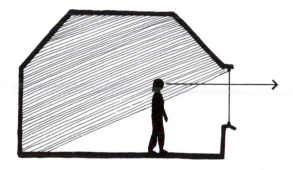

We experience plan, section and elevation differently. Plans tell us about relationships of one activity to another; sections tell us about the spatial quality, views from and light into that place; elevations we see when they confront us; normally they don't and we don't see them.

My own priorities in design are place, relationships and sequential experience. Walking the site, plans, sections, clay models (form), sketches (mood and sequence) and card models (space) are all involved in the design process. Elevations, my main concern as a student, are only the servant of the experience I wish to create.

We're now getting near to a mutually agreed design, but it's never too late to step to the side and try a *completely different* layout. With this technique, most projects develop several families of plan before we decide on just one.

At the end of this session we're all rather tired! But what we've done is to design something *together*. It isn't my design, nor is it anyone else's. Each of us has brought something individual, from our own unique biographical stream of development, but it has been *given* to the whole. The design has arisen out of the conversation *between* us. The result is much better than I could possibly have achieved on my own. That is why I say that I depend upon the client, and why I must be confident that we share fundamental, usually unspoken, values – even if outwardly they live a completely different style of life.

At the heart of the process is listening – one of the most difficult things in the world to do! For to listen you must put your thoughts and opinions aside and listen acutely to what the other person means but is perhaps unable to say properly – even if you don't like what you hear. *Listening* is the opposite of *argument*. Arguments polarize people's positions until they can't listen, but they don't produce anything. I have never convinced anybody (nor been converted) by an argument whether I won it or lost it. But out of listening, the right questions arise. Conversational design depends upon the right questions.

I find this an obvious way to go about design. In fact, I find design impossible without users to talk with. For this very reason, I just can't make any headway with competitions. In isolation I can't ask anyone questions, so have no way forward – only my own ego-trip ideas.

Conversational design is easy to practice in pairs. One person takes the user's part and answers straight from the heart. The other – 'the architect' – must hold back his or her own preferences and only offer 'what if ...?' or 'do you mean like this?' suggestions. The client speaks with words, the architect supports everything with sketches – the less words and more pencil the better. To make the sketches meaningful, you can measure the sizes of rooms and chalk them on the floor.

Conversational design is about finding appropriate qualities, adjectives (even if the user at first asks for objects, nouns), and – with imagination, sensitivity and experience – giving them possible forms. It is not about imaginatively thinking up qualities and combining them to make individual statements. That is how I work with owner-users who comprise only two or three people and buildings that are reasonably small. Larger groups of people require a more structured technique.

Larger projects usually will have lots of people working or living there. However much I think I know, it's only users who really know how buildings are used. Cooks know more about kitchens, and caretakers about maintenance, than administrators and designers. I'm therefore keen that anyone both involved and *committed* to the project takes part in design. Commitment means committing *time*. If they're too busy to co-design but only want to object to finished proposals, we'll maximize only the negative aspects of participation. I want the process to be positive, to be consensual.

Where two or three people can agree things, with four, however, it's twice as hard. With ten, a hundred times! There's also the problem that some people come to one meeting, agree something, and then other people at the next meeting want something different! How can, say, 30 reach consensus?

Buildings don't float around. Every one is built in a place – even if it destroys that place as it was. Environment involves the interaction of building and place. We may not be able to agree the sort of building we want, but we *can* agree what the place already here is like. So I start with the only thing beyond dispute: what's *physically* there. This we study together. Not what we feel about it, how we'd change it, why it's as it is, just the incontrovertible facts, visible to all. The self-discipline such objectivity requires is more exacting than it sounds.

We can't understand places – or people – however, without knowing them in a time context. They haven't always been as they now are. Their biography has shaped them. We therefore now study the place's biography. How was it last night, season, year, decade, generation, century – and beyond? But no place will *stay* as it is now. We now, therefore, extrapolate this stream of time into the future. How will it change next year, decade, generation, building lifespan, century? We also consider hypothetical interventions, like new drainage, gates, roads, buildings. How do these divert this current of change? This tells us much about what places can or can't accept.

Again, like people, places don't *mean* much to us until we *feel* something about them. We, therefore, still as a group, consider what moods the parts of a place have. What feelings do these sub-places induce in us? We can now make colour-mood 'mood maps' to supplement biography maps and physical description annotated maps. Through these three layers, a place begins to reveal its essence, its spirit-of-place. We are now ready to ask how, in human terms, the place would describe itself.

This is about what the place says – the subliminal message *everyone* responds to, though few are conscious of. And we, as a group, have reached this conscious recognition through consensus. This brings us

to the obvious question: 'What should the *project* say?' Whether thought about or not, this value-message lies at the heart of every project. If we can't agree this, nothing will ever get off the ground. We try, therefore, to encapsulate it in a few words.

What activities will take place? Each activity has a different mood 'colour'. This mood is further differentiated, so an exclusive cellar restaurant feels different from a fast-food bar or a Rembrandt-like library from one like a Mondrian. How would the 'colour' of the activity benefit from and contribute to this particular place? Orchestrated in one or another combination, these mood-colours enrich – or negate – spirit of places. Medieval towns had streets of shoemakers, saddlers, jewellers, cloth merchants, haymarkets. This isn't about zoning: a street you can walk through in a few minutes – a zone you must drive through.

To support this spirit-of-project, what moods should each activity-place have? From what we now know of the whole place, where would each mood – hence activity – feel at home? We can peg out 'mood boundaries' on the ground. These form the limits of mood-places. But the actual *form* of each place needs a gesture that will support the chosen mood. Because this gesture isn't about personal preferences, but is servant to mood, which in turn is servant to spirit-of-project, it's easy to agree.

We peg and string this gesture on the ground, then record it on a scaled plan. We now lay room- (or building-)scaled bits of paper over this gesture. These are rectangular, but the gesture probably isn't. When we trace this layout, gesture has paramouncy; the rooms therefore lose their rigidity. This brings us to a rough plan.

Next, we take clay rectanguloids, scaled to room volumes, and lay these on

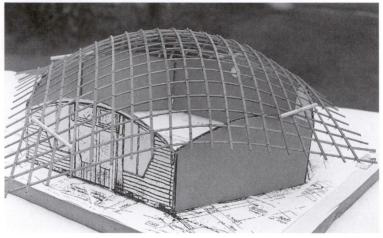

With clay, the form of buildings and their larger external spaces can be rapidly developed and continually altered. Though the clay model is unlikely to be precise, it's adequate to measure drawings off. These must then be adapted for dimensional, constructional and other requirements.

A working card model simulates the constructional limitations of carpentry. You can make any sort of curved surface in clay, but in cardboard you must make rafters and other shaping pieces just as though you were really building the form.

All models, however, have the limitation that, being frequently viewed from above, it's hard to remember that in reality we won't experience form and space as a whole; also, minor elements like climber-overgrown trellis fences which hardly show on models will block view and enclose space. Then there can be seasonal barriers – a few bare twigs in winter but a wall of leaf in summer. Similarly, volume and speed of traffic can turn a dimensionally inconsequential open space into a major division and focus attention on whichever side of this invisible barrier we happen to be.

Using the consensus design process enables even large buildings to fit comfortably in sensitive sites.

a tracing of this plan. Again, rectangu-loids don't fit non-rectangular gestures, so need squidging into forms that speak to each other, speak with a language quality that serves the moods needed and agreed. Clay models are invaluable as they're easily reshaped to explore how alterna-tives look. Card models, however, are inflexible and tend to fix our thoughts. The time for them is later when we need to see structure or interior space.

From the clay model we can draw more meaningful plans and sections and integrate organizing diagrams, such as daylight or ventilation sections. With the form so substantially in front of us, we need to ask what materials suit form, gesture and mood. Also how different sub-places and buildings relate to each other. Should you see one from the other? How should paths and roads lead and flow? What barriers, invitations and pivot points should there be? What passage-ways, portals, steps, turns and changes of textures to articulate space?

If projects are phased, we must now take 'buildings' away and go through the process in the probable construction sequence. Does the project grow properly? If it never completes its final phase, will everything still feel 'right'?

When we're just modifying existing buildings, the process is the same in principle, but differs in some details. Instead of biography, we concentrate on how *we* meet the place in time – the sequence of experiences we encounter and how they breathe and flow. When designing, we therefore ask: 'What sequence and flow of movement would support the moods that support spirit-of-project?'

By listening to the needs of a place, the new (here: additional buildings) can feel like it has always belonged there.

All this we do by consensus. While not problem free, it's much easier than it might sound – and quicker! I've done this about 50 times, mostly over the course of a weekend. Fundamental to this process is listening to the meeting of the idea, the 'colour' it will give a project and the place already there: listening to the spirit-of-project coming into being, that invisible ideal which is so much more than the sum of its individual components and functional requirements. It's possible to cultivate this listening ability by looking at places and thinking: what activity – and therefore what qualities of building or landscaping – would add to them, help them grow, become something even better than they are now?

By approaching places like this we're no longer thinking of them as opportunities to impose great ideas, but of developing what's *already there*. In the same way

that we convert existing buildings, this is about converting *places*.

Sooner or later these buildings we've designed actually get built. Now what were previously thoughts recorded on flat paper, or – at best – seen from above and outside as models, become actual spaces. As they grow to completion, all sorts of things begin to show up.

What previously we could only imperfectly imagine we can now see! Users can start to see the ways they'll use their rooms – and also our mistakes! We can now see lots of things we could previously only guess at: views past and sunlight through trees may only require selective pruning. These just can't be anticipated or even identified on paper. Nor until we stand in the half-built building can we see the views from new floor levels or the ways walls, ceiling planes, doors and other architectural elements meet. To

Hand construction allows builders to become artistically involved in their work. It allows on-the-spot design so that, as here, the ceiling shape can metamorphose from one situation to another in a way that paper design can, at best, freeze into a lifeless diagram. If labour costs can be

freed from conventional time = money formulae by more creativity-enhancing contractual arrangements, the costs need not be penal. This school (left), built by volunteers and therefore with free labour, cost approximately a seventh of estimated contract price.[2]

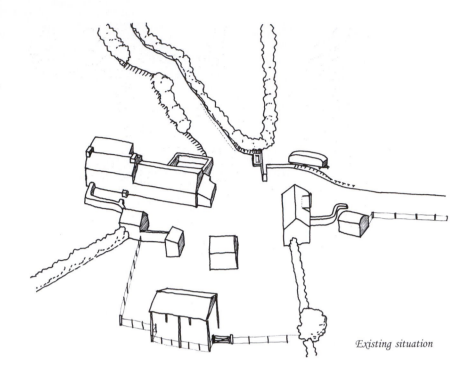

Existing situation

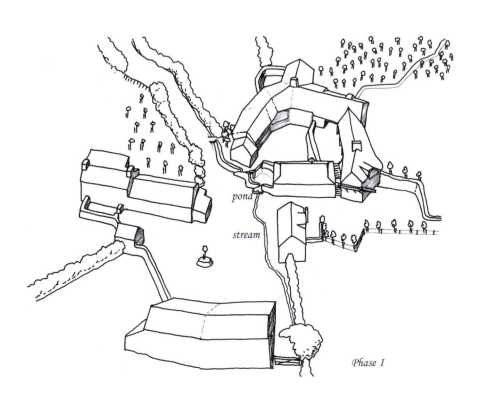

pond

stream

Phase I

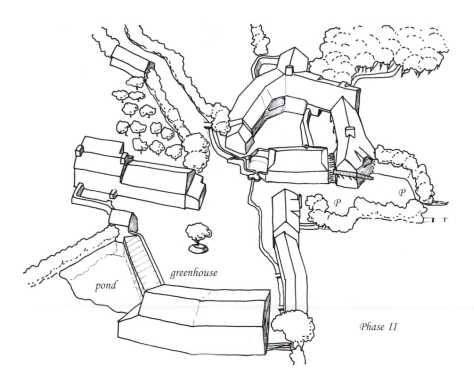

pond

greenhouse

Phase II

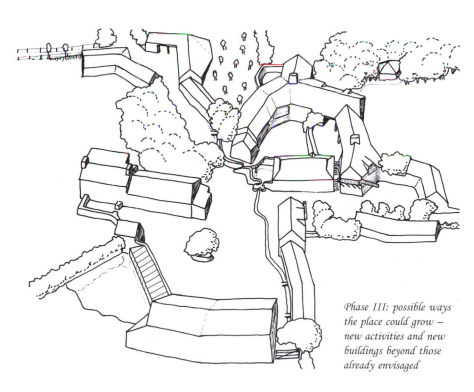

*Phase III: possible ways
the place could grow –
new activities and new
buildings beyond those
already envisaged*

bring these meetings into conversation we can try out different shapes by nailing up battens. This way of listening to how places want to develop is something easy to practice. When I pass half-built projects, I can question how these forms, spaces and meetings of elements now emerging ask to be developed.

As building progresses we can actually experience entry and movement sequences, the ways views are focused, sunlight penetration at particular times of day and year, and many other things we had no way of visualizing before. We have the opportunity to emphasize or moderate these experiences.

Once we think of the creation of places as a process, it is obvious that for places to develop in a healthy way, every stage needs not only to be healthy but to add something beneficial to whatever has gone before. While the purpose of architecture is to fulfil and harmonize people's and places' needs, this is a *process*. It doesn't stop with design. Building construction, then occupancy and use, further develop this process. Each stage builds on the one before and opens itself to the one after.

Architecture is about bringing place and project, background context and the life of future users into relationship. If it can weave together what has come before – the environmental context – and what *will* come – the users – and through the process of designing and making raise the ingredients artistically, it can find in a *new, conscious* and *relevant* way the organic process on which the evolution of places depends.

Notes and references

1 There were also planned villages and towns, but prior to the industrial revolution, these were very rare.
2 More details about how this was built, the potentials and problems of gift work are given in: Day, C. (1990) *Building with Heart*. Green Books, Devon; and Day, C. (1998) *A Haven for Childhood*. Starborn Books, Dyfed.

Pages 154–5
Helping a place come into being: at every stage, the place needs to be both complete – have a quality of belonging, of eternity – and also allow opportunities for future growth. The present, grown out of the past, needs to be both complete in itself and open to the future. I have designed too many buildings shut to the future; now, more concerned with place and the life within it, I try not to, for living, growing places are founded on the meeting between activities, users and environment. This is a farm course centre for city children and others with special needs.

Chapter 10

Ensouling buildings

Stand in front of, or go into, a new building and it usually feels empty, a spiritless shell. It waits for someone to come along and give it love, coziness, individuality, to put curtains in the windows, flowers on the balcony, life in the rooms. And so it should! Until that happens, however, many buildings are lifeless. They offer nothing other than spatial constraints and architectural qualities, like proportions, materials, colour and light, to build upon. Such buildings haven't yet started the process of being ensouled.

By what process do buildings acquire soul?

Soul can incarnate progressively into a building with each step from wish, through idea, planning, constructional design and building to occupation. Each stage develops, deepens and extends that which had come before. These stages don't alternate from artistic to practical but, with these aspects inseparable throughout, make a continuous process of incarnation into substance until architects complete their task, leaving a shell for the life which will further grow its soul.

It's conspicuous that buildings designed and built without care, or whose tenancy and management structure encourage tenant dependency on faceless or exploitive owners, rapidly deteriorate into slums. A generation ago, slums used to mean buildings with physical deficiencies. Today's slums are buildings from which care is absent.

Old buildings are rarely just museums of a particular historical period. They have physical elements from many dates right up to the present; also the imprint – both visibly and invisibly – of the many occupants, lifestyles and values that inhabited them. When this has been a harmonious progression, the new built upon the past, old buildings have charm and appeal – one reason they're so popular. Where new brutally rips out old, trampling it without respect, both new and old are compromised: inefficient, unloved and un-enriched by time.

This also applies to townscapes and landscapes: everything new that we build will be set in a place *that already exists,* a place formed by a long historical process. What we call *sites* are already *places*, places

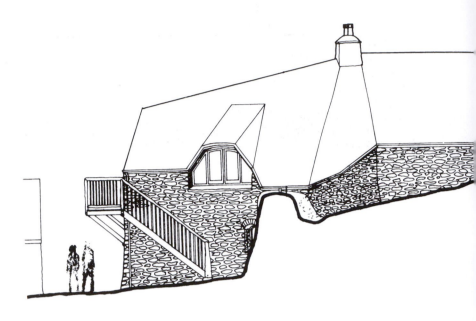

to which their histories have given soul and spirit.

The soul of a place is that intangible feeling – made up of so many things – that it conveys: sleepy, quiet lanes and pine tree scent, or vibrant activity, bright lights and hurrying people. Upon this composite of sensory experiences, reinforced by historical associations ('under this clock is where couples always met, even my grandparents', 'here the great ships were built', etc.), we begin to feel that there's something special about this place, unique, living and evolving, but enduring beyond minor change. It is a being in itself – the spirit of the place. Every place has a spirit – though not always benign.

Children know every corner of the little piece of land they play on. It gives them happiness and health forces they'll carry into later life. To the small child it's a whole world, every part a spirit-rich individuality and large in area. Revisit it as an adult and it seems tiny. Revisit it as

a site manager and 'here we can stack the concrete units, here the reinforcing steel; we need only to level the site first'. Nowadays so much land is *used*, so little *appreciated*.

Large projects – urban redevelopment, housing estates, motorway junctions, oil terminals, airports – how many places with a special, unique, valuable and health-giving spirit do they obliterate? Subtler things like through traffic and brutally unresponsive buildings can also destroy places and their long-embedded spirit. Whenever we build something new we have a responsibility to this spirit of place. A responsibility to *add* to it. To the Ancient Greeks the sense of place-spirit was so strong that in some they could say 'here lives the god'. This being they enclosed and strengthened with a temple.

Today our buildings serve different functions – inside and outside ones. *Inside*, they house *ideas*, like clinic, shop or home. *Outside* they bound, articulate, focus or alter an external space, adding to or

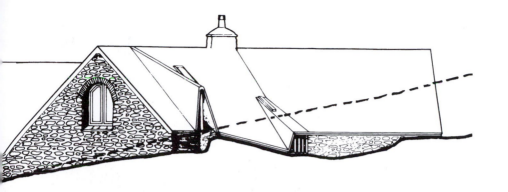

detracting from what is already there, the spirit of place. Many outside spaces serve both functions – an 'idea' function (like a meditation garden, private courtyard or car park) and a 'response to place' function.

Because the inside space, activities and qualities of a building and the outside surfaces and appearance are interrelated, the whole building and all the activities it generates need to be involved in this great conversation. The conversation between idea, usage and place, between what will be and what already was; between physical substance – the materialization of the idea – and invisible spirit-of-place – the spirit emanated by the place's physical substance. This is a fundamental responsibility in any architectural action. I've described techniques by which spirit-of-project can condense into material buildings. This lets place and project symbiotically reinforce each other. Through this process, soul moods suggest physical form and materials. Buildings subjugate to landscape, for instance, may

need to minimize their scale, so have eaves below eye-level, be tucked into landform and extend hedgerow lines. Townscape issues include finding the right visible-activity intensity while minimizing shading, noise or other consequences impacting neighbours.

The spirit buildings emanate colour the *activities* within and around them – activities which may well have greater impact on their surroundings than buildings themselves! Construction materials influence what buildings say. On the whole, we don't look at these. We breathe them in. Architecture provides an atmosphere, not a pictorial scene. Look at a photograph of somewhere attractive and you'll notice how much of it is ground surface. Our field of vision usually includes more ground than sky. Our feet walk on it. Its materials are *at least as important* as those of the walls.

Traditionally materials found in the surroundings were raised artistically to become buildings. Today we're free to

Existing features, like roads and hedgerows, not only tie a building into a place; they can suggest, even ask, that it be there.

use anything. But to fit, the materials need to feel right for the place. When you study place (as described in Chapter 9) the right materials become obvious – stone or wood, earth or brick, glass or vine-cloak either fit or clash. Some buildings need to blend, others to assert themselves a little more, others again be more urban, contemporary, extrovert in character – though never without respect for context or they'll be *anti*-social, *anti*-community.

Every building needs forms and shapes – outlines – roof and eaves lines which relate to (not necessarily copy, perhaps contrast with) its surroundings. These, combined with plan shape, create appropriate gestures: of welcome, privacy, activity, repose and so on. These in turn

are part of the experience of approach and entry. Roads, paths, boundaries – from walls and fences to permeable woodland edge – and topographic features, like the junction of sloping and level land, tie buildings into landscape.

The 'keyline' system of erosion control and irrigation is generated from the 'key' contour where steep meets flattening slope.[1] Though developed for dry climates, the principles of water interception make it equally relevant to flood control, showing (in combination with soil permeability) the most effective places for swales, seasonal ponds and water-absorbing woodland and pasture. This isn't just pragmatic landscape design – its authenticity has aesthetic implications. Such sensitivity to landscape-

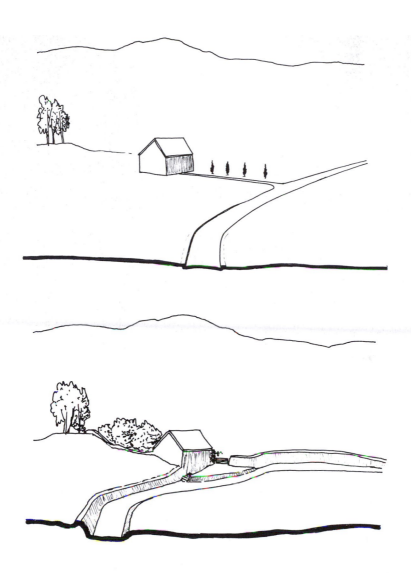

quality 'meetings' also helps find 'at home' places for buildings.

I notice that, quite unconsciously, I often locate buildings on the edge of a site where there's something out of which they can grow – a wall perhaps, or meeting point of different qualities of place. Also, instead of just bits of leftover space around buildings, this leaves more open space to do something attractive with. In built-up areas where open space and sunlight are at a premium, buildings placed to dominate the site are spatially – and in this commercial world, monetarily – an extravagance rarely affordable. Buildings sited to give priority to the place they bound make better environmental and economic sense.

Approaching a building, there comes a moment when you become aware of the influence of its *activities*. This is a threshold – the place for a gate, bridge, steps or archway, either built, formed of trees meeting overhead or implied by buildings compressing and focusing space.

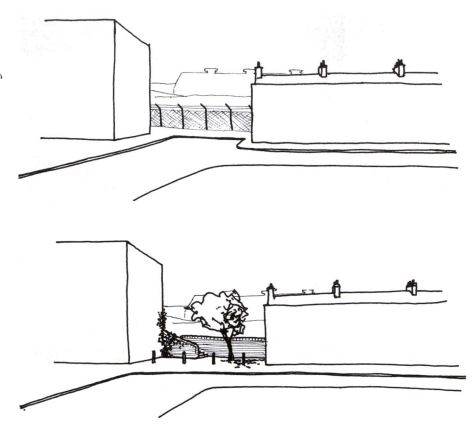

Other ways to emphasize this threshold include turning paths around building corners, groups of trees or land-slope, a change in ground surface such as from long to mown grass or gravel to brick paving, or in acoustic texture as with plank bridges or echo-confining walls.

For something new to improve, not compromise a place, artistic quality is vital. Art starts when inspiration struggles with the constraints of matter. When the painter paints, any pre-formed idea has to give way to what is developing on the canvas; matter and spirit become interwoven into a single whole. The idea on its own existed outside the sphere of earthly reality or life – the painting process gives it reality and life.

This process applies as much in architecture as in any other art. First someone perceives a need; then (conventionally) comes the idea – how to satisfy this need; then an architectural concept; then a building plan, constructional design. (In the system I use, design condenses without any pre-fixed ideas – but both processes involve increasing materialization.) Now comes a period of building longer and more energy and money demanding than all previous stages; then use – even longer and with daily building–occupant interaction.

Even in a small country like Britain, much land is wasted. Too many
forgotten spaces: behind the garden shed, the other side of the factory
fence, behind the dustbins. Some are miniature wildlife havens but most
are just places of squalor. Children need such hidden places, but not the
ugliness, the excreta of society. Turning our backs on things, pretending
they don't exist, is quite the opposite from not interfering with places.
Britain can justly be proud of its tradition of backs to houses: many
countries have fronts all round. But a house back is the front to more
private and less conformist activities. It is the lifeless backs that I
lament – so much land in despair that could be home to life.

Conventionally, artistic design stops at or only a little beyond the design stage. But most of the work is still to come. If any product is to be artistic, the people who make it must be involved in the artistic process. Of course, few builders have gone through the long aesthetic-sensitivity development architects have, but there are other ways to look at it.

It's often said: 'What is wrong with this region is that there's no overall planning!' We live daily in localized experience, all influenced by a regional structure. Our local world is the victim or beneficiary of mega-decisions: after Regional Planning comes District Planning (we begin to *see* the consequences here) – then architecture. Then the textures, loving craftsmanship (or otherwise) with which things are built, then furnished and maintained. Then homemaking – both at home and at work – perhaps the most important stage of all, as it is this that makes places welcoming and our lives a pleasure. Leaving this out undoes all the good built up so far.

Generations of care and life give old buildings their charm; lack of it turns them rapidly into slums. Architectural qualities have but a small part to play in their spirit, as I'm reminded every time I see a holiday home, attractive but empty. Yet it's everything that has gone before that influences whether places will be loved and cared for, or resented and abused. Only for about a century has this whole process been compartmentalized, restricting aesthetics to the architectural stage. Yet great ideas badly, carelessly, lovelessly built are awful to live in! Many qualities depend upon *how* they are made.

Many of the finer qualities of a space – the complexity of meeting forms and planes, metamorphosis of one shape, form, space into another, effects of natural and artificial light – can only be

The attitude, artistic and care-filled or otherwise, with which a building is built makes all the difference to the end-product.

Much more than the architecture, it is the materials and play of light upon them that make the atmosphere of this place.

approximately and inadequately anticipated. They must be made.

Dead-straight lines are so *dead*. To give
them life they need to be not wobbly,
random or weak but made with a feeling
hand. Made. This is the sphere where *only*
the building workers can make or break a
building. When you make things with
your own hands the same form doesn't
satisfactorily convert to different materials. It feels different, needs a different
structure and form.

Making and building things is the
stage at which idea meets material. They
can either compromise each other or,
through their fusion, reach a higher level.
Sculpture in the mind is pointless.
Without art, stone fresh from the quarry
is little more than a pile of broken rock. It
is, however, a *little* more than just a pile
because each material already has
something in it waiting to find an appropriate place and form. Not every stone
has Michelangelo's David in it, but every
stone has a quality of 'stoneness'. The
violence of the quarry leaves it with sharp
split surfaces, but the quality of enduring
rock can be refound.

All materials have individual qualities.
Wood is warm, redolent of life even though
the tree is long felled; brick still has, to
touch and eye, some of the warmth of the
brick kiln; steel is hard, cold, bearing the
impress of the hard, powerful industrial
machines that rolled or pressed it; plastic
has something of the alien molecular
technology of which it's made, standing
outside the realm of life and, like reinforced
concrete, bound by no visible structural
rules. It is out of these qualities that materials speak. It's hard to make a cold-feeling
room out of unpainted wood, or a warm,
soft, approachable one of concrete.

Beyond individual personal preferences, we respond to the history and
'being' of materials printed into their
appearance. Our feelings aren't random

*Ground texture and vegetation are often
the most expendable items of an
architectural budget. Yet they can be the
most economical and effective elements in
making a place.*

The structural integrity of this gridshell ceiling/roof gives it authenticity and firmness without compromising gentleness and grace.

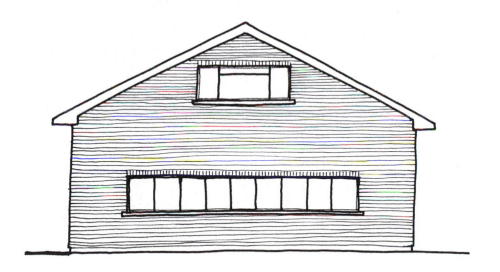

Timber allows long horizontal openings to appear quite natural; not so masonry, where vertical openings make better structural sense.

171

but relate to how appropriate this 'being' is to our needs of soul. They also are closely interwoven with the effects that each material has on the body. Materials are the raw ingredients of art. But they themselves affect our emotions. Mediocre architecture of non-oppressive scale is really quite pleasant in timber or a well-chosen brick but a disaster in concrete or fibre-cement panel.

Biologically and emotionally metal, reinforced concrete and plastic aren't good materials to live within, but wood is – very much so. Nowadays we rarely picture wood as the curving branches and forks chosen by the shipwrights and cruck-house builders but as machine-extruded strips. These lend themselves well to planes but poorly to curves – the opposite of brick, where curves can give such strength you can't push over a tall narrow wall. In brick, curved walls look – and are – strong. Not in wood. In wood, I usually make curved gestures out of straight lines. Three-facet arches and polygonal spaces suit its softer, more approachable surface and give firm forms. Curves can look silly faceted from planks – they have no strength. But curves of firmness, of structural meaning – as in planked boats – look wonderful. If you steam or shape wood into curves by hand, the limitations of tools and materials give this strength. Jig- or band-saws give freedom to make any shape, but unless you've first learnt with hand tools won't make strong curves.

Wood allows longer horizontal runs of windows without any visual loss of structural strength. Sometimes, even, the windows *are* the structure. Wood is for life above the ground. It needs a masonry base to root it in the earth – a heavy inward-leaning base, preferably part-covered with vegetation. The linear characteristics of wood can be exaggerated or softened by colour and tone – white (and yellow and orange) fascias and corner boards most emphasize shape-enclosing lines. Low pigment stains and, particularly, unstained natural weathering soften the effects of shape. Even very square buildings blend gently into landscape when weathered grey: though not always the best thing for wood it's such a life-filled grey, quite unlike grey paint!

It's natural to feel at home with 'natural' materials. Humanity has grown up with them; their source is life. By 'natural' I mean of course modified nature. The tree is sawn and planed, earth baked into bricks and tiles, but there's still a strong link between finished appearance (and sometimes feel and smell) and natural origins.

Natural materials are 'natural' for a human environment. They help to give us roots. The need for roots has led to revivals of past architectural styles. But, however skilfully recreated, revivalist forms built in modern materials – concrete, glass-reinforced plastic, imitation stone, wood laminates – look as fake and hollow as they sound when you tap them.

One aspect of traditional building materials is that they're all bound by the scale of the human body: bricks are sized to be laid by hand, prefabricated panels by crane. Compared to ordinary concrete paving slabs (not my favourite material), concrete pavements cast *in situ*, sectioned only by expansion joints, are a huge step away from human scale. A large, simple roof can be at least acceptable, if not attractive, in subtly variegated tiling but dominating and place-sterilizing in uniform asphalt. Swiss farmhouse roofs[2] are huge but don't look it; metal warehouses do.

Anthropometric measurements like the imperial system, and even more so the ell,[3] imprint bodily measurements into

Ageing is a process by which forms and materials are modified by the forces they're exposed to. Impact and frost damage hard edges; ground movement and compression under load soften geometric purity; photochemical reactions bleach colours; water saturation encourages mould, moss, even tree growth. We can pretend ageing will never happen – or accommodate it, letting the passage of time mellow, rather than tarnish, our surroundings.

173

Congruence of structural and aesthetic requirements is typical of vernacular architecture. The necessary is inseparable from the attractive.

buildings. Our main concern, however, is how many body heights something is, how much above eye-level, how many paces away, how much within or beyond our reach. Small measurements in relation to eye-level are critical to views and privacy. A few inches difference in wall height profoundly alters our spatial experience.

When we design things on paper we tend to consider dimensions arithmetically: 2.2 metres is a mere 10 per cent longer than 2 metres. In life, however, we experience them anthropometrically. A standard door opening is around 2 metres high. Ten per cent higher, it's almost at (common) ceiling level; we hardly notice passing under it. Ten per cent lower and – at least psychologically – we need to duck under it. These few centimetres, hardly noticeable on drawings, make all the difference. Arching the opening so it's high enough to pass through but feels lower achieves both safety and threshold

Buildings of comparable volume can have markedly different perceived sizes: walls confront the observer and imply used space within much more than do roofs. Furthermore, perspective effects can reduce the apparent height of roof ridges.

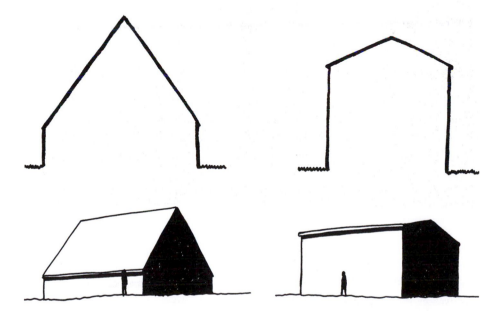

experience. Similarly, an inch more or less on the rise of a step makes a dramatic difference to the experience of going up or down stairs.

We also experience objects anthropometrically. We can experience a sugar cube within the hand, and something larger within our arm encompass, but something just a bit bigger that we need to walk round to understand, we experience quite differently. Even the smallest buildings like bus shelters are in this scale, but when designing it's hard not to draw, model, experience and think of buildings as immediately comprehensible objects.

How big a building appears in the landscape is affected both by the proportion of roof to wall and by the time of year. Walls confront us whereas roofs slide away and also have perspective reduction. The gesture of a steep roof can tie a building down to the ground whereas a shallow one with deep eaves (and hence shadow) can frame and emphasize a wall.

In towns, views are often so hemmed in that, unless looking *along* streets, we're not aware of the upper parts of buildings. Other factors like textural scale, distance between events and comparative sizes of building units, vegetation and visible sky affect perceived scale. Parapet skylines tend to increase apparent size and therefore 'urban-ness'; visible (hence fairly steeply-pitched) roofs do the reverse. To reduce *apparent* density, pitched roofs are effective; for city centre stimulation, they're less appropriate.

Seasonal growth or snow banks can make a striking difference to the apparent scale of things. The low doorways and eaves of traditional buildings were lower than some annual plants. In some three weeks of early summer or one night of snowfall, such buildings could change from focal points to the barely visible. Human life also, in its relation to the

Snow banks can make a striking difference to the apparent scale of things.

The apparent size of a building appears to vary with the seasons. Annual plants can grow to human height in barely a month; leaf transforms a branched stick to a heavily laden tree able to completely conceal something dominatingly large in the bare winter. Snow can also change the scale and focus of things.

forces of nature, used to be subject to the same dramatic swings. Nowadays we've evened out these experiences; enlarging buildings, raising eaves, cultivating low gardens – often only mown grass – and fixing regular patterns of work regardless of season.

Nowadays many people seek to find roots in tradition, in tracing their family histories. The life-renewing rhythms of nature root us in time and place. But how many urban children even know that grass can flower? Every half month has a definably different quality to the preceding and following ones. Almost every week of the year is distinct, yet in many places you can only experience seasons. When I lived in London the months had no individuality – they were just summer and winter.

It is the progression of nature's rhythms in one place that is so rooting, centring, stabilizing. Travelling to find seasons – especially out of season, like winter holidays on Tunisian beaches or summer skiing in Northern Scandinavia – is like buying vegetables out of season, and as crazily driven by economic reasons. Farmers and market gardeners try to produce food out of season when prices are higher. Moreover, food often reaches the kitchen hardly recognizable as anything that ever grew in the land – and neither is the tourist hotel in a fishing village or ski resort on summer pasture. Farms where city children can experience where food comes from, what happens at what time of year, how it's done, how they can do it, help redress this – help re-root them in life. When designing these, I've always concentrated on consciousness-awakening experiences like doors opening to focused views and under-roof journeys instead of indoor passages.

Places give roots to people, anchors so necessary today when codes of behaviour, established institutions, ways of looking at the world are increasingly called into question. Personal identity, marriage stability, job security – all seem so much less certain than they did to our parents.

For buildings to benefit places, their first responsibility must be to nurture – or heal – their spirit. This spirit nurtures us. The interiors of buildings create inner places. Each room has a spirit. It starts with the architecture and develops through usage.

In the dark we can go into two rooms in a strange house – one a bathroom, one a bedroom. We know instantly which is which; we can hear the acoustic difference. The architectural differences start with the senses. But there can also be rooms with similar spatial characteristics – say two identical prefabricated buildings in an army camp: a chapel and a lecture room – one a place for peace, one for war instruction. A difference in spirit begins to be noticeable. When a building has been used for generations – a church or torture chamber, for instance – this feeling is stronger. The place becomes imprinted by a spirit. However much it becomes a chrome and plastic city, who can visit Hiroshima without remembering?

As places develop soul atmosphere to support a spirit of place, so too do rooms within one building: this room, or even part of a room, for instance, is a hearth, the warm social heart of a *home*, not just the centre of a house. Other rooms are haunted by past traumas. Working on a school converted from a mental hospital, I found children would rush past the former electrotherapy room, never dawdle there.

Nowadays space is expensive to build. We design therefore in time and space; some rooms are multi-used. We think of time–space management. Indeed, sometimes I tell my clients that what they need is not more space but a different timetable. Most built spaces are empty more than they're in use, but we need to think first about the spirit of these places before making any decisions about multi-use.

If we work sensitively with light, texture and space, even mundane rooms can be ensouled, can become welcoming, supportive places. They won't need to be personalized and enlivened by adding objects, decorations, possessions. If we don't work consciously with these soul qualities we can hope to provide no better than the everyday norm: architecture that needs things to humanize it, so encouraging the tendency to acquisitive materialism.

Some of these 'spirits of place' are resilient, allowing places to be used for many purposes. Others are more fragile. A cross-country cycle race doesn't do much harm to woodland and farmland, but to a wild, empty, lonely mountain it leaves a long echo of use; not appreciation, but exploitation! Even amongst people who won't admit to anything spiritual in our surroundings, many recognize that gambling machines feel wrong in a meditation centre, even when it's not in use. Similarly, the protective tranquillity of a kindergarten is threatened when used for excitable evening debates about economic survival. In the morning, children pick up the disharmony echoes.

Architecturally, what can we do to help nurture this spirit of place? Externally, it's a matter of conversation between what already *is* and what we bring afresh with a *new idea* – an idea inspired out of the future, inspired from beyond the physical earth. Internally, room occupants are confined by fixed physical restraints – walls, floor, ceiling. We need to bring in something enlivening, changing, renewing, something with a cosmic rather than just a human-usage rhythm; and that, of course, is natural light.

We tend to think of architecture as substance, but this substance is just the lifeless mineral vessel. Light is the life-giving element. Both in quality and quantity it's absolutely central to our well-being. Light affects all aspects of mind and body, but, just as warmth is related to activity and will (as you notice if trying to work in an overheated room), so light's effects are most pronounced upon our feelings. So much so that we often describe light in terms also used for moods, like 'gloomy' or 'gentle', 'harsh' or 'warm'.

Though inadequate light causes depression, we mustn't just think of light as a matter of physical quantity but as a life-bearing principle. We can enhance this life by how we texture, shape and colour the substance that frames and receives the light, for we can't see light itself, only its meeting with substance. Some quite attractive materials drink up light so even bright windows can't dispel gloom. Misplaced or shallow-set windows can lack tonal transition; harsh geometry and gloss reflection tend in the same direction.

Light gives life to a room. There can be too much – window walled classrooms used to be the fashion – or too little. Rooms without natural light – worst of all, classrooms with no windows at all[4] – can have very disturbing effects upon physical, mental and social health. Laboratory rats in these circumstances attack each other or damage themselves. Some observers notice similar behaviour in those windowless schools. Daylightless living (like night-shift work) is also linked to increased cancer risk.[5]

The window area needed for particular lighting levels varies with orientation, climate and surrounding vegetation, buildings and topography, as well as room design and window placing. The amount of light we need likewise varies according to where we are in the world. City dwellers need more, so do those in northern latitudes or under predominantly grey skies, while further south, slatted shutters are used to darken rooms, creating quiet, cool sanctuaries from the outdoor heat. In Holland, windows are often big but, with lots of shrubs and trees right outside them, rooms are gently lit.

Sunlight through vegetation gives gentle colour and modulation to the light in a room.

Candlelight gives life to a dark room which, poorly lit by an equivalently weak electric bulb, would be depressingly gloomy. So do sunbeams reflected off whitewashed walls. To give life to a room it's much more a matter of quality than quantity. The human spirit needs this life-filled light. The soul needs it. Even the body needs it for physical health.

Sky light from different directions and sunlight at different times of day have different qualities which breathe into our states of being throughout each day. Quantitatively, west light may be the same as east. In quality they're distinctly different. The light of the seasons awakens us physically in summer. In winter its withdrawal awakens us to more inner activity.

Religious buildings – temples, cathedrals, stone circles – were built to correspond with chosen points in these great cosmic rhythms. Even today, we orientate windows for spring sunrise or low-angle winter sunbeams. We can also work with reflection. Water-reflected light at midsummer noon brings soul delight. Reflection needs care, however; from snow it can warm solar collectors or lighten dark rooms, but the light is cold and there can be dazzle and glare problems. Mirrors can increase light, but confuse us with deceptive space. Fun to play with perhaps, but being deceived doesn't help inner security.

All surfaces reflect light, which brings up issues of material and substance. The right materials make a building. In the days of black and white, if I photographed an attractive village street the photograph would often show mediocre architecture. The colour, light effects of sunlight and materials, not to mention its unphotographable sensory richness, *made* the place.

Materials and light are two completely opposite poles – but they belong together. Thick walls with sunbeams through deep windows, dark rocks in luminously still water, trees fringed with light against the sun: these joy the heart. They are unphotographable because they are alive. Light and matter is the greatest of architectural polarities – the polarity of cosmos and substance, one bringing enlivening, renewing rhythms, the other stable, enduring, rooted in place and time. This polarity is the foundation of health-giving architecture, for the oneness of stability, balance and renewal underlies health.

The ancient druids worked with this polarity with rock and sun, for in the tension between them health-giving life arises. I also try to work with it in a qualitative way. Rather than thinking my way, it's sensitivity to qualities that has led me in this direction – I started just by having a *feeling* for these things. I've therefore made a lot of mistakes, but the process I've gone through is an important prerequisite for spirit-of-place nurturing design.

It starts with asking what a place should say, then developing a feeling for the appropriate mood, then building a strong soul of a place with materials and sensory experiences. It starts with the feelings; architecture built up out of adjectives – architecture for the soul.

Notes and references

1 This system, developed by P. A. Yeomans for Australian climatic conditions, has been widely and successfully used to reclaim and improve dry land prone to infrequent but destructively heavy rain.
2 Bernese farmhouses in particular. In other areas, they're smaller.
3 Ell: fingertip to elbow measurement. Particularly useful when laying stonework as a quick guide to the size of stones needed to complete a course.
4 This was thought to increase concen-tration. It became a movement in the 1960s. Later, it was promoted for energy conservation. Later again, people realized what social, psycho-logical, developmental and physical harm it did to children.
5 Electric light, lacking the full spectrum of daylight, decreases melatonin production, increasing cancer risk. Paper at the American Association for Advancement of Science, Denver, 14 Februrary 2003; reported on BBC Radio 4 *Today* programme, 15 Februrary 2003.

Chapter 11

Building as a health-giving process

Many people regard building as just something that happens, nothing to do with health. In any case, health of what? How can its *process* be unhealthy?

Building work is predominantly one-sided. It involves little more than intellect from managers (and all too often, architects) and physical strength and manual skills from workers. Not surprisingly, buildings built like this are sterile.

The whole process is one by which ideas are materialized, often too fast and too far: too fast because ideas often become concrete and inflexible before they've met and conversed with the requirements of surroundings and people – hence, however architecturally 'good', are imposed on them. Too far because decisions become dominated by monetary considerations. So do relationships – indeed, conventional building–industry relationships are governed by the principle of gain. The natural tendency to try to get the best out of any situation, to get as much out of anything as possible, leads to exploitive relationships. Nobody likes being exploited; nor does anyone ultimately gain.

It's a human need to be meaningful, whole and nourished. To be meaningful involves giving benefit to others – *giving*; taking can't make us meaningful! Giving is not the same as imposing, taking not the same as receiving. One is a selfless outward gesture, the other egotistical. In land- and townscape, as in human society, a nourishing gift gives meaning to a place or a person whereas exploitive taking denies it.

Yet neither what we give nor what we experience through our work can be healthy unless we can effectively involve our whole being. Healthy work engages mind and heart as well as the hands. Also, for the ultimate users of our product this has repercussions.

The extent that builders understand and care about what they're building shows up in the performance, quality and feeling of the end-product. It's often said: 'You can't get good workmanship these days ...' But should we expect good workmanship when we offer nothing to inspire and nourish workers? Volunteer and self-build building provides opportunities more or less denied under the contract system for work to engage mind and heart as well as hands. Elsewhere,

clients can rarely afford an artistic input, and when they do this is provided by specialists. The contractor makes profit by using tradesmen[1] who know what to do so well that they don't need to think. Their feelings have nothing to do with the job.

To be whole the aspects of one's being must work together; intellect and physical actions be brought into harmonious relationship by artistic and moral feelings. Balance and harmony is vital to health – whether in individuals, society or ecosystems.

Harmony can't occur when polarities clash. Just like unrelieved planes meeting at right angles without mediation, there can be no harmony when fully-formed inflexible ideas are imposed onto places, disregarding their evolution from past through present. Just as harshly-meeting architectural planes or building and surroundings can be brought into conversation with each other, so can architectural intentions with the ideas, sensitivities and skills of the building workers. Both internally and externally, roof and window shapes need to speak to each other. Internally, ceiling shaping, view focus, light and all the rest of the room need to join in this conversation. Externally, a whole range of elements, shapes and spaces will be involved. Naturally, I try to design this sort of thing well before building starts, but I can't see everything on paper. I consistently find that the fine-tuning can only be done on the spot, at full scale, involving the people who are working there, using the building as its own constantly evolving model.

The fixed idea imposed as object: the individuality of place, the users and the stream of time through past to future are of no concern to such a building.

Every building situation is unique. The building's relationship to its surroundings is unique; its users, even if we don't personally know them, are individuals. If designers live up to their responsibilities, they must listen to the unique requirements of each individual environment, each particular set of users. If not, we've seen enough mass housing repetitively and brutally imposed! Once we listen like this, it's quite clear that no two sites, no two users are the same. They may share similar characteristics, but they're not *the same*. No one design can fit in different surroundings; only in one can it be appropriate. While we can look to historical precedents or places we like to inform us and broaden our experience, we can't merely repeat them.

Every client, occupant, user, even those not yet born, is an individual, a human person, not a feelingless statistic to be packaged. They need their own places as houses for the soul, not as boxes for the body.

An important characteristic of models is that they can be adapted. We can see how something looks this or another way. It's quicker and easier when design models are small, but there's much we can't experience. Models show form, not space. We experience them from outside, not from within – as objects, not volumes within which to live. Only at full scale do so many things become apparent. There's no undue difficulty in modifying design as you go along. Prior to paper-based design, this was normal. Within structural, constructional and legal limits, it always feels to me the natural way to go about it: the problem is to find opportunities to be able to.

The historical development of building into the contract process has been one by which designs become frozen. Everything has to be defined by the contract documents, and these are confined to what can be described on paper or screen – namely, shape and words. Not space, not sensory experience.

In the conventional building process, time costs money. Flexibility takes time and, by making rigid pricing difficult, adds financial risks. So everything has to be fixed and put on paper – and, as a matter of course, we accept the disadvantages.

There are other forms of contract. A lot of small builders will only work on a time plus materials basis. If honest, it's fairer all round than a fixed price; builders need neither take risks nor cover unknowns by the 'double-it' rule. (For example, non-standard door: double the price. Hang and fit: double again. Total price: 400 per cent. *Actual* costs are 150 per cent labour on door; no more on anything else.)

Time plus materials contracts depend upon trust, honesty and flexible budget limits. There are, however, no monetary incentives to tighten management efficiency, shop around for materials or subcontract to more competitive specialists. On the other hand, achievement-related bonuses put quality of work at risk. Piece-work and quotas are virtually synonymous with shoddiness.

Between these contractual extremes, I've developed a pricing system whereby the unknown costs of quality work needn't bring disaster to client, contractor or workers. What I call target pricing is calculated on a time plus materials basis:

Estimated time @ rate per hour = target price

If work takes more or less time than estimated, the rate can be decreased or increased up to a mutually agreed margin, although, if work is quicker than expected, actual price may not exceed target price nor be less than target price if slower. This restricts undue profit or loss to a level mutually agreed beforehand.

This system is only a start and, being dependent on honesty and accurate records, isn't problem-free. Contractual systems aren't very exciting to get involved with but they do have a signifi-cant influence on working relationships and the quality of the end-product. There is a real need for innovative forms of contract to release creativity and work as an (albeit paid) gift from their present day straightjacket.

All contractual systems, however, to some extent deter workers from involving themselves artistically. But there *is* another way. If time isn't given monetary cost, it can be used to allow the design to evolve on site, to develop potentials that only become apparent at full size – indeed, in every way to improve quality, visible and invisible. If inspired by beauty, self-built buildings have this opportunity – one client of mine described his work as 'building sculpture to live in'. Where motives are pecuniary, however, the opportunity doesn't exist for, in that world, 'time is money'!

This opportunity is enhanced in voluntary projects as time spent is money saved, and time spent can be used artisti-cally. A group of which I was part bought a building, derelict for 20 years, to convert to a Steiner school.[2] After purchase, we had only some £36 to finance major repairs and alterations,

---

Target pricing examples

Estimate: 100 hours @ £5/hour = target price £500
            margin: £1/hour

Actual job:

A.   140 hours @ (£5 − £1 =) £4/hour = £560

B.   105 hours @ (£5 − £1 =) £4/hour = £420
                          or £500 = £500

C.   85 hours @ (£5 + £1 =) £6/hour = £510
                          or £500 = £500

D.   75 hours @ (£5 + £1 =) £6/hour = £450

without which it was totally unusable. We had only two options: start work on those jobs that were 95 per cent labour or give up the whole project.

We started work, initially two of us, and through working opened the door to donations and help from people we had never even met. Without the gift of work the school couldn't have come into being. An unexpected result was that financial stringency fuelled artistic work.

In this project the flavour of the brief was established by the qualitative and economic requirements. As with the education, the building environment should nourish the children. The architecture shouldn't force them into a mould but give the possibility to move, live, imagine in their own child-worlds and to receive attention as individuals. The building should therefore show individual attention throughout, all woven together to create a harmonious, gentle environment. This then required individual attention from the builders. It isn't possible to design for individuals without individual attention. Imposed standard details have no place in such a building.

But what does 'individual' mean? If made by a discerning hand, no two door handles will be the same. Similar, perhaps, but not the same. Nor will two doors. Each is the result of the conversation between wall shape and opening, between one space and another, meeting at a portal, a punctuation point to our movement and progressive experiences, an open or closed eye – a door.

The economic requirements were more straightforward: build at minimum cost! This inevitably meant voluntary work. Labour therefore was free, allowing us to incorporate much labour-intensive handwork, to give every element its own individual attention, to take time to bring it into conversation (even song) with other elements. Interpreted in this way,

Once we recognize that every situation is unique and once builders work not as mechanical executors of other's orders but as artistic individuals, even every door handle will be subtly different from each other.

the economic requirements thus supported the fulfilment of the aesthetic requirements.

Working in this manner has profound implications for the people involved in the process as well as for the building. It soon became obvious that gift work is sustained by inspired will. It's vital, therefore, that this inspiration is nourished or soon there'll be no volunteers! While gift work is commonly seen as a one-way process of giving, it actually required the work situation to give *to* the volunteer, and the organizers have the special responsibility to arrange the work to enable this.

As foreman of volunteer building projects, I learnt to present even small jobs so that their part in the performance of the whole can be seen and so that workers can understand why they're doing something in a particular way. I explained, for instance, *why* as well as *how* intricacies of damp-proof, thermal or acoustic detailing are so important, why some jobs must be done in a specific order and so on. It's important that each day is marked by visible achievement – this often requires organizing work on a teamwork basis so that everyone, regardless of skill or strength, can contribute and at the day's end clearly see something achieved. Blocklaying, for instance, can absorb seven people: one carting, one cutting blocks, two mixing mortar, one laying it on the wall, another placing blocks, and someone setting out ties and checking plumb.

Perhaps most important, however, is cultivating artistic involvement. *Cultivation* because the seeds already lie within each of us. Building is essentially an artistic process on a large scale with more parallel functions than painting a picture or modelling a sculpture. It is out of our artistic attunement that *how* to do something – plaster a wall, for instance –

emerges. A plaster surface can be dead, limp, without strength, or as life-filled and harmonious as the firm forms of landscape. I can describe how to do it in words but only the experience of actually *doing* it can make it live inside yourself, enlivening the artistic sense.

This perhaps is the greatest gift to the volunteers, that they develop in themselves, in addition to manual skills and meaning in work, a sense that *any* work can be artistic.

The benefits for the building itself are no less significant. Fundamentally, gift work is the reversal of the normal contractual approach. Normally, inspiration (the idea, the client's and the architect's vision) becomes progressively more and more materially defined (drawings, specification, bill of quantities) until it's solely a monetary description – the contract. The contractor seeks a profit, the workforce a wage; the project is coloured by the principle of monetary gain, yet it started as inspiration. Spiritual values have become reduced to material values, qualities to objects, adjectives to nouns. In biblical terms, bread has become stone.

With gift work, it's the other way around. Building materials can, through gift, be raised to a work of art. I don't believe it's possible to create works of art without gift. We give ourselves. It is possible (often necessary) to be paid, but this is always secondary.

Raising is the key element. For buildings to nourish the soul, their material elements must be raised, by artistic means, to the spirit. We can look at food in the same way: to be nourishing, mineral elements are raised through the processes of life to become nutrient substances. If only half-raised, protein is poisonous, as for instance is spinach grown in warmth but inadequate light. They're then further raised in the kitchen

to provide a truly nourishing food – half-raised they're uneatable! Cooked without love and delight, they only fill the stomach, they don't *nourish* us. Nourishment from the environment is the same.

This approach imbues material substance with spiritual values – art, inspiration. And this has benefits, visible and invisible, for the building, those who work on it and its future users. The visible benefits are obvious in the qualitative, aesthetic sphere. The intangible, invisible quality of a building is also quite different if it has been built for profit or gift, without or with love.

Buildings cost time. If you build your own house with all its components it may take two or three years. If you buy it built by others the price is comparable in the time taken to earn the money. We take it for granted that people built beautifully in the past, something we can't afford today. How could they afford it?

Perhaps half of the cost of a building goes on services and fittings, something our ancestors never thought of. Many of these comforts have been bought at the price of artistic quality, for today we can't afford to do without the comforts but we can't afford the aesthetics – or so it's often claimed.

To the practical 'realist' these benefits aren't materially measurable, but there are also economic benefits. The school I described was built at approximately 17 per cent of estimated contract price; sometimes this 'impractical' approach is in fact the *only* practical course. Indeed, in this case lack of money actually reinforced the artistic impulse. Not a complete absence of money, but certainly no surplus! Lack of money had its negative side too – much needless drudgery like mixing concrete by hand, inefficient sequences of work and many delays – but it never restricted the real *wealth* of the project, the extent to which artistic, spiritual values can raise matter.

What can be merely structural problems on paper can, on site, be seen to be opportunities for artistic development. Here the builder designed the details.

When people say, 'There isn't the money to make a building artistically satisfying', it's just not true. What they mean is that there isn't the will or priority. Money for them is the first priority, aesthetics follow – and we all know what happens!

It's not that supportive money is unimportant – far from it. However, when it becomes a ruling consideration, when a project is for the accumulation of money, practically the only purpose (because it rapidly becomes the dominant one) is the pecuniary one. Users and environmental responsibilities become secondary – and, insidiously or overtly, the results are inevitably destructive.

The approach to work as gift not gain is less easy, though always possible, with paid work. The concept of measured exchange, of buying, tends to enter in. 'I do so much for so much pay' – 'You're expected to do this because I'm paying you ...'

In every sphere of society, in every sort of work, it's the *approach* that is crucial: art or profit, service or exploitation, need fulfilment or market opportunity, material or spiritual value. Just as the gift principle can be applied to all work, so can the ideal of all work as an artistic – a sacramental – act. But unless we've travelled this inner road, most work doesn't encourage this attitude.

Gift-work projects provide a more supportive framework to this inner growth process. The benefit charities bring to society isn't limited to the services they provide; they also give their volunteers opportunities to experience work as meaningful gift and creation as service rather than indulgence – triggers for the reappraisal of values. Anyone in any situation can go through these growth processes, but without support far fewer will.

The opportunity for artistic involvement is a cornerstone of this supportive framework. To maximize this aspect, projects need to be managed differently. The emphasis needs to be more on the artistic consequences of work than on high productivity. Since work is given, this is *essential,* for it supports inspiration, upon which all voluntary projects depend. There are, therefore, very practical reasons why wholeness must replace atomism in management thinking and working relationships.

How does this work out in practice? Converting old buildings gives plenty of scope for mocking up, chalking out, listening to sound transmission and so on, as I've described; we can *see* what needs to be done next. If we listen to the needs of the existing building meeting its future, work can be the artistic response to the situation. New buildings at first sight seem more constraining. On paper, design integration usually appears complete and fixed, but the paper design need only be the starting point.

On the Steiner kindergarten I built with volunteers, I found the exact plan shapes, curves of the walls and size of play alcoves could best be established when laying the first bricks.[3] Only at this stage did lines on paper become boundaries to space. Only by daily observing sunlight did it become clear which trees to fell and which to retain. Only by standing at future windows could we know exactly where they'd be best for sunlight and view focus. Just where and how the different roof geometries should meet was much clearer on site than on the model.

Allowed to evolve on site, a building now starts to take over. If it didn't, we could build nothing better than a good plan. What work of art of any worth is an exact, larger scale model of smaller sketches – how can it be art if it's merely a fixed idea? The painter's sketch, sculptor's maquette, architect's drawings are only a way in. Thereafter, buildings start to grow

as real living beings – with their own suggestions and demands.

There are a lot of things which can only be brought to fulfilment by design on site. This means that builders *must* be brought into the design process. In fact, I consider it vital that they're involved artistically. Indifferent architecture built with care and artistic involvement can become a beautiful, soul-nourishing environment. Excellent design built without care or concern *never* can be.

In any case builders often know a better way to make something than does the architect. But we must be careful here – sometimes they know the *easier*, not the *better* way. It's only a step to go from how to make something to how to make it look as we want it. Together we can discuss, gesture, draw, mock up, the *exact* curve, the view from a window, sort of quality of a door latch, of plaster texture and so on.

Architects tend to think large. Unless details are standardized for repetition or individually described – involving an uneconomically huge mass of drawings – it's up to the building craftsperson to make the little bits. But it is just these little bits that are the contact points between users and buildings. For small children especially, they give the opportunity to 'use' the building in their imaginative world.

There's no better way to prepare yourself for these conversations than making things yourself. Here you learn how the material and the act of making suggest the way that appearance, feel and so on should go. Also, when builders say, 'It can't be done!', you're in a better position to say, 'Yes it can: I've done it – and I did it like this!' After all, all builders know that all architects know so little about how to make things that they design things that can't be built! It shouldn't be a case of passing down orders but of *agreeing* things together. If we disagree I can give an order and the builder will do what he wants to anyway as soon as I go away!

This isn't the conventional way of doing things. Conventionally, the architect's great ideas are executed by others and in the process compromised by constructional requirements, by builders, by users, and eventually by ageing and weathering. Buildings can be completely ruined by this process. I take the unconventional view. I feel that the life history of a building from clients' need to well-used old age should be a history of *continual improvement*. It should get better and better at every stage.

Constructional design brings our attention to the details people will actually touch, sit on, use, bump into. Building construction allows us to see what we couldn't visualize on paper and to develop its potential. Building craftsmanship brings care into a building and gives it a soul. Users bring life and spirit into a building. Time brings maturity, richness and increased harmony with surroundings. But none of these are isolated compartments: each stage brings something new to add to what's already there, a conversation between what has become and what is becoming.

Design is the process by which needs are worked out as practical solutions. It

Even before occupants breathe life into a building, even before it's finished, the process of ensouling can be well advanced. Had the (contracted) building workers not been artistically involved in their work, I doubt that it could have been so.

depends on this conversational principle to maintain balance, otherwise it becomes a compartmentalized activity in itself unrelated to place or people, to builders, users or initiators. I've certainly missed this balance far too often and done things on my own, neglecting conversation when it was most needed. To be balanced, design needs both overviewers and localized involvement. Neither overall planners, specialist consultants, builders nor users can be left out.

Looking at the process as a whole, we can see it as a cycle through spirit and matter. What starts as an abstract idea becomes increasingly condensed into substance – a building – and this in turn is increasingly filled with life, by its builders, then by its users.

At least, that is how it should be. What we often see, however, is a progressive descent of that which started as inspiration into more and more lifeless material form: the architect's inspiration ossified into contract documents, quantified in monetary terms and eventually built as an exchange of building substance for monetary reward. But it need not be like this; an interweaving upward stream can also flow. On the one hand, the inspiration finds its feet on earth; on the other, matter is imbued with spiritual values by being raised artistically. Both matter and spirit need each other – neither is whole without the other. But this can only happen when the work of *building* is approached artistically.

It isn't usual for builders to bring artistic values to their work, but it *is* possible. In my experience, however, it's *only* possible if they're involved in the artistic process. Certainly, the less they're involved, the less can they be expected to care. Yet it is the artistic sensitivity of the making hand that is *vital* to the process of ensouling buildings – at least as vital as the architect's skill. Just as it is the archi-

tect's task to bring soul qualities into the rational world of regional planning, it is the builder's hand that gives life to the architect's plans.

An important effect of letting the design evolve as potentials become apparent and are developed is that the building process and the building itself develop a kind of life. Hands which work with loving feeling imprint a kind of soul into a building. You can go into an empty unfurnished building and already feel 'it has a soul'. Go into an unoccupied machine-made one in which the workers had no artistic involvement: it waits to be given soul by its future occupants, and they will plant their qualities upon no foundation – it won't be a conversation, part of time's continuum. It will never be as much a 'home' as if the building started out 'ensouled'.

This is not to say that some people don't interpret this process as freedom to depart from the design or, deaf to the incarnating theme, impose their own personal preferences. In every building that I revisit I'm acutely aware of those things which weren't done as I would have liked them. But it is only *I* who notice them. What others see, appreciate, and misdirectedly give me credit for, results from *how* the building has been built, the work in which others have *gone beyond* what my design only started off.

Any credit for *how* a building has been built is due to the building workers. Yet how many get a mention on architectural prizes? Recognized or not, however, what this process means for them is that more even than completing the physical building (the noun) they are building the qualities (the adjectives). As best they can, they're building something beautiful, nourishing. Just as, for instance, to poison others with words poisons myself, so to make for others something nourishing brings unlooked-for nourishment to the building workers. Good nourishment is essential for good health. But no product will nourish either makers or users unless it has been made out of the spirit of artistic gift. To find ways to make this spirit accessible in the daily working situation is a task vital to the health of society.

We have come to take for granted that buildings are provided ready-finished by others. The less we are able to do ourselves, the more dependent we become. Dependency is a step towards social malaise. The wealthy can buy their way out, commissioning others to design and build their homes and workplaces. The skilled can do their own building. Self-builders currently build more houses than any firm in Britain, though very few start low on the ladder of privilege. My experience with volunteer building, however, demonstrates that even with no previous skill and with low expense it's possible to break the links of individual-suppressing dependence, to afford and achieve surroundings that nurture the soul, build self-confidence, community and, almost coincidentally, learn employable skills by the back door.

Notes and references

1 Unlike Russia, there are very few women builders in the UK or US.
2 Photographs show this school throughout the book (see List of photographs). For a fuller description of this project and discussion of gift work, see: Day, C. (1990) *Building with Heart*. Green Books, Devon.
3 More on this building, its design for children's needs and its construction by volunteers can be found in: Day, C. (1998) *A Haven for Childhood*. Starborn Books, Rhydwilym, Dyfed, Wales.

Chapter 12

Healing silence: the architecture of peace

Healing is a process that can only take place from within ourselves, but this process can be triggered and supported by things and actions outside us. We can, therefore, talk about healing environments and healing qualities of environment. Of all the healing forces in the God-given world around us, silence is perhaps the greatest. We've discussed the health-giving effects of processes, activities and material qualities, but silence is neither process, activity nor object. It is ... silence.

But what is silence? Is it complete absence of sound? Where can we go in the world and find no sound – no wind in grass, no distant clink of rock, no lap of water? Sound means life; in quiet places, the ears sharpen to listen for it. We even start to hear the sounds of our own body.

There's a lot of difference between a resting and a dead body. A dead animal looks different to one lying down; the wind stirs its hair as a lifeless surface on something immovable. This is the silence of death. To experience literal silence you must go into a special sound-absorbing chamber – a strange feeling. Sensory deprivation experiments have shown that if all senses are denied stimulus, so acute is the crisis that within seconds a risk to life develops. Literal silence is not life supporting: it's the opposite.

Or is silence the absence of noise? Even noise is hard to define: is it insects on a quiet summer's day, waves on rocks, wind in trees or over snow? But there's plenty more noise than that around us. The average house is full of noise-producing equipment – from freezers, furnaces and pumps to barely audible electric clocks and lamps, all dead mechanical sounds, not sounds of life like speech, music, crackling fire, wind in chimney, rain on glass.

We live in a noisy world. In cities, you can't get away from noise. Even in the countryside how far must we go not to hear cars, chainsaws or aeroplanes? When you listen, there's mechanical noise almost everywhere, most of the time. Silence – freedom from mechanical noise – has become a threatened species, extinct in many areas.

Whether we notice it or not, noise affects us. Physiological effects start at

65 dBA with mental and bodily fatigue.[1] This is typical urban noise level.[2] Mainroad kerbside noise, typically at 75 dBA, is over twice as loud and motorways nearly double again at 83 dBA.[3] Street noise can reach 90 dBA, causing heart stress.[4] Much lower levels, like background fan noise, interfere with sleep, digestion and thought.[5] We soon stop noticing ambient low-level noise, but it's an insidious stress-builder. When it stops we're struck by the sudden tension release.

Noise, in other words, is harmful to human health – a recognized environmental pollutant. There are well-established techniques for noise-abating design. Distance, obstruction (as by walls, banks, buildings), absorption (as by vegetation, which also filters fumes), zoning of sensitive and tolerant areas, and masking (as by rustling leaf, moving water, birdsong or other living sounds) can all mitigate outdoor noise. Where noise is bound to aggressive movement, like fast traffic, visually screening this often helps. Intermittent noises such as trains, however, are less of a shock if you see and hear them approaching. Noises from living sources like school playgrounds can be less irritating if you can see what's going on. Outdoor noise gets indoors mainly through openable windows. When noise and air pollution sources coincide, as is common, windows facing this way need to be sealed (and double-glazed, absorbent lined, etc.) and ventilation drawn from a cleaner façade. Indoor noise can be reduced with absorbent materials, room shape and, particularly, control of noise-making at source.

There is of course more to noise control, but however thorough our measures we can't hope to achieve silence. With triple glazing and absorbent indoor surfaces we can make acoustically dead

environments, but that's not the same as silence. Yet silence is something we need to have access to, for while noise is stressful silence is healing.

Where in the world can we go to find this sort of silence? And for those who can afford the expense, how much noise does travelling there cause? One place to go is within ourselves. Many seek inner silence through meditation, but it's not easy to keep inner noise at bay. To design healing environments, however, we need to create qualities of holy silence accessible for all, not just globetrotters and meditators, but especially for those who lack the outer or inner means.

Even if we can't define silence, we can recognize it. Gentle, unobtrusive, calming, life-supporting, holy sounds allow us to be quiet within: eternal sounds, like the breath of air, the quiet endlessness of water. Sounds of the ephemeral moment can be calming, but never tranquil. Cows chewing the cud and bumble-bees droning are almost soporific, but they're not eternal. Silence, tranquillity and the eternal have a lot to do with each other.

It's even harder to *define* silent architecture – but easy to recognize. There is dead silent or living silent architecture. To create living silent architecture we need to understand and work with the essential qualities of living silence: the gentle, the unobtrusive, the tranquil, the eternal, the life-supporting, the holy.

As a foundation of tranquillity we need balance. This often means focus and axis. Symmetry is rigid; rigidity excludes life. Balance is life-filled and breathes from one side to the other. Balance is also a matter of scale and proportion. Rooms can be quite small – monks' cells were often little more than the space to lie and stand in. The smaller a room is, the more modest, plain, ascetic and quiet it can be – furniture is an intrusion. Such a room is

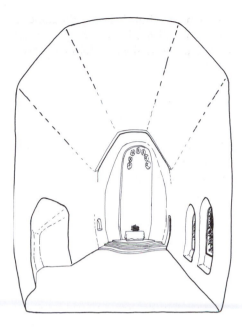

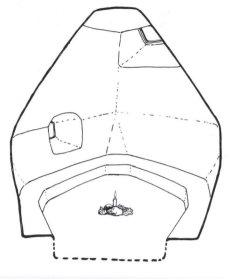

Chapel – different elements on either side of the axis balance each other.

Meditation room – different light sources to enliven a central, almost symmetrical space.

for a specific purpose, but not a silent place *within* the stream of daily life. If the proportions, textures, light and other qualities aren't just right, a small room is a trap; larger ones aren't, but you can rattle around in them, and their silence feels oppressively empty. Too large a space can be too awe-inspiring. We feel too insignificant beside the power of architectural scale. Those cathedrals that are places of silence (there aren't so many; most are places of awe) aren't the largest ones. Their scale is usually reduced by being built of tiers of elements or, in Romanesque churches, gestures tying them firmly down to the earth. Imagine such a cathedral plastered and painted

uniformly – in simplicity, its size would be too strong to be silent!

Proportion determines whether places are at rest or have a directional dynamic and the feeling that goes with it. Upward, forward or all-round horizontal emphasis can induce awe, expectation or soothing. Proportions at balance reflect balance in the human body, inducing a mood of balance in the soul.

Proportions too high, too wide, too long – like lines that are too dynamic or spaces too strongly focal – risk being too compelling. I want to leave occupants free. I try to be careful, therefore, not to have too strong an emphasis. Indeed, for a place of silence I try to underplay the

architecture generally so it's not intrusive. This means a certain simplicity. Simplicity, though enshrined in the modern movement, is often just boring. Some buildings need to be less simple, some more so. Places of silence need to be simple – but how can reverent simplicity be achieved without boredom?

I approach simplicity like this: generally, sacred spaces need to be entered and focused axially, but slight variation from one side to another, slight ambiguities in form and, most particularly, living lines (like flare at the base of walls, curved qualities in the almost straight and straight in the curved) give them a quality of life. So too do life-source textures like wood, even with its colour variation muted by staining or lazuring. This life is further enhanced by the light. Where the windows are placed, how they're shaped, how the light is quieted (for instance, divided by glazing bars, reflected off splayed reveals or filtered through vegetation) can enhance the interplay between daylight, sunlight and reflected light – so crucial to the mood of a room.

Light needs texture to play on. It's most alive with life-filled, but unobtrusive, gentle textures. I commonly use hand-finished render.[6] This can bring gentleness, life, conversational softening of plane changes and – as it's practically impossible for plasterers not to get artisti-

Textureless rooms need wallpaper or colour schemes to give interest, to paint a superficial individuality upon their surface. I use colour for a different function, so different that when I'm told, 'I have these curtains, I want a colour scheme to go with them', I'm at a loss to know what to do: I use colour to create a mood. My starting point, therefore, isn't 'Which colour do you like?' but 'What mood is appropriate?' Particular colours emphasize particular moods, red for instance bringing warmth, stimulation, passion and aggressiveness.[7] Yellow can bring light to sunless rooms, also vitality and cheerfulness. Green is calming and refreshing – the colour of surgical gowns and actors' 'greenrooms'. With all colours, associative qualities are bound up with physiological effects upon the organs and metabolism. Cold things are often bluish; blue light slows pulse and blood pressure.[8]

In therapy, coloured light is more effective than pigments.[9] Light can be coloured by reflection – so floor, walls, ceiling and outdoor ground affect mood. I use light reflected off natural materials a lot. Like lazure, self-coloured materials aren't normally as forceful and dominating as opaque colours. Brick, tile, timber and dark rich weavings bring warmth. With lazure, even grey – from thin veils of red, blue, green – can be alive. We chose grey for a theatre interior to create a focal, unobtrusive space. As a *free* mood needs light and levity, I usually use lazures. Even too delicately thin to notice, they're very effective mood-setters. Look from a lazured room to a plain white one – it looks so cold, so dead.

Nonetheless, for silence, I often use white. With light reflected off wood, tile, fabric and foliage, it's no longer plain white. White is commonly used when designers can't think of anything else. But it's the colour I use when I don't *want*

Where windows can be deep set into walls, light reflected off their reveals not only adds to room illumination, but intercedes between the brightness outside and the shade within, giving a calmness to the light. A frameless window, softened but firm and balanced in shape, with soft plaster texture can add to the mood of calm silence.

cally involved – soul is impregnated into the room. Requiring more sensitivity than skill, this technique has the additional advantage of being cheap and well suited to gift work or self-build.

I've been in spatially simple rooms which lack any life in their texture. Smooth-plastered, smooth-painted rooms, even the woodwork gloss painted. To be alone, quiet, in such a room is to be in a prison. You need a radio, CD player or television for company to fill the empty space, to bring a kind of life. I aim to make rooms in which you don't need these supports, rooms that will be alive whether by sunlight or candlelight, grey dawn or twilight, birdsong or silence.

anything else, when I want silence. Some think it isn't a colour, but the right white (there are many, also many mediums, from limewash and emulsion to gloss) can sing! White is the mother of all the colours – it has the potential of all moods – it can be calm, life-filled, joyous, timeless, whereas blue can only be calm and risks being cold or melancholic; orange can be full of life, welcoming, but risks being too forceful, even discordant; yellow can be joyous but risks being too active.[10] I've never seen more eternal qualities than in Vermeer's paintings, yet brown risks being too heavy, dark, oppressingly entrapping.

However, where room or window shapes are rectilinear with smooth surfaces and sharp arrises, white would be altogether too hard. It would also emphasize noise. Research on colour and perceived noise shows white rooms sound loudest.[11] They therefore need especial attention to qualities of shape, texture and light. The quietest room colour has been found to be purple. In ancient times purple wasn't a colour anyone could use; its use on clothing was restricted to a certain spiritual rank. Even today, less sensitive to the 'beings of colour' as we are, it doesn't seem quite appropriate for everyday use; a purple kitchen doesn't feel quite right.

I try to make silent, sacred rooms *plain*. They need to be somehow above any more specific mood. When the circular meditation chapel (see pp. 106–7) was nearing completion its exposed radial rafters looked so attractive that many people wanted them left in view. I felt that they created a warm cozy atmosphere – appropriate for a living-room perhaps, but not a chapel, especially not the silent, spirit-renewing focus of a retreat centre. I offered to pull the ceiling off if nobody liked it: fortunately I didn't have to.

Just as even attractive colours can be inappropriate, so can materials. Some feel

Gesturing of unfinished form.

In any line, curved or straight, there is a dynamic.

There is also a dynamic in the shape and tension between two lines. Responding to one crisis often produces another! To peacefully resolve these unfinished movements can take hours of effort!

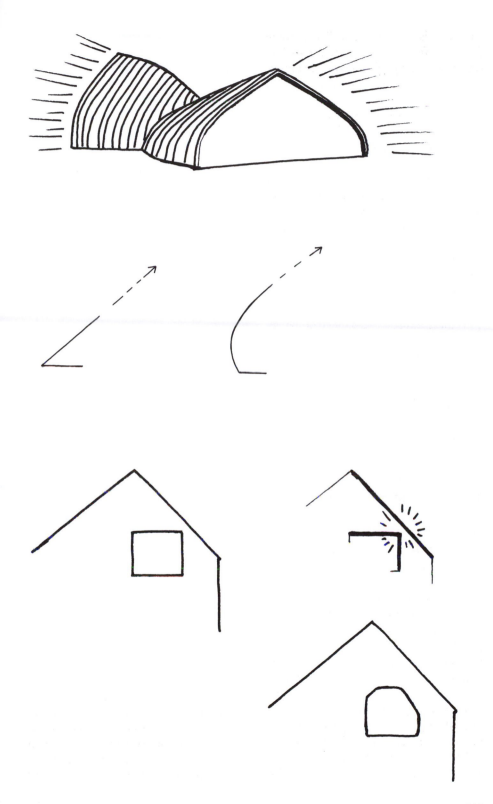

right for a place, others don't – usually because they're not practical, durable or local. In some countries, brick, stone or timber is the only suitable choice; anything else is alien. While I've experienced wonderfully sacred places in diverse materials, too many generally makes places busy and assertive. Often I use only three: walls and ceiling of the same finish, running without break into each other and unified by a single uninterrupted colour; wooden doors and windows, unpainted but possibly stained or transluscently lazured, and a texturally inviting floor of a colour to warm reflected light – usually wood, brick, tile or carpet.[12]

Unified materials and colours have a quietening influence – so quietening they need a life quality or the whole place will slide into lifelessness. Shapes, forms and spaces need, therefore, to have gentle movement. The static resolution of the right angle lacks life, but dramatic or dynamic forms and gestures have an excess of force. For both movement *and* stability, gesture needs to answer gesture in a life-filled, harmonic conversation – not repetition but resolution, transforming what the other says so it's just right for its particular location, neighbours, material and function. Quiet harmony is the product of a quietly singing conversation.

Perhaps the most essential quality is timelessness. A painting can be timeless, so can a building. Obviously the painting has to avoid anything that finds its resolution in time outside the moment – like someone kicking a ball. The same with a building. This doesn't only mean qualities at once traditional and modern; it also means resolving sculptural forces – energy and implied movement, gesture, gravity, structural and visual tension. Dead things are stable, immovable, but they're left behind by time. The eternal lives in every moment.

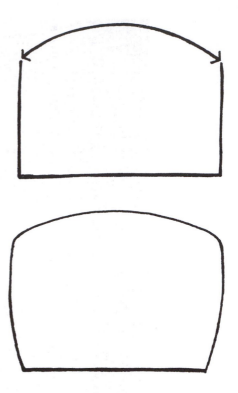

Even a quietly enclosing curve still has a visual force – reflecting its structural force. The meeting of the moving against the rigid can appear unstable unless resolved by moderating neighbouring elements, angles and meetings.

I try to make buildings which belong in the place they are, which are rooted in the earth, which give us the feeling that they always have been and always will be. Places which have this eternal mood can convey stable yet life-filled tranquillity in a way that those bound to a transient moment of style never can.

It can help to practise timelessness exercises. I like to paint uneventful balanced landscapes (of the soul imagination – not real ones) bathed with peaceful light, trying always to find that which is eternal, not momentary. This is about balance: stability and permanence without rigidity. Buildings which are *rooted* in the earth can be developed to be timeless, eternal. Buildings which aren't never can be. As well as shaping walls and ground, plants at the building–ground junction and climbing on walls can help.

As far back as I can remember I've looked closely at how rocks rise out of land. Some are half-buried boulders, some are the protruding bones of the earth. Some mountains are the earth itself pushed through, but now at repose – sometimes bare, sometimes draped with living covering. It is where they're firmest rooted and least dramatic that they're most eternal. This, the landscape I grew up in, greatly sharpened my feeling for timelessness.

To be timeless something needs to feel inevitable, right – so much so that we can no longer imagine it other than the way it is. Buildings, therefore, need to be in the inevitable place on the site. I used to do this intuitively, but sometimes places ask for something somewhere, sometimes they don't. The hardest site I've ever had was flat, featureless, with only short-lived caravans (trailer-homes) on it; nothing to grow from, nothing to create a place between, nothing to relate to. Usually, however, listening to the place gives a progressively strengthening conviction that this building should be *here*. Nowadays, I use the more structured consensus design process described in Chapter 9. With this, building location either condenses naturally, effortlessly, or its unsuitability becomes clear to all.

Buildings don't exist in isolation. We can develop the whole entry progression so the building we eventually reach feels inevitable. Indoors we can continue this preparatory experience until we reach the place to stop – a sanctuary of rest. Wherever there's a change of mood, we can enhance the experience with physical thresholds or darker, lower, narrower passages, cloisters, tree-overhung paths and suchlike. A substantial door with heavy latch makes a strong portal. This makes it a conscious step to pass into another place, a place to stop. For de-stressing tranquillity, this needs to be calm, protected, enclosing. A glass box can wash you inwardly clean with the forces of landscape – but it isn't somewhere to find inner calm in silence. In more densely settled surroundings you can feel displayed in a goldfish bowl, certainly not at peace!

This experience progression is built of the same vocabulary that's available in most homes and workplaces: thresholds, emphasized by portals, doors and latches, places to move in and places to stop. It can be enhanced by making these more *conscious*. I like hand-made wooden latches that you really feel and whose movement makes opening or closing a door a conscious bodily experience. Also, low doorways (or broad, so lower-proportioned, ones) with arched or shaped heads; low, dark, arched or shaped ceiling passageways, slightly twisting, leading to quiet light-enlivened (not necessarily bright, certainly not dramatic) stable-proportioned rooms.

Such daily rituals, repeated thousands of times, can have a healing effect. Even in places of work, and especially in homes, architecture has the function of providing rest for the soul.

When we come home from a stressful day, the home and the night are for renewal. If they don't provide it, stress builds upon stress and physical or psychological collapse follows. When we go to bed at night we pass into another world and are reborn each morning. How

Our ancestors knew well that the places we pass through affect our inner state of being. Typically a church wasn't entered directly from the busy street but after a series of threshold experiences to support the necessary inner preparation.

much care and worry can be washed away by sleep! We enter each new day with hope – how otherwise can we survive?

But what haven of calm do we come home to when its inmost sanctum is full of refrigerators, heating pumps or fans, TVs or radios? How do we bring the nightly renewal of rebirth each morning when wakened by mechanical or electrically created sounds? The issue isn't gadgetry, but rooms that need noise to keep you company. Many houses, many rooms need noise. To make places where we can live in health, places where we gain rather than lose strength, grow rather than wither, we need to make places where silence can be a welcome guest, where silence can fill the space with its renewing, healing power. This doesn't just mean good sound insulation; it means places of silent quality – to sight, touch, smell and so on – not just noiseless places, but places of healing silence.

My office as a room is a silent office, even though we talk there. It is not oppressively empty when it's empty, but peacefully at rest. It's an office more like a church than a factory – and so it should be, for I want the work that comes out of it to have something of the same sacredness.

If we think of work as the raising of matter, as provision of food for the human spirit, then places of work need this sort of atmosphere. I think of old carpenters' shops in the days before they became a screaming tension of dangerous machinery. Not silent rooms, for there were too many interesting things in them, but places of magical reverence.

What sort of a world will our noisy sheds with dead avenues of fiercely powerful machines or cosmetically zippy offices create?

Notes and references

1 Szockolay, S. V. *Man–Environment Sonic Relation* (Course notes: E 13), p. 9. Polytechnic of Central London.

2 Typical values, 10 per cent of the time 7 a.m.–7 p.m. all use zones in Inner London. *Traffic Noise: Urban Design Bulletin 1*. GLC, 1970.

3 Every increase of 10 dBA represents a doubling of apparent loudness.

4 McHarg, I. (1971) *Design with Nature*, p. 195. Doubleday/Natural History Press, New York.

5 Wyon, D. (1987) In *Det Sunda Huset* (Dawidowicz, Lindvall and Sundell, eds), p. 196. Byggforskningsrådet.

6 Ratio of 9 coarse sand : 2 lime : 1 cement, or lime or clay plasters, applied not by float but with a round-nosed trowel so as to obtain gentle undulations without tool scoremarks, finished with a (gloved) hand when it has started to firm upon the wall (about an hour later, but depends on conditions).

7 Bayes, K. (1970) *The Therapeutic Effect of Environment on Emotionally Disturbed and Mentally Subnormal Children*, p. 32. Gresham Press.

8 Birren, F. (1978) *Colour & Human Response*. Van Nostrand Reinhold, New York.

9 Bayes, K. (1970) Op. cit., p. 32.

10 Blue can of course be warm, yellow cool. This is both a feature of hue and context. To work with colours like this requires an artist's sensitivity, experience and attunement.

11 Bayes, K. (1970) Op. cit., p. 33.

12 Loose, washable carpets. Fitted carpets make too good a home for dust mites.

Chapter 13

Children and environment

Small children drink in everything in their surroundings, both animate and inanimate. Everything they experience is reflected in their state of being; indeed, much is imitated in play with penetrating accuracy. Harsh, immobile, imagination-suppressing surroundings are hardening and damaging to children's inner growth. They need soft, fluid and wonder-filled places for their imaginative world to blossom. (Play alcove, with coloured glass windows, for four- to six-year-olds.)

When children draw their first maps they start and end with home. Home and their range outside it are their whole world. The qualities they meet there, just like those they observe in people around them, they bring into themselves. Small children have no defences, filters or ability to process what they experience. They just drink it in unselectively. Hence its influence on developing personality, and even – as they're still physically maturing – their bodily organs. Hardness has a hardening influence. Aggressive or dishonest surroundings do them harm. Rigid forms and spaces have an entrapping, sterilizing effect on development, fostering rigid-category thinking in place of mobile openness.

Unlike sharp-edged buildings, greenery is soft, its spaces too fluid to define. Plants germinate, grow, flower and seed, wither and die; they need other life – insects and animals – and, though resilient, do best if appreciated and looked after. Just like us. As younger children don't learn intellectually, they subconsciously connect deeply with such experience-metaphors. Natural, living, surroundings stimulate their creativity unconstrained by category thinking. They recognize how cycles are renewals, hopeful even in death. From caring for animals, they learn communal relationships, care, responsibility and gentleness to others. Quite different from what they learn from computer games – here, if things go wrong, you just switch off! You can't just switch off a pet. If children never play on grass, amongst leaves, care for animals, will they necessarily grow up hard, uncaring, rigidly thinking? No – but they'll have to work harder to overcome such tendencies.

A conical roof on a (rounded) square(ish) plan forms low-ceilinged alcoves for play, child-scaled kitchens and fireplaces to gather round.

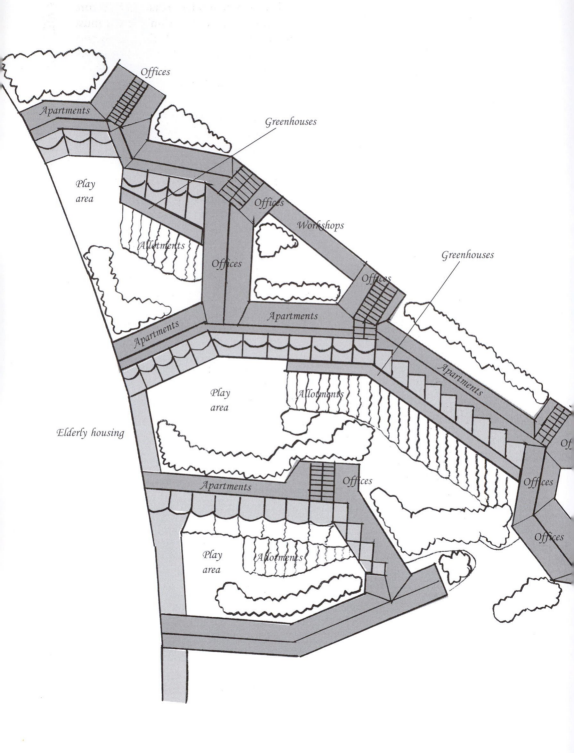

Offices

Apartments

Greenhouses

Play
area

Offices

Workshops

Allotments

Offices

Greenhouses

Offices

Apartments

Apartments

Play
area

Allotments

Apartments

Elderly housing

Offices

Offices

Offices

Apartments

Play
area

Offices

Allotments

Play
area

Allotments

220

If we blame modern harsh architecture for opportunist crime, think how it must be to grow up in it! High-rise apartments trap small children indoors. When they fight or grouch you can't just send them to play outside without going with them. Larger ones can go out on their own, but building height and project scale often mean they're free of supervisory eyes. When their world is predominantly hard, they're also disconnected from the rhythms and life-sources of nature. This is *new*. Since the birth of humanity, we've grown up in natural surroundings; until a century ago, even large cities were small enough to walk out of. Urban pressures mean high densities, but need not preclude greenspace territorially 'owned' by small communities of neighbours and in visual and access contact with every home. For children, even more than adults, living nature is a deep archetypal need – even if they don't know what to do there, or how it works.

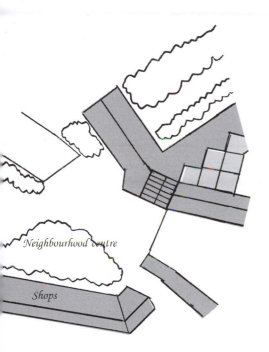

Neighbourhood centre

Shops

Cul-de-sac play space, easily accessed and multiply overviewed.

It's not just growing up not knowing that milk, cows and grass have anything to do with each other; one-third of city children don't even know eggs come from chickens ('don't cows make them?'); two-thirds think cotton is from sheep.[1] Nor knowing where the moon or even sun will be, nor varying play according to season, never hearing silence, perhaps never experiencing wonder. Many grow up in an environment with a high level of aggression – social and sensory.

Suburbs aren't the answer. They cover vast areas with uniformity, roads and private property, so children can't roam as they did even only a generation ago. With less spontaneous play space, they make fewer friends so social development is inhibited. Research has linked this non-socializing aspect of suburbs with increased psychiatric illness in later life.[2] Another reason for play-streets, court-yards, greens and secure and overviewed common spaces.

Even inner city childhood doesn't have to be child-unfriendly. It isn't hard to design places that are human-scaled, community-sized, soft and green; places that enjoy, savour, the different qualities of sunlight; places which vary signifi-cantly from season to season. Deciduous trees and shrubs that flower for shorter, not unnaturally long, periods maximize seasonal progression through different plant varieties. When breeze-stirred, different leaves move in different ways. Rain boosts plant growth and brings puddles with magic reflections – for children, a delight to splash in. Channels, cascades, water-spouts (but not drench-ingly high above you!) dramatize rain. In places that offer such benefits, even rain can be something to enjoy. Elsewhere, by exposed bus-stops, in traffic spray, lashing wind exacerbated by high-build-ing turbulence, on mud-squelched playing fields or in any damp grey –

Rainwater – millions of gallons – disappears instantly, often causing flooding down-river. Yet it could course through streets and courtyards in broad shallow streams, drawing bickering indoor children to play in the open air, making rainy days something for them to look forward to.

especially concrete grey – place, it can be a misery.

What childhood experiences do you remember of urban places? For me it's the smells, textures, sounds and space of different streets. I remember the long straight ones, dusty and hot or rainswept and open; the more interesting curved ones, leafy and quiet or rich with varied shops and people. I remember the dull dead places and those sensorily and spatially alive.

Growing children need life-rich food. They don't grow up healthy on deprived diets. Nutrition doesn't only enter us by the mouth but through all the senses. The importance of living lines instead of dead, of mobile forms and spaces instead of rigid, of metamorphosis and poetic conversation instead of repetition and imposition, of child-friendly scale and touch-inviting materials, is too great to be left to practicality – or, too often, profitability – criteria. Such qualities aren't just good architecture but are health-giving, formative influences for growing children.

Mid-childhood is the age of dens and wilderness play. Children are naturally drawn to learn through exploratory play, to stretch their boundaries towards independence, to develop resourcefulness and creativity. As unstable dereliction, unfinished demolition, guard dogs and discarded syringes make urban wasteland increasingly dangerous, this frustrated creative play finds less and less socially acceptable forms on the street, from skateboarding and supermarket trolley races amongst sedate adults to mischievous damage, breaking trees, vandalism and arson. There's plenty of need for chosen, manicured landscaping, but children need something they can adapt, something more of a wilderness garden with places they can't be seen in (but not dangerously far from adult earshot), branches and

A swing, climbing frame or rope bridge above a slope feels more dangerous because you look down a long way. A fall, however, would be no further than onto flat ground. Design for adventure play – and this is everywhere children are, not just adventure playgrounds – needs to maximize apparent dangers, reduce real ones and, insofar as possible, eliminate unseen ones.

stones to build things with, water to dam and divert, steep slopes to run, roll and slide down, opportunities to scare themselves without serious danger. If these places aren't there, roads, building sites and railway lines are ready magnets for more 'creative' – major risk adventure. Even more adventurous is experimenting with glue and worse! Adventurous places, street-hard or vegetation-soft, competitively aggressive or creative cooperation dependent, have a very formative influence.

Teenagers need to break out from the protective claustrophobia of home life and find adventure in the real world. It can be morally inspired adventure; protest movements offer such opportunities. It can be existential, exposure to a flood of powerful new experiences. In the super-stimulated time we live in, existential adventure can be much more dangerous to the personality than it seems.[3] You can't protect people from themselves, but just as adventure playgrounds are designed to *feel* more dangerous than they *are* in contrast to playing on the street – which seems tame until hit by a vehicle – it's possible to create environments which maximize excitement but not risk.

Adolescence is the period of growing towards your own personal identity, of becoming aware of yourself as separate from family, from institutional groups (like schools), from others. Peer-group conformity protects against the insecurity and loneliness this separateness opens up. The entertainment and clothing industries exploit this as marketable fashion, changing fast to stimulate new sales. Conformity – so effective as a defence – can easily become an obstruction to the ideal-inspired development which marks entry into adulthood.

For teenagers, newly-found sexual desires, powerful emotions and adult bodies are unfamiliar and unsettling. It's easy to hide the tenderness of this new emotional self behind acting tough and insensitive. A lot of money is made from catering for desires, but the characteristic of desire is that it can never be satisfied. You always need more ... and more. Desires are natural, but to be ruled by them is never to rise above the animal. It is the transformation of desire from masters to servants, from sex to love, from personal status to inner resilience of character, from craving to independent discernment that marks the development of an inwardly free individuality. Market forces feed the former state, extending enslavement by desire back into childhood and far into adulthood. Toy, computer game, fashion and car advertisements exemplify this well.

To design, therefore, for what young people *need* is to transform what they *want*, to provide environments where they meet more as humans than as sex objects, working relationships where mutual responsibilities are more meaningful than prestige, and where socially inspiring necessity calls forth self-sacrifice, hardship and adventure. Such situations strengthen individuality development.

It's easy to see where inspiring *projects*, like work for the community, environment or the arts, can play their part, but what about architecture? Especially, what about architecture *not* associated with inspiring projects?

We all, but young people especially, need buildings and places *welcoming* to the soul: places that aren't exploitive, places that, in the way they're conceived, planned and built show love – that most needed and least supplied quality – that can transform the social delinquent into a crusading rebel or the competitive success figure into the servant of a great cause. Easy? Obvious? Then why doesn't it happen more often?

What sort of a place do teenagers need to nurture the development of inner freedom? Firstly, of course, it needs 'youth appeal'. With inevitable time-lags between planning and completion, anything 'provided for' them won't be in step with current fashion, so risks being seen as philanthropic institutionalism. Scope for user adaptation is therefore important. Flexibility doesn't mean providing empty sheds but places with varied qualities which can be enhanced, styled and used as required. Even better are opportunities for young people themselves to build, adapt, furnish and decorate. For this, old, 'unsuitable' premises are often better than new, purpose-designed ones.

Whether in schoolroom, café or youth centre, different qualities of room will support different aspects of adolescents' inner growth. Depending on our picture of the human being, we would design quite different rooms. Imagine a room with dramatic centrally directed lighting – perhaps stroboscopic, multi-coloured or ultraviolet-rich – focusing attention on people moving so you're hardly aware of the many protected niches with seats and small tables, their privacy enhanced by semi-darkness. In contrast, the drinks counter is glitteringly, invitingly lit. The whole room would feel, if possible be, underground. A lowish ceiling, and strong, dark, opaque colours – black, brown, dark red – reinforce this mood. Windows – if there are any – you don't notice. A narrow passage entry makes this a 'special' place, separated from the everyday. This is a room of the night with the privacy of darkness contrasted to dramatically lit self-exhibition. With loud music this makes a successful club, also a certain sort of café. But when morning sunlight streams in through open fire exits, the place seems hollow, disenchanted, fake. It is an environment for only *part* of the human being.

A room to encourage teenagers' questioning social awareness would be different. It needs more natural light: windows with views of *things going on*; perhaps sitting or sprawling window alcoves which aren't private from the main space. The architecture would have cleaner lines though not simplistic forms: perhaps gentle curves but with open, not protective, gestures. An openness reinforced by light-enhancing pale colours, perhaps blue–grey veils enlivened with tints of green. At night, gentle differentiations in light, heat and comfort individualize areas. So do lights above circular tables in corners, alcoves and window-bays. Cushions on the floor near the fire and hand-made music give 'ownership' to its inhabitants. This is a room to foster society based on friendship, on the whole human being.

When designing a hostel for urban teenagers in a spectacularly beautiful rural site, I was asked to include a social room with an (alcohol-free) pub atmosphere, a night-time place, yet located where the views and sunlight were best. I questioned whether the project should bow to consumerist expectations or encourage creative and participatory activities. Would a group tea-making corner be more appropriate than a bar and vending machine selling manufactured drinks in disposable cans? What about a cooking, baking, open fireplace instead of a purely amenity one, sunset and candlelight instead of a dark-walled electrically lit cellar atmosphere? Could we encourage live music instead of a jukebox? Could we make the place wonder-filled in a way these teenagers could never experience at home? The project was postponed (or perhaps they got someone else to do it), so who knows whether this would have led to a mass exodus to the pub each evening or to a waiting list to stay there.

*Kindergarten: circular rooms have a
singular social focus but 'imagination
worlds' are dispersed. These are corner play
alcoves at various levels with tiny low
deep-set coloured windows.*

Naturally, a room for 17-year-olds would be quite different from one for five-year-olds. They're not only taller, with higher eye-level and more interested in the world beyond their immediate surroundings, but also more alert intellectually. Five-year-olds need a more protective environment, opportunity to live actively in a world of imagination and imitation. One room would be more upright, firmer in its forms and spaces, more outward looking, and structurally and constructionally legible. The other would be warmer in colour, softer, lower, snugger in space and form. One more skeleton and muscles, one more womb and mummy's lap. For buildings and play spaces, one would have the quality of an eyrie observatory, the other of a fairy-enchanted woodland glade.

While teenagers, though few admit it, crave inspiration, wonder is essential for small children. To them, the world is new, vivid and wondrous – something to explore, revere and delight in. But things that don't change, don't respond to weather, seasons or life, don't stay new so long. Simple, hard-edged rectangles don't leave much to explore. Sensory dullness doesn't provide much delight. Ugliness doesn't encourage reverent appreciation. Children need a life-filled, life-formed and life-enlivening environment – vegetation, fluid forms, sensory richness. Without this, childhood is impoverished.

The sense of wonder – that most valuable and fragile of human faculties – is essential to healthy childhood.

Without wonder nothing is new except the dangerous, nothing is inspiring, nothing worth putting our own interests aside for. But wonder doesn't sell. It can't easily be commodified. Stimulation can. Like 'super-sell', however, 'super-stimulation' squeezes individual freedom. But architecture can support the sense of wonder, by maximizing the 'soul colour' of places. For this we depend upon its full sensory palette to make different qualities to flavour, enhance and encourage many different 'activity colours'.

Transformative delight, place-creative opportunities – it isn't only teenagers who need these. All-engrossing wonder, sensory delight, living forms and spaces – not only small children need these. All of us do.

Notes and references

1 A survey in a Scottish city, reported on the *Today* programme, BBC Radio 4, 2 May 2002.
2 Lantz, H. (1956) Number of childhood friends as reported in a life histories group of 1000. In *Marriage and Family Life*, cited in Thomas, D. (2002) *Architecture and the Urban Environment*. Architectural Press.
3 Cannabis, as everyone 'knows', just makes you harmlessly dopey. Its effects on mental development, weakened concentration and will, also links with schizophrenia, don't show up till later.

Chapter 14

The urban environment

Sustainable values, urban pressures

Is this book just impractical idealism? Is it relevant to the sort of projects most architects work on? Is this way of working commercially viable? Is it expensive, for the privileged only – or affordable? Most particularly, is it applicable to the urban situation?

A decade of mostly urban work, much with developers, has taught me that economic, social and ecological sustainability depend upon each other. They're as irrevocably linked as is short-term profit to high economic risk and social and environmental exploitation. Indeed, something *not* financially and socially viable won't last – however ecologically responsible, it can't be *sustainable*. For this reason, I *always* listen closely even to anti-sustainable developers (but would never work for them). What they see as profit-drivers I see as social and environmental forces to harness for other ends. Nowadays, even from a commercial perspective: 'Sustainable retail projects

are profitable, in good measure, because they are pleasant environments that tenants and shoppers prefer.'[1] Nonetheless, economically, socially and ecologically motivated projects have different agendas. Singular objectives, even ecological ones, aren't holistic – nor sustainable. Only multi-objective symbiosis is.

But first, what are cities? 'City' means different things in different parts of the world. The word conjures up widely varying images: caverns filled by traffic; intense experience of human activity, both stimulating and stressful; jumbles of decrepit buildings used in ways they were never designed for; clean-edged, bland-surfaced rectanguloids; squalor, poverty and tension, as well as luxury and affluence; industry, offices, shops, apartments, people. There are all kinds of cities, most offering many kinds of experience. Vegetation-rich, traffic-free, human-scaled winding brick passages, decaying workshops, houses rich in history, vandalized multi-storey blocks in bleak grassland deserts or brand-new prestige symbols may be next door to each other.

In one project, we found inner city shops couldn't even buy wholesale at prices urban-edge warehouses sold retail. Only by offering attractive environment could they compete. This meant clean, cool air and life-dominated soundscape – hence vegetation, water, natural ventilation and cooling, and noise screening. Places delightful to linger in increase trade. Multi-use, multi-size units, population and activity diversity, overlap and symbiosis improve resilience, a cornerstone of proprietary community. All this improves street safety – hence economic success.

Natural systems, resilience through multiple activity and scale, proprietary occupants, symbiotic relationships – is this a description of a healthy ecology or of how sustainable economic, social and ecological aims feed each other? (California)

Despite endless diversity, urban benefits – economic, cultural and social – tend to be common to all cities. So do problems – and not only traffic, air pollution and crime. Generally, these increase with size – as every city that's joined two riverbank towns by a new bridge has found.

All sorts of factors – social, demographic, logistical, economic and ecological – interweave to create the living, vibrant and imperfect miniature world that is a city. All of these are influenced by its built substance: some beautiful and good to be in, some the reverse. Unfortunately, many parts of many cities have been distorted from places of convivial vigour to alienating, life-suppressing, hardening and unwelcoming ones – but that is not what city life is about!

Urban life is overlaid with emotive associations and values, many contradictory: urban living – good; inner city – bad; downtown – exciting; business district – boring; suburbs – bad; garden city – good. Some people enjoy, some hate, cities, but their centrality to civilization is beyond dispute. They're the places where economic activities, ideas, cultural and social diversity symbiotically interact and cross-fertilize each other to a high degree. Unfortunately, however culturally vibrant the parts outsiders think of, there are usually also areas of social, economic and environmental decay.

Urban life: urban needs

Humanity is now urban. Almost a third lives in large towns or cities.[2] Like workplace smells and industrial toxins on workers' overalls, we bring home the experiences of the day each evening. Some are stimulating or enriching, some stressful. Homes have a renewing function: the greater the stresses and imbalances brought home, the more does home need to be a place of healing.

Homes for renewal, for healing from stress, need the right balance of privacy – traditionally obtained by front gardens, yards, basement 'areas' or living half a level up. Steps or bridges across sunken areas emphasized thresholds. Step-free wheelchair access requires other means, like inset front doors, flower-bed obstructions outside windows, or window-sills raised above passer-by eye-level by sloping ground. Even token front-garden gates are realm markers.

Some cultures have a whole series of buffer thresholds from the noisy, impersonal and public, to the quiet and private haven: community, street, yard, staircase, home. Even with 'an Englishman's home is his castle' attitude, imagine living in a caravan (trailer) in a city: you go straight from outside – with one set of behaviour expectations – into the living space – with another. You can survive in it, but its renewal characteristics are small.

A dark low tunnel leading through into light is both threshold from the outer world and the first step of an important ritual experience – a real portal. The protective womb-like enclosure of the bedroom is also important. How can we be born afresh each morning from a box?

Places for inner renewal need uncluttered space. But to be spacious, rooms needn't be large. I've stayed in smooth box-shaped bedrooms, twice the volume of my own but half as spacious. Layout, furnishings and light, extent, focus and shape of window, shape of space, texture, colour and vegetation can transform a small room into a spacious calm one.

Urban homes have to resolve greater conflicting requirements and constraints than elsewhere. They need more privacy, but also more spacious, calming, tranquil

views; more light, but also more protec-tiveness; more space, which land price makes impossible; they need quietness and clean fresh air – both rare.

Between home and the wider world lies the home *area*. Suburbs appeal to families with young children just *for* their quiet streets, lightly enough populated to get to know neighbours. Houses have gardens and ideally space to 'walk all round my house'. But low density denies them convenient public transport, tameness makes them claustrophobic to young people, and their mono-use dormitory nature – exacerbated by driven-to supermarkets instead of walked-to corner shops – can be socially isolating. Hopefully suburb building is over, as there isn't the space, nor the air to dilute their traffic fumes. But what about those already built? 'Village centres', where more things happen over longer hours, bring life, variety and area identity, and increase public transport viability.

attempts to relate these findings to human communities founder in the complexity of human life. Many think stress is proportional to crowding,[3] but crowding isn't easy to quantify. Culture, surroundings, noise, air quality and climate all affect tolerance. Attitudes to density are coloured by historo-cultural factors. In continental Europe, a millennium of foraging armies made walled urban (or nucleated village) life the norm, whereas New World settlement brought an 'expanding into open space' attitude – protectively closed or generously open gestures.[4]

Reducing city densities have led, in the Californian extreme, to situations where roads and parking dominate, often eliminate, pedestrian life, so 'chance meetings' feed road rage, not community. More stress not less! Density versus sprawl issues won't go away. As sprawl is environmentally, socially and climatically disastrous, how can we maximize the advantages of lots of people living close together while minimizing the adverse effects?

Density figures imply a contour map of human activity – hence noise, generated traffic, limited space and sunlight, along with requirements for paving, play space, shops, services and public transport. This suggests what uses, atmospheres and densities are appropriate for each other. Some activities, uses and sorts of places are compromised by cramped space, crowds, lots of things going on and background noise. Others are tolerant. Some even benefit by them. Silent, empty or over-broad, a shopping street becomes a ghost.

After matching sensory load to activity mood, come sun, vista and perceived space maximization strategies, and noise reduction, zoning and screening. This takes a lot of pressure off high-density design. The more conventional 'stack

Even in densely built-up cities it's possible to create havens of peace. To enter this courtyard you must pass through a tunnel under a former factory, then turn along a narrow mews.

This means gathering shops, workplaces, health clinics, playgrounds and suchlike into one place. But where? Grant, tax and land-value inducements can help densification. Also, traffic-calmed roads blocked to through-traffic liberate significant land.

Is density a stress or slum factor or just a measure of how many people can be packed onto a particular site? Certainly, too many animals on limited territory cause diseases and social aberrations, but

Quiet back but busy front (Scotland).

Perceived density in homes and public green-spaces minimized by:
- *stepped façade;*
- *long view 'corridors', greenery dominated.*

Perceived density maximized for urban buzz in neighbourhood centre by:
- *maximum scale of buildings with visually prominent vertical circulation;*
- *compressed public space and 'closed views';*
- *location astride route from transport (light rail, tram, bus, electric-car depot, cycleway) to nearby shopping centre 'magnet';*
- *entry doors, paths, workshops, shops and other activities focused into public 'square';*
- *retail and market stall opportunities.*

Photovoltaic
roofs

Solar collectors
double as shades

Wind pump for rainwater
harvesting system

Balconies edged with planters
ensure visual privacy

Play area   Allotments   Greenhouse   Apartments   Solar hot-air ducts
double as privacy walls

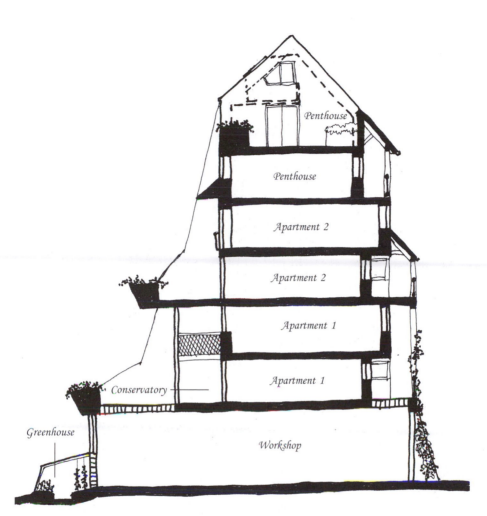

High actual density, lower perceived density: mixed-use development with 440 people (180/acre) and 3800 m² workplaces, shops, etc. per hectare. Zig-zag façades accommodate awkward site orientation and enable socially-focusing layouts. Every flat has a garden, sun in midwinter, long(ish) views, visual privacy, acoustic flank-walls, easy access to secluded, resident-overviewed play spaces and a songbird-rich acoustic environment (Scotland).

them up tall' approach doesn't reap any advantages, avoid any disadvantages, or indeed address such issues at all.

High density doesn't have to mean high. Nor does it have to be crowded or stressful. These are consequences of *perceived* density. A third of all people in Britain want to live in bungalows. But if they did, there wouldn't be much Britain left! What makes bungalows so attractive? They provide visual privacy, (reasonably) quiet, (reasonably) spacious views, all day sun all year, individual identity, connection with the ground, gardens, secure play spaces for children. All achievable at high densities.

Cities as places

Cities lack full meaning if they don't condense and fertilize the spirit of a region. This doesn't mean architecture *copying* local style but that the mood of a region can find expression in the built environment. When you go from countryside to market town you feel this intensified spirit, even with towns swollen and distorted by industry. Although range increases yearly, migration from surrounding areas still ensures kinship links between city and region. Trans-continental immigration creates individualized enclaves: new blood, new cultural riches, new identity, but still within continuum context. The huge conurbations no longer respond to their surrounding regions, they dominate them. But Paris, Moscow or Washington have the unmistakable spirit of France, Russia or America.

Chainstore architects' departments with more allegiance to company image than place individuality, and ubiquitous international-style 'downtown' imports, de-localize the very heart points of a region – the condensed core of its economic, cultural and social life. Outside these centres, national speculative building companies and standard-plan designers continue this process. Imported glitz architects for urban regeneration and prefabricated housing from different climates and traditions don't help either.

Life vigour enlivens places – but also drives up property values till old buildings aren't as profitable as newer, larger ones would be. But if these impose new space language, new scale, alien materials and diminished sensory variety, they easily destroy place individuality. Large developments stifle diversity. Brand-new places won't change for several decades. Their newness gives an impression of optimism and energy, but until they fill with life and this life matures into diversity, optimism is *essential* for they're only half-alive. Also everything will age all at once – especially glass and steel buildings, as these depend on short-lived components like silicone jointing. We should learn from the rapidly expanded industrial revolution cities. Simultaneous ageing (and lease maturity) turned large areas of housing into slums. Not something to repeat.

Spirit-of-place is fragile! Organic growth feeds it. Imposed projects attack it. The thoughts that shape these have originated *outside* the stream of place biography – no wonder they destroy. In only a few decades many places of soul-warming character and human support have ceased to exist: they may be there physically, but in spirit they're unrecognizable. Human scale feeds street life. Prestige scale doesn't. It makes gusty wind, permagloom shade and street boredom.

Yet development needn't be like that. Cities are made up of human activities. The places in them are given individual-

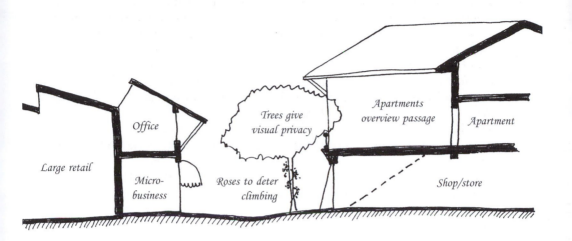

Labels in figure:

Large retail

Office

Micro-business

Roses to deter climbing

Trees give visual privacy

Apartments overview passage

Apartment

Shop/store

Micro-businesses wrapping dead faces of large stores.

ity by the colour mixed from these activities – and there are thousands of colours! New activities *of the right colours* add to a place. Hence, listening to what it needs isn't only beneficial to place. As 'place-hunters' hunt places nourishing to employees, buildings that feed not compromise, spirit-of-place make good commercial sense.

Unfortunately modern buildings, even highly glazed ones, often withdraw activity from the street – or even windows – and shut it away inside. When I grew up, a footpath led *through* an ironmonger's shop – life-richness rare today! The greengrocer's or ironmonger's street display, fishmonger's water-sluiced window, shoemaker seen at work, baker's oven smells, clatter of printing press just glimpsed within, the dark tunnel into the glowingly lit fabric shop, these are increasingly shut away. A whole street block can be just one supermarket.

With Northern European climate and culture conducive to closed walls and streets taken over by motor vehicles, we tend to forget that it's human activity that makes cities alive.

Despite the variety of goods and people to watch, often all that's visible are receding ranks of fluorescent lights above discount price advertisements. Chainstore conglomerates increasingly replace small family businesses. But even here, *architectural* arrangements can reinvigorate dull buildings. Where we look *down* into stores, we can see what's going on. Individualized displays and entrances express departmental individuality, without compromising interior inter-relationships. Attractive, interesting, descriptive window displays sell products, but the broader each shopfront, the less variety for passers-by. It's quite a different experience to walk through an alley of little shops or between two department stores. Unlike *long façades,* deep *narrow* plans maximize activity face, hence life vigour. Blank walls are dead, but they're good opportunity to let for micro-businesses or other human-contact activities. Like upper-floor leases, 'wrapping' makes more work for developers, but façades are higher value than interiors and increased activity means more trade for all.

In pre-industrial towns, buildings were built onto each other. With increasing individualization, we're possessive about plot boundaries and don't like our buildings touched by neighbours. Individual-building consciousness isn't social, doesn't make streets. But, however independent, individualistic and asocial, we're a gregarious species. Individuality without a social context is lonely. *Social* activity needs places to happen in. Replacing building-consciousness with place-consciousness allows architecture to transcend the constraints of atomistic plot boundaries and insular economic criteria, making places people *enjoy.* This enjoyment is key to economic success.[5]

Shops, cafés, entertainments and street-visible activities bring life to towns, but what about offices? Victorian factories expressed their varied industrial processes in their purely functional buildings. Unlike modern factories they were interesting to look at, though pollution made them unpleasant neighbours. But even in those days, offices were just big blocks with lots of windows – as dull to look at as the work for the clerks inside them.

To office-building boredom, town halls often add a prestigious grandeur inappropriate for 'servants of the people'. To walk past, this just makes them boring, a sterilizing influence right at a town's heart. As urban regulatory organs, however, they perform three functions:

democracy, administration and public contact activities. Administration is necessarily internal, but democracy demands transparency – hence the recent move towards all-glass civic buildings.[6] Public contact activities are less bureaucratically institutional at a building's face, opening off the street, not 'somewhere' down long Kafkaesque corridors. Democracy, being about representation and social pressure balancing, can enrich the streets the building bounds with advisory clinics, immigrant cultural centres and the like.

However boring or buried under bureaucracy, profit, prestige, institutionalism, elitism, their precedents, we can ask of any projected building: 'What is its true essence? What *positive contribution* can it offer society and place?' Likewise, viewing its site as a place, ask: 'What does this place, and its community, *need?*' This is about marrying the *inspiration underlying any project* with the *needs of the place* to fertilize a whole district, town, city.[7]

What about purely commercial projects? Where short-term profitability is the sole aim, people, place and project share no responsibility bonds, so there's little resilience when circumstances change. Hence even *economic* sustainability isn't likely. Profit may be an unstable – and asocial, anti-environmental – *driver,* but it can also be a *consequence* of responsible design. Meaningful staff involvement in office redesign boosts morale, reducing staff turnover and 'stop at ten-to-five syndrome'. As well as improving surroundings and showing people they're valued, it's profitable. Moreover, attractive workplaces help 'attract' staff. This doesn't only apply indoors. Buildings which improve area attractiveness also themselves benefit. (It's called: 'location, location, location' – but this is *added* location value.) What's right for people and for place is also economically sound.

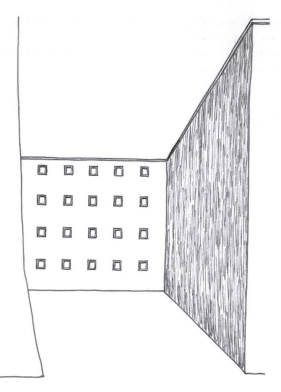

The extent to which buildings reveal what's going on inside them makes all the difference to whether somewhere is interesting and alive or the opposite. This is more a matter of surface treatment than architectural form. Just add ground texture, a tree and its shadows or a pool and its reflected light, and somewhere that felt like a prison now invites entry.

Looking at projects *from the viewpoint of place* shows up all sorts of potential benefits – both environmental and economic – that aren't obvious when thinking of them as *buildings*. 'Office block' conjures up an image very different from 'street face' or 'courtyard and passage complex'. Most urban building design is – or should be – about enhancing public realm as much as designing private buildings. Iconic buildings, competing in image projection, hardly help here.

Whatever the design, some places will lose more than they gain from some sorts of buildings. Unlike building-consciousness, place-consciousness makes such situations quickly apparent. It requires sacrifice to refuse work, but doing things against one's beliefs destroys people. Fortunately, it doesn't have to come to a choice between prostitution or starvation. Place-consciousness, by showing what places *can't*

accept, shows at the same time how this is unviable.

Nonetheless, my first reaction is often that places would be better undisturbed. Almost everywhere, however, their charm is due to human activity. We can continue this process of improvement but *if and only if* development can take part in those organic process by which places come into being, grow and change. Here the fundamental questions are: Is the project founded upon a need in this place? Is its scale appropriate? Will its underlying motive raise or debase the place?

Techniques for liberating latent place potential centre on 'mood mapping'. Those for aligning with currents of change – usually externally driven – centre on place biography, as outlined in Chapter 9.[8]

In almost every city, old residential areas have been demolished and replaced by new. We now know the cost to neighbourliness and community, and that

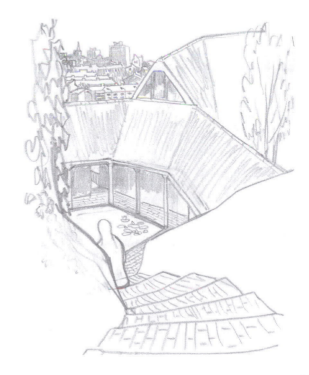

Why should offices be blocks? Why should work drain energy, not rebuild it? Where can you reflect, relax, wash away work pressures, de-stress? To step outside your workplace is often to encounter heavy traffic. Yet buildings shield from noise: they can create tranquil inner courts.

slum problems like mould growth and structural deterioration reappear whenever buildings don't match users' lifestyles. What the demolition ball smashes isn't just buildings but that web of long matured personal relationships, memories and thoughts which makes the spirit of community. Most towns are at least several generations old. They have historic roots: places known from childhood, in grandparents' stories. These give stability when skylines, streetscapes, usage patterns and local 'atmosphere' change bewilderingly quickly. Hopefully urban redevelopment by demolition is behind us, but there are other threats to places.

Every four years cities compete to host the Olympic Games. The winner gains prestige. The immense inpouring of money stimulates a ferment of demolition, building, motorway and parking construction. The economic benefit is mixed. Money is meant to – and does – breed money. But large inputs often breed money-making projects, not wealth distribution – the bigger the investment, the worse the damage. The *environmental* price leaves a lasting mark on a whole region.

This sort of thing happens in miniature all the time. But there's also the problem of *migrating* money: new wealth at the fringe, dereliction left behind. Both large-sum injection and migrating money exploit undeveloped opportunities. Neither develop existing seeds of latent vigour. New situations create new opportunities – profitable, but often unidimensional. In town centres, shops and businesses traditionally grew organically, spreading outwards from activity-places where separate (walking-speed) roads came to a single destination. Motorized shopping, however, occurs on urban edges. This sort of focus reversal is even more extreme in Norway where, prior to

oil wealth, many towns were only linked by sea, so commerce and cultural focus edged the harbour. Now all-season arterial roads from inland have spawned road-based shopping centres.

There aren't many accountants, chiropractors, cobblers, repair workshops or sign-makers in shopping malls. Nor even many local shops; most are chain stores, dependent more on brand recognition than individual character. This sort of development isn't just local character-robbing, but also place-weakening. Moreover, many places, once the coalescence of community spirit, have been obliterated by traffic. This starts by turning a shopping street *focus* into a barrier, a *boundary*. Life withers here. As roads widen, this boundary hardens and blight intensifies and spreads.

Traffic isn't the only place destroyer. Some places feel threateningly surrounded by boxes to accommodate statistics – so many hundred, or thousand, people; not homes or work or meeting places for individuals and social groups. Others by new uses – hence types of people – changing character and focus beyond recognition. Others again are just too boring to walk around in. How can such places again become living magnets, inviting to linger; places to enjoy, to love and care for?

Places can't acquire life unless they invite us to *stop*, not just *pass through*. This means multiple reasons to be there, a symbiotic mix of activities and many inducements to linger – from cafés to back-protected low walls for sitting and watching the world going by; from flowforms and fountains to idle by to street exhibitions and events. Delight is also vital: climatic delight, multi-sensory delight, visual delight. This means suntraps in cool season, leaf shade and sparkling water in warm. It means focus on life sounds – people, birdsong, leaves, water and street music (often, inexplicably, illegal) – not mechanical ones like traffic. Also enticing aromas – baking, coffee, garlic grills, fruit and flowers; attractive qualities of light – sunlight, sky exposure, reflected and filtered light, textures, shadows and colours. Such delight magnets are the precondition for enhanced activity, the foundation of social magnets. Life breeds life. This means life *qualities,* life *activities, socially* interactive life – to look at, take part in or to provide informal meeting opportunities. This *qualitative atmosphere,* combined with *physical draw,* like route between activities, from transport node to destination, or between 'anchor' activities, is key to sustainable *economic* life.

Life is speeding up. You need only read an old novel to notice the faster pace we've got used to. A characteristic of over-speeding, whether driving, eating, speaking, at work or in daily living, is that we don't notice it. Stimulation increases until it crosses the threshold of stress. Some people consider the number of psychiatrists in New York in direct ratio to the pace of life – a pace immediately visible to outsiders even in the speed at which people walk. For health, high-speeders need holidays in slow-moving places. All of us benefit when places give inducement to stop. The development of *places* as distinct from *routes* doesn't just make shops viable, and cities nicer, but is fundamental for the health of their inhabitants.

Big cities were, and to some extent still are, made up of little places. Sociability, founded upon re-meeting the same people in different circumstances, is much easier in small communities than large. Chance meeting is inverse-scale related. It's unavoidable in hamlets, rare in cities, impossible on the Internet. Locality and identity can depend more on social and sensory character, colour,

scale and spatial characteristics than on shape or style of buildings. Analysis of random photographs shows how much stylistic variation can exist in an apparently uniform area. Materials, constructional and spatial principles, however, are usually more consistent. Important as such visual characteristics are, however, they're only part of identity. This depends on magnetic foci, boundaries – sometimes barriers, sometimes just quality change – and activity gradients. These – and their space, scale and tempo of life – typically change by a heirachy of steps, making *large areas* into a pattern of *smaller places.* Different activities – shops, factories, houses, apartments – street width or sectional proportion, also changed scale, textures, lighting, and softness or hardness confirm places' identity and character.

Gated estates aim to exclude non-residents; pedestrian through-route closure to deter undesirables. After all, strangers might be coming to rob! But when I'm in a strange city, I want to walk wherever interesting, to experience its differentness – not feel a trespasser. Threshold markers, like archways or ever-open gates, don't shut anyone out, but by making strangers aware they're conspicuous as visitors, that the place is 'owned' by an identifiable community, are significant crime deterrents. Walking routes that lead to a centre – whether hard courtyard, soft park or social building – reinforce this proprietary identity. Routes that just go *through* a place, dilute it.

Crime and private property are growing phenomena. They feed each other. There are two broad schools of thought about architectural means of reducing opportunist crime.[9] One is to enhance *private* realms so every place is guarded by its owners. The other is to develop *public* life so places are always full of life and never abandoned. Both have

social and political implications. Personally I don't doubt that the current exaggerated advocacy of privateness will, locally, lower robbery statistics. However, by stressing *private* ownership it's feeding a tendency to take for yourself whenever you can. In society at large, therefore, it undermines ensocializing values and may well be counter-productive. Private ownership and gated estates least guarantee safe *public* spaces!

To be safe and vandal free, public spaces need also to feel 'owned' – valued and cared for by their community of users, not just leftover property. Places of individual character enriched by the 'colours' of life around them are places of spirit, places worth valuing and caring for. Ubiquitous bleak grass fields aren't.

Through arched passages you can enter another realm: an unexpected courtyard, a quiet street, a residential area. The scale, darkness, texture, shape, slope and twist of the passage can help reinforce the change of inner state that accompanies the change in outer place.

But even these are improvable. Shrubs, trees, berms and buildings can define distinct areas, each used and 'owned' differently.[10]

Improved places, however, are good property bargains, so are often taken over by new, better off, occupants. Gentrification invariably improves appearance and land values – making houses too expensive for locals. The very success of environmental improvement risks social erosion. The same differential buying power that turns Welsh communities into English holiday houses, mostly empty, unsupportive of community facilities, yuppifies urban areas so nurses, firemen and essential workers can't afford to live there. No schools, no shops: no community. No plumbers, teachers, street cleaners: no functioning town.

Appropriate tenancy structures, levies on resale price increases and community-specific improvements, like centring areas around workshop facilities and play-streets, can moderate these effects. There are also financial devices, like split purchase. Here, purchasers pay the full building cost and 'borrow' the site cost. This is high and revised annually in line with local property index. If they sell to locals, this price component is again deferred; outsiders pay full price.[11] Some countries, like Austria, long the poor neighbour to Germany, restrict land ownership to nationals – something many Eastern European countries wish they'd thought of earlier!

Environmental quality is inextricably interwoven with economic cause and effect. There's a view that new businesses are necessary to initiate any spiral of environmental improvement. These need new 'executive-class' people. To attract them, depressed areas need a new image. They need environmental improvements to stimulate the economic recovery that will *really* improve the environment. But

what sorts of improvement? And who gets pushed out?

New cultural facilities, like concert halls and art galleries, can indeed reverse urban decline – as 1980s Glasgow clearly demonstrated. Beyond attracting 'the right people', they boost morale. But high-profile projects are expensive, can be socially exclusive and – not having grown organically – economically risky. The cheapest way run-down districts improve is by settlement by artists. Invariably, where artists start – *because* property is cheap – up-market values follow. The artists are then pushed out. Suitably managed with anti-eviction safeguards, however, cheap studio space can both culturally reinvigorate a city district *and* initiate economic and social recovery. This is the other way to invest in the arts.

Cities for people

Cities are about diversity. All sorts of people – occupation, culture, race and income level – live (almost) side by side. This means people different from ourselves: alien groups to fear, not see as individuals. Once you get to know people, this is reversed. They're individuals foremost; differences in race, occupation and background merely make them more interesting. But even getting to know next-door neighbours isn't easy. Cities can be lonely places, with informal meetings strangled by alienated inhibition. I doubt anything contributes so much to social malaise as anonymity – the feeling that you know nobody and nobody cares whether they know you. Certainly it's easier to shoplift a department store than a shop where you know the owner.

Opportunities to meet partly depend on appropriate facilities – especially

places to *do* things together. Doing things
together, from child care, work, study or
sport to participatory entertainments –
particularly with the same small community of people – breaks down barriers.
Tenant-managed community rooms,
kick-about football areas, motorcycle
repair tool clubs, food buying co-ops and
allotment plots all give such opportunities.

*For urban footpaths, 'inviting' doesn't
have to mean garden city rural.*

To quite a large extent *how* people meet is supported or hindered by surroundings. If I wanted to obstruct this community-building process I would design apartments where I wouldn't dare let my children out to play, where the only places for casual contact with others are concrete access balconies, impersonal corridors, lifts and refuse chutes, none conducive to relaxed meeting. For the better off, separate housing units with private, self-contained gardens and *en suite* garages may be desirable, but if you drive to work, to shops, friends and entertainments, how do you meet your neighbours? Dutch, German and Danish studies show how parking restricted to *ends* of streets builds community.[12] In walking to your car, you meet neighbours. With automatic garage doors, you don't. The more activities overlap in the communal realm, the more chance meetings.

Local shops don't only depend on housing density; destination-focused short-cuts bring more housing within walking distance. The more inviting are footpaths, the more used so safer, and the better they compete with driving. Otherwise, once you get into a car, you might as well go to somewhere bigger. Many urban housing projects have village-sized populations, but being *housing* projects, provide this only; everything else – everything with social-building potential – is somewhere else.

Stopping places from laundrettes with tea-making facilities to bridges where you can idly watch the stream beneath also need to be inviting. If not they won't help to make friends any more than will a concrete parents' bench by a sand pit in draughty shade or fierce sun, unprotected from traffic's noise, fumes and aggressive movement, and surrounded by ugliness. Plenty of landscaped roundabouts have park benches – always empty! Daily life is full of little activities that, in welcoming surroundings, encourage meetings between strangers. In hostile surroundings they won't. In such ways, environmental *quality* powerfully affects social health.

It is in the poorer parts of cities that 'weed' trees grow up on abandoned land, yet it is they that make the surroundings, however dull or lifeless, bearable.

In every city live many dispossessed and underprivileged, unemployed, materially poor, even homeless and social outcasts.[13] Poorer areas typically have the worst environmental conditions – and naturally so, because the better off buy their way out of them! It is here the environmental, architectural, social and personal problems of cities are most acutely visible. Financial poverty may be greater in the countryside, but it's bleaker in cities. Without monetary buffers, environment is often life-sapping: traffic, squalor, shabbiness, abandonment, decay, unapproachable materials and hard, dead forms. Walking through mass housing projects, it's rare to experience song in the heart – yet we live by the heart! No wonder stimulus is a saleable commodity.

Places built for poor people need to be cheap. With little money, nothing is left over for 'beautification'. But imprinting spirit into matter costs no more than does building containers for statistics. Love doesn't cost money, nor does user involve-

freed from its shackling equation with money.

Sadly, construction processes that involve people as human beings, rather than mechanical repetitive producers, usually make buildings cost more. Cost-wise, they can never compete with mass-produced dressed-up boxes. Self-built buildings, however, are much cheaper than anything from any producer's system. Projects by organizations like Habitat for Humanity, architects like Archetype, and housing and community associations prove this many times over. Yet it's still an uncommon path. Could it be councils and governments are obsessed with control?

Self-building, whether doing every-thing or just painting or landscaping, doesn't just increase affordability – at least as important is self-esteem. Unlike employed builders, tenants and occupants involved in construction and maintenance are free to build environ-ments of love.

Individual design can be a licence for an individualistic free-for-all and the disputes that follow. The techniques described in Chapter 9 overcome this. To balance responsibilities to community with freedom for individuals needs a structured design sequence from overall community through local area quality, with communally-responsible building exteriors to family-controlled interiors. Listening design unlocks thinking from imagination-blinkers so people can build the places they deserve. Consensus design harmonizes conflicting viewpoints, agendas and pressures. This is an effective first step in community building.

Cities are for all: children as well as adults, poor as well as rich, yet the decisions that shape them are largely made by a restricted social, income and age group, mostly men. Designing for people we've never met, though undesir-

Hand-made textures bring so much more life to a place. They are something more easily afforded by the poor than by the better off.

ment in design and construction – in fact, things are cheaper that way! Cheapness needn't mean poor environment. Cheap – sometimes even free – materials can be the most attractive, approachable and alive. Poor districts of older cities are often graced by ivy, plants and moss on walls, roofs and paving. Buildings carefully patched, not renovated, age gracefully. Materials like brick, wood or colourwash aren't expensive: some, like the vegetation, cost nothing but take time to maintain. Where labour is free, time is

able, is sometimes unavoidable. Only by trying to project ourselves into their life and state of soul can we meaningfully ask: what would support these (unknown) individuals and what hinder their inner growth? Outer analysis only lets us react to what already is, what has been brought into being by financially disproportionate pressures. Reaction causes counter-reaction, breeding bitter divisions. To heal we need insight, and insight means stepping beyond our own narrow boundaries. Real insight, because it is concerned with the human being, is always spiritual.

Cities for life

Urban problems aren't confined to the poor, to minorities, children or any other under-represented groups. Alienation is a fact of urban life – too much is too big for

High-density inner city housing (13 two-and three-storey terraced houses) built by tenants from short-life housing.

In summer, inner city air can be 10°C (18°F) hotter than surrounding countryside. Topography and differential warming create diurnal air currents. With clear air paths, these can cool and cleanse city air. Being delicate airflow, however, road embankments, forestry, tall or misplaced buildings can easily obstruct these.[17]

us to open ourselves to. Things and systems don't relate to each other, nor we to them. Large communities have lost their 'translucency'.[14] Unlike village life, we can't easily see the systems – social, ecological, economic – that flow through cities. Daily personal encounters aren't part of a social pattern; urban growth isn't a visible organic process but a series of unasked-for impositions unrelated to previous social form. Cycles of materials, food, waste, water, air and energy are complex, invisible, incomplete and technology dependent. Topography, watershed, ecology and climatic zones aren't legible. Waste heat and light so blur seasonal and diurnal rhythms that month or time of day often aren't obvious without thinking.

Experiencing growth and change as organically developing processes helps root us in time and place. This is about the working of the *living* on the *enduring*. Rooms where sunlight creates significantly different moods at different times of day and year, buildings that glow with life in rain or dark, places with different appeal each season, allow rhythmic changes to play over physically durable place. Despite ground slope and microclimatic variation, we can rarely see topographic form as a whole. Stepped or steeply-sloping squares, unexpected vistas, short-cut steps up hillsides and streams cascading down them can recreate a coherent sense of the earth's shape beneath our feet.[15]

That such things give rooting security is easy to observe in small communities; they know where they are, where they've come from and who they are. A health-giving theme is no less relevant to larger communities.

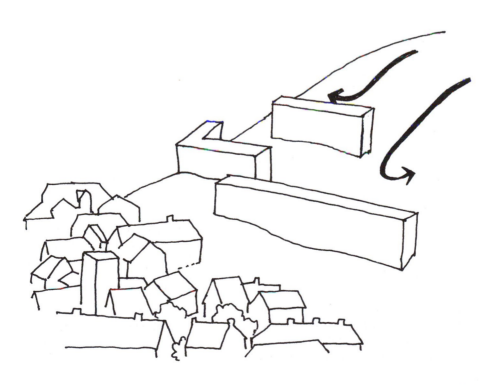

Different topographic, moisture and sun-orientated situations produce markedly different microclimates. Windy ridge, sun-drenched slope, sleepy hollow are essential to *whole* place experience. Though central to landscape use both agricultural and recreational, they're rarely considered in urban design. Yet these link us to source – a de-alienating influence. Also, they're *economically* significant: in temperate climates, shops and businesses dependent on customer mood prefer the sunny side of streets, while banks and cinemas accept the shady side.[16] Street trade grows up around sunny steps, not in shady, draughty ravines. In hot climates, shoppers avoid afternoon sun. Traditional designs, like Middle Eastern covered markets, respond to climate; so do things that 'happen' organically. Most modern design doesn't. Sun- and shade-sensitive design isn't just vital for soul uplift, but also economic viability.

Cities depend upon *mechanical* support. This grows exponentially with size and speed-of-life – and these feed each other. Cars, lorries and construction machinery are noisy. It's hard to find silence anywhere in the world; cities in particular are always washed by background noise. Quiet is so strikingly therapeutic, think what noise – and the unnoticed tension it brings – must be doing all the time.

Anything which reduces noise improves urban environment. This starts with traffic reduction. Public transport, water buses, cycleways and, especially, walking routes all contribute. In many European cities cycle routes – distanced from traffic – link traffic-calmed 'home zones',[18] and networks of passages and stairs weave between main thoroughfares, well served by trams or electric buses.[19]

Traffic may be the lifeblood of cities, but it also kills them. *Through* traffic may

Acoustic sections: noise is intensified by echoes from buildings or cutting walls (left). Inclined surfaces of absorbent materials can reduce this (right).

Non-noise-sensitive buildings and continuous obstructions as noise screen. As porosity would compromise acoustic efficacy, a broken skyline or plan helps reduce wind turbulence. This also breaks up noise pattern.

serve other places, but does nothing for those it goes through. Sometimes it's avoidable. I used to live outside a small seaside town. Over the years the road leading to it grew from sleepy and winding to a four-lane trunk road, cut through the landscape. It led to a densely built old town with minimal car parks, on a headland surrounded by sea! Roads are expensive to build; car parks destroy towns. I wondered how much cheaper out-of-town parking (on fields, as demand only existed in fine summer

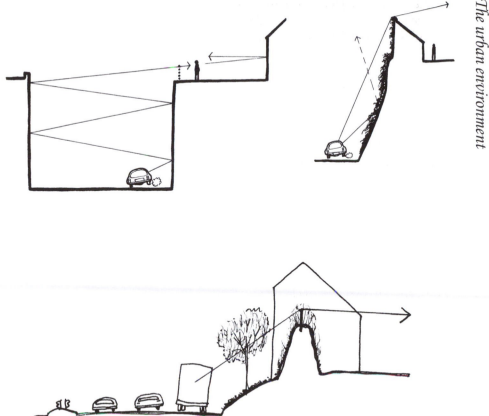

weather) and a free bus service would have been. Thirty years later, this did happen!

Psychological issues being more intransigent than physical ones, few cities have found traffic problems easy to solve. Sometimes places need to turn a strong back to traffic; a barrier to noise, fumes, speed and risk. As exhaust is heavy and doesn't travel far, distance from, or elevation above, roads helps air quality.[20] If roads can't be sunk in cuttings, buildings can function as traffic screens. Both work best with echo-minimizing sectional design, and surfaces cloaked by noise-absorbent plants or fronted by trees. This foliage also helps clean air.

Showing a strong back doesn't help retailers dependent on passing traffic. They need inviting views in, preferably from traffic lights and places where traffic is slower. Glimpses are enough, if sufficiently intriguing. Trees pruned for open view at windscreen level and water-features, street musicians or other noise masking can mitigate the noise that accompanies view-lines.

Street life, buildings as traffic screen,
inviting view, leaf shade, rippling water
(California).

In the semi-protected world of an arcade, the focus of attention and sensory climate can be more human-orientated than in the busy street.

It was of course traffic which brought into being places to stop, buy and sell. With iron wheels on cobbles, a horse (plus dung) for every horsepower, such streets were more crowded, noisy and smelly than those today, but street life was coloured by people, not fast-moving pressed-metal containers. Cities designed for traffic are too spread out; nothing within walking distance, eight-lane roads you can't cross. Slow speeds and road crossability are vital: 20 m.p.h. for streets and residential 'home zones', 5 m.p.h. for pedestrian-priority areas and 'play-streets'. Even 200 vehicles per hour start to turn roads from commu-nity spaces into barriers, compromising neigbourhood sociability.[21]

When pedestrianized streets first appeared, shopkeepers resisted them – but they proved to increase trade. Streets where pedestrians have dominance over vehicles invite relaxed ambling, alfresco dining or shopping at outdoor stalls. Likewise, congestion charging, though widely resisted, has proved highly successful, with journey-time and stress-reduction benefits as well as air-quality and noise-reduction ones.[22]

In traffic-congested cities, cycling is usually faster than driving – hence

When we look at old photographs of
familiar places, we can often see
how little has changed. Yet
everything has changed. What were
then sociable places, bounded by
buildings and hedges, are now linear
– hence unsociable – corridors of
motorized movement. Squeezed to
the side are narrow bands for
pedestrian movement.

*Places once coloured by human meetings
are now compartmentalized strips,
dominated by the noise, speed and latent
aggression of motor vehicles. Yet the actual
material alterations are small and subtle –
in many cases too small to show up on a
1:100 scale plan.*

London's cycle couriers, even ambulances. In rush hours I used to find walking time comparable to public transport. But vehicular noise and fumes along the main road bits of my route undid all the calm of dark, quiet canals or the interest of delivery-men manhandling goods in narrow alleys. Civic investment – minuscule compared to road building – could open up pedestrian exits from vehicular cul-de-sacs, so linking walkway fragments into routes free from main road stress.

To encourage walkers, routes need to be reasonably direct, attractive and *safe*. Crossing roads typically halves urban walking speeds. Less, and slower, traffic eases this. Slower speed limits aren't only safer (kinetic energy at 20 m.p.h. is below

Even a three-step (60 cm) raised pavement considerably reduces sensory assault from traffic. Railings add further security. When, as here, the pavement is at upper floor level, traffic noise, fumes and visual impact are noticeably less and we're more aware of people, displayed goods and place than of vehicles. Devices like this, together with arcades and passages, can increase the level of human activity, hence urban buzz, while reducing the stress-inducing qualities increased density usually brings.

Walking routes for topographic drama (Edinburgh).

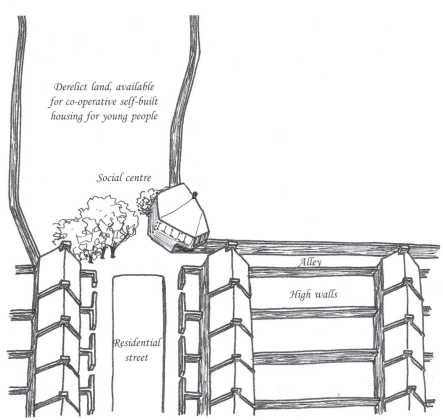

Derelict land, available
for co-operative self-built
housing for young people

Social centre

Alley

High walls

Residential
street

half that at 30 m.p.h.) but reduce stress. The more appealing and faster is walking, the more people do it. This doesn't just reduce noise, improve air and personal fitness – it's also cheaper than building and maintaining roads. Raised pavements protect pedestrians from traffic. Colonnades, with their enclosing gestures, additionally focus attention on people and shopfronts.

Pedestrian, railway or river bridges, sometimes stairs, alleys, cliff-edge-like footpaths or arched tunnels under buildings, are experiences I seek out on any walking route. Concrete road underpasses I avoid. Also, they're a lot less safe. Lamentably, city walking, even cycling, involves safety issues. As risk increases when there's nobody around, continual casual observation is a significant deterrent. Sight lines are straight, but straight-line streets and alleys are uninviting to walk along, so self-defeating from the safety point of view. Magnet activities, from late shops to clubs, 24-hour services and all-night cafés, can keep danger spots populated during risk hours. Sheltered housing, upper-storey restaurants and other situations where people typically look out of windows make premium 'observers'. The greater the mix of activities, the longer are the life-hours of public spaces and the more interesting they are to look at and walk in – hence the safer they are.

Walking isn't always rejuvenating. On even pavements through even activities in an even textured environment, punctuated only by main roads, it's life-sapping. Sometimes the contrast between commercial faces and stark sterile parking and loading areas conveys exploitationist motives. Sometimes the economic forces behind entrepreneurial vigour are visibly dominant. Huge financial and administrative institutions express their power as imposing buildings – forceful icons but

'Murder mile': many parts of many cities are desolate, unloved – spiralling into despair. Yet imagine small changes: occupied buildings on the derelict plot; the self-sown trees ten years bigger; pedestrian-priority streets; rainwater as a landscape feature.

In this project, one of the site's few visual assets was a narrow brick-walled alley which, however, had a record of sexual assaults. We proposed that the housing association social centre be located as 'gatehouse' and double as a public café to improve social and financial viability and draw more people over longer hours. A cantilevered upper floor lets windows look down the alley, bringing this former danger spot into public view.

What messages do our surroundings convey? Do they make us feel valued as individuals?

their lifeless blank faces starve passers-by of living experience. Some are even mirror-faced. To get a feeling of what's going on inside is like trying to read someone's thoughts through mirrored sunglasses.

Places given over to super-sell make us feel exploited, unfree. Shop displays may be acceptably low pressure, but the *architecture* forces focus upon their wares. Much depends upon scale: short alleys, streets or arcades are *routes* fortuitously lined by shops, but longer ones, destinations in themselves, are shopping *zones*. You enter them not to taste freely but to buy! Just as casinos have no clocks to remind you of the real world, indoor malls focus on goods for sale, not the life of sky and season. Sometimes even shop thresholds are removed, making displays seem unowned, unguarded, there to take. This is architecture to encourage shoplifting.

Shopping malls are, effectively, pedestrian streets – but offering unidimensional experience. One activity – shopping – has, despite 24-hour opening, one life-period and pattern of peaks. Offices have another. Entertainments, residential areas, service workshops – each have their own activity periods. None, on their own, make balanced, whole – or safe – places. Also, each needs enough parking for peak demand. Add all these peaks and it's a sea of parking. Time-share them and it's only moderate. Extensive parking isn't just bleak and expensive, it so decompresses urban life that it becomes car dependent – and doesn't even feel urban.

Mixed use was natural to pre-industrial cities; people made things and sold them from where they lived. Today, with mobility, specialization, industry and *compartmentalized thinking*, it isn't. But the *demands* for many uses, side by side, still exist. Urban living, work near home, shops and service workshops near workplaces are all popular. Telecommunications has given such impetus to work/live arrangements that 55 million Americans now work (at least in part) from home.[23] Rush-hour traffic is an industrial era phenomenon – first by foot, cycle and train, then, with spatial dispersion, by car. Flexitime and 24/7 disperse congestion peaks, but only work/live proximity reduces traffic.

After decades of zoning, mixed use is now recognized as vital to social wholeness, security and urban colour, as well as traffic reduction. Not all uses are compatible, so nuisance (noise, fumes, traffic, etc.) parameters are important.

Slaughterhouses aren't good neighbours to housing, nor nightclubs to chapels of rest. Commonly, 'mixed use' means shops, housing and perhaps offices. But what sort of shops? Most developers want high-status brand-name stores, but few residents buy shoes or perfume daily. Such uses are mixed, but don't feed each other, so places feel fake. Organic commerce takes a different form. In post-*perestroika* (actually *un*structuring) Moscow, ground-floor apartment-block windows became (not quite legal) shops – supplementing pavement, subway and kiosk vendors. They weren't cheaper than proper shops (Vodka cost more and was less certain not to be petroleum based!), but they were in the right place and selling what people needed. *Favela* traders, and indeed all unplanned, non-car-dependent commerce, grows up like this. This symbiotic 'rightness-for-place and -purpose' isn't just essential for economic viability – it makes places *authentic*. Impromptu traders can't pay for high rent locations, so need great sensitivity to life currents. For viable *development*, this is equally vital. Not living in this tenuous-survival world, few designers have this, but the unfolding biography and mood aspects of the consensus design process (see Chapter 9) offer a different route to the same end.

Whereas traffic needs planning, life vigour thrives best where development is organic. This doesn't mean a free-for-all, where the richest, biggest, most prestigious – *and place-deadening* – building wins, but creating situations that invite shops and entertainments to grow up. With careful listening to where conditions best favour them, the locations and levels for offices, shops, workshops, even parking, suggest themselves.

This approach gives an opportunity to adjust 'perceived density' so small commercial centres can feel busy enough

Typically, towns adapted for vehicles have large parts dominated by traffic. Often, 80 per cent of the visible space in which we move is flat road surface and aggressive horizontal movement, while buildings rise vertically to contain our vision. Towns for people traditionally enjoy a much more lively interplay between horizontal and vertical.

and large ones be diffused into less pressured human-scale passages and squares. Places can come into being where sociable commercial functions organically grow up – quays, streets and larger squares where it's natural for all sorts of commercial interchange to take place; off-street courts and upper-level arcades and passageways. Rather than suites within large, place-deadening buildings, offices can be 'personal-faced' around peaceful courtyards. If this sounds unprofitable, think of rents in London's Inns of Court! Moreover, high buildings don't improve density; they just cost more to build! Their real justification is Freudian.

Activities 'colour' places, but single activities are monochrome. Concentrated, varied and *visible* human activity is central to urban vitality. But as unrelieved stimulation can cross the border to stress, we need places to rest, to 'take a break' from pressure – from people-watching seats to havens for soul recuperation. The greater our need, the more personal space required to rest eye, ear, nose and soul. We need quiet places with 'difference-in-sameness' ambience, places of respite from 'involuntary attention' – all those situations demanding continual alertness – nature permeated places like sun-filled and dapple-shaded walled gardens, set apart from busy streets by archway entrances. Also, places near water, the greatest of all calmers – fountains, flowing or calm water, pools, rivers, canals, large expanses.

Almost every city has grown up around water, its commerce, power or bridges bringing them into being. Yet all too often riversides are just major roads, car parks, warehouses and inaccessible industrial zones. Even riverside parks aren't relaxing with fast roads at your back. Most small streams are now underground sewers, their disappearance a major loss

to topographic understanding. Most cities – but not their children – turn their back on ponds, canals and streams. Out of adult sight they're not only squalid but dangerous. Others fill docks with rubbish. Yet in some cities streams rush beside streets, cleaning air and enlivening mood. In Freiburg each shop door has its own bridge.[24] Water is perhaps the greatest environmental asset any city has, yet how rarely is it developed!

Sky – its space and quiet clouds – is a healer everywhere available. Visible sky, natural light and sunlight all powerfully influence mood. Many indoor workers so crave sunlight that they spend their whole holidays to get it. Dead, grey, polluted air induces similar grey moods in us. As morale affects every kind of activity, this makes a stronger economic argument for pollution control even than the cost of corroded building fabric. As looking over building cliffs means neck strain, we see less sky so easily feel trapped – another stress and depression pressure. Fortunately, even in heavily built-up areas there's some sky. How many psychiatric hospitals would domes over cities cost?

Low, widely spaced buildings dilute urbanism so even vast cities just feel suburban. Selective 'view windows' focused on skyscape and distant views are more effective. Spanish colonial streets, designed to 1573 *Laws of the Indies* specifications and still occasionally found in the south-western USA, terminated in landscape views.[25] Cities on hillsides can enjoy squares ending in balustrades, steep passageways pointing out into space, unexpected galleries, staircases and ramps in view and wind, amongst treetops or overlooking rooftops.

Urban experience doesn't work in less-than-urban space. Traditional European shopping streets are often as high as wide, medieval ones three times as high.[26] The smaller are streets, the more human their

scale. Trees, awnings and curb-edge arcades narrow them. Bends, road-ends and out-jutting buildings 'deflect' or 'terminate' them, closing the space to a scale we can relate to and making inhumanely long strips into a series of smaller places.[27] But 1:1 proportion feels quite different in a two-storey street or a 15-storey canyon. Low buildings can be in shorter blocks and twist for human-scale closed views. High buildings closing views can feel like prison walls. Short-plan ones are just blocks, not street-faces. High tends to be grand and long; low, short and informal. Broaden streets to 1:2 proportion, and three storeys makes a market street, six and a half a parade avenue. Both have the same building density, but in one all the people are in a narrow street, in the other there's so much space for traffic it takes over the mood. There's also a dimensional aspect. Twenty-three metres (75 ft) being the limit of face and voice recognition,[28] Christopher Alexander and colleagues[29] consider 70 ft (21 metres) the maximum width for small public squares, and 60 ft (18 metres) the optimum.

Close-walled streets and courtyards, so effective for urban experience compression, make ground-level rooms dark. Good for indoor-orientated or night-mood activities like pubs and restaurants, but not to live in. Daylight at street level depends upon reflection off materials (including the ground) as well as visible sky. Damp concrete paving can make the whole world seem grey; brick makes it warm. Whitewash (especially if a warmish, soft white) can brighten even a north-facing yard, but paints need careful use. Singing, light-bearing colours are easily sullied by grime; quieter or earthier colours are more tolerant.

Cities are concentrations of people. Multiple interactions invigorate life, social, cultural and economic. But

Like dead giants, large buildings can tower over us, dominating place and person: 23 storeys, 1 km (3300 ft) long – not comfortable to be within its embrace!

High-density juxtaposition of different activities is at the heart of urban living. Though attractive places to visit, inadequate sunlight, play space and greenery, cramping neighbour proximity and street noise can be claustrophobically oppressive to live in. At certain stages of life, the social and cultural richness of dense urban experience outweigh the disadvantages. For families, however, we need to find ways of combining this with the renewing qualities of light, air, greenery, quiet and space to feel free in.

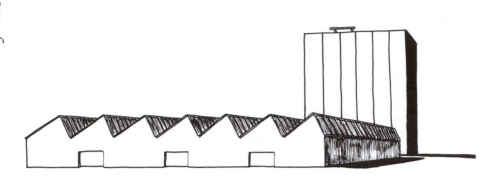

How many square miles are covered by buildings which try to avoid sunlight? Painters seek north light to not distort their colours, whereas office and factory designers seek it to minimize variations in indoor climate. In doing so they eliminate the element of life which can breathe vitality into otherwise sterile places and joy into human hearts.

The conflicting requirements of urban compression and sunlight can sometimes be resolved in section. Where street sunlight isn't critical the space can be narrowed, concentrating sunlight on building faces. Where sun on buildings is a problem (for glare and air-conditioning load – which says something about these sorts of buildings!), turning them can maximize sunlight to open spaces. These simple functional responses to need-of-sun produce a language of compressed and contrasting open spaces with sun avenues and pathways, twisting according to cast shadow; sun and light matched to peak use times, much as we place windows within rooms. Yet so many gables lack windows!

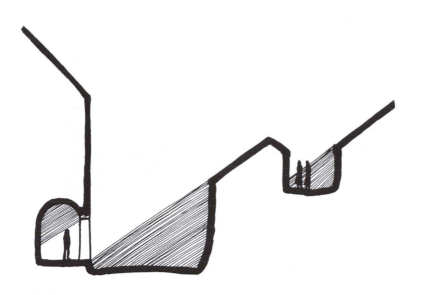

unrelieved dynamism can be stressful. Unless we design for soul nurture as a first priority, maximize nature's life-renewing potential, tranquilizers and worse are inevitable.

This isn't about soul nurture versus profitability, society versus economy, aesthetics versus practicality or jobs versus sustainable ecology – these all depend on each other. Nor does it mean designing buildings for practical uses then making them look nice, but of doing it the other way around. It means starting by asking what a place should say, what spirit it should emanate. Then asking what sort of moods-of-place and sensory experiences would support this; then how current processes and latent forces can be harnessed to bring these into being. It means starting by listening, by thinking not of privately delineated buildings but of communally experienced place.

Eco-cities: Utopia or practicality?

I've never designed an eco-city, but urban eco-projects I have. Urban planning is largely about infrastructure and strategy. Eco-projects aren't, but they highlight what's needed. All cities used to be bound to local ecology, enmeshed in local cycles, limited by local carrying capacity. Meat can walk hundreds of miles,[30] but vegetables too long in an ox-cart aren't fresh. This limited city size; disease limited density and population. Modern cities are different. Though unavoidably enmeshed in *global* ecology, consequences are too far away to see to trigger self-correcting feedback. Typically, cities' relationships to their 'host' ecosystems are parasitic not symbiotic: they *take*

rather than *exchange*. Their systems are linear, open, not cyclic, closed. Does this mean sustainable cities are impossible?

Challenging, certainly, but I've never been quite convinced of the meaning of 'impossible'. With two-thirds of the world's population urban, we can't afford not to try. It's definitely not hard to go a long way towards this ideal. The technologies already exist; also, in places, the systems and, even – more rarely – the consciousness and (some) political will.

A first step has to be localization. Unless consequences, feedback and cycles are visible, good intentions are no guarantee of good results. In nature, small cycles link into bigger ones, but locally, they're substantially whole with multi-path links, so flexible and resilient. *Planned* ecosystems are never so rich. Complication, ambiguity and undefinability don't go with planning. Even mixed use and multi-role have, until recently, been much resisted. For resilience, planned systems need robustness to misuse and highly visible (preferably economically significant) feedback.

Obviously eco-cities assume integrated multi-mode transport. The mode interchange points – tram to bus to foot, train to rickshaw and cycle hire, land to water – make obvious activity nodes around which shops, entertainments and service offices thrive. Eco-buildings are also assumed, though many so claiming suffer from 'the bigger the name, the grander the claim' syndrome. With photovoltaics and wind power (but not vibration-transmitting generators mounted on buildings!),[31] these can also contribute electricity. Weather-powered systems don't necessarily match demand, but the diversity of urban opportunities tend to balance this out. Wherever energy is needed as motive power or heat, I prefer lower-technology systems like wind pumps, CHP[32] or solar water-heating –

more efficient, less to go wrong, easier to link cause and effect.

For cool climates, eco-building means solar design – but not at cost to social layouts. Zig-zag façades or 15° (about one hour) variation from optimum orientation allow non-parallel buildings so more socially-focusing gestures.

In hot climates, shade – especially in late afternoon – is critical. This means no east–west streets without kinks, taller buildings or trees to block low sun. Generally, spreading trees are best to the south, for shade beneath; bulky ones to the west for long cast shade. As vines grow fast and far, these make excellent shaders, vertical to the west, horizontal for noon sun.

Zero-energy, CO_2-neutral buildings are achievable even at high densities. Bedzed housing and workplace development, London (architect: Bill Dunster Architects).

South   South-west,   West, east (if required)
               south-east

Hot climates: shade for different orientations.

Urban life depends on imports of food, water, air and power, and exports of sewage and wastes. But these life-giving flows are largely out of sight and out of mind, separating us from nature's life-giving cycles and weakening awareness of the effects of our activities (Hydroelectricity works).

Most buildings produce heat. Air-conditioners deliberately dump heat – downwind it's warm. Even in hot climates, why waste it? This brings up issues of heat *matching*. Like industrial waste heat, that from freezers – whether supermarket cabinets or ice-rinks – is reusable for fruit and timber drying, heating buildings, greenhouses and swimming pools, and for low-temperature industrial processes. Heat matching needs proximity, making it a design as well as a technical issue.

It's obvious that ecologically healthy supply and waste cycles are vital for planetary health. The more local these are, the more complete, more resilient and self-correcting, and more *visible*. This visibility encourages proprietary steward-ship. Connectedness is also important for *human* health.

How many people know where water comes from and goes to beyond the limits of tap and plughole? While cholera in nineteenth century London proved the undesirability of urban wells, most water

Greywater treatment as amenity feature in atrium.

doesn't need to be potable. Rainwater is normally piped away, adding to flood risk. Harvesting needs collection strategies like roofs and paving to multiply volume, surface channels and ground levels regraded to direct flow to trees, ponds and cisterns.

While sewage is conventionally treated by biological systems, these needn't be conventional sewage farms. Flowforms,

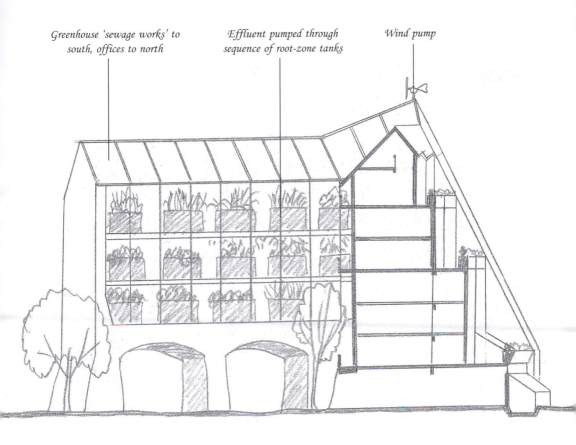

Greenhouse 'sewage works' to
south, offices to north

Effluent pumped through
sequence of root-zone tanks

Wind pump

'Living machine'-type sewage works.

reed-beds and wetlands can make attractive, even artistic, watergardens and tropical greenhouses. Greywater is much easier to treat – perhaps by watergardens in parks or between roads and cycleways or cascade-linked planter troughs on walls – till clean enough for irrigation and toilets.

Unless they're just overblown suburbs, cities can never grow all their own food – but, as 1970s pioneer projects and, more cruelly, besieged cities demonstrate, a surprising lot can. Food growing is more an issue of consciousness than of design. Few city dwellers have contact with the food cycle, but rooftop gardening, green terraces and window greenhouses bring at least some aspects within almost universal reach.

Landfill dumping is expensive. Many European cities both undertake municipal composting and encourage householders to compost in gardens or worm-bins. This doesn't just close the food cycle, but through the act of separating compostable and non-compostable material raises consciousness. Farmers' markets with their unprocessed seasonal produce bring a stronger sense of yearly rhythm than supermarket Christmas displays.

Urban horticulture isn't problem free. Vandalism, crop robbery, even waste dumping, are common. Private or community supervised plots minimize such abuses. In countries like Russia, Germany and Sweden, allotments double as places of sensory delight where families live all summer. In dense cities, land cost and space scarcity have made loft conversions common. Many include roof-gardens. Fork-depth planters maximize food-growing opportunities. While public-realm edible landscaping risks soft fruit thrown around, blackberry hedges are multi-functional: providing fruit, bird-food and habitat and thorny security. Some soils are too contaminated for edible crops, but cities need plenty of greenery for clean air. Linked greenery makes 'greenway' wildlife corridors to tie in to the many scrubland wildlife reserves every city has.

All this is relatively easy for new districts, but what about old buildings, old roads and old cities? Land is rarely a problem; defunct, underused and brown-field sites abound, though many are small or awkward – so need imaginative design – or contaminated, limiting their uses. Most old cities already have well-developed public transport, often with cycle-way networks. Many are so congested, traffic reduction policies, however unpopular, are unavoidable. Though building upgrading for energy conservation can be complicated, it's nonetheless widely done.

All the ingredients of eco-cities are already common practice, but not co-ordinated, not common and rarely with sustainable intent. This makes them *very* achievable, even in old cities; even more so in new ones.

Notes and references

1 Altoon, R. (2002) Green retail. In *Urban Land*. November/December.

2 Figures cited by UNESCO spokesman (1995) *Eco-Villages Conference*, Findhorn, Scotland.

3 McHarg, I. (1971) *Design with Nature*, pp. 187–195. Doubleday/Natural History Press, New York.

4 Other factors include seaports ('humanity at last!') and agricultural centres (a paddock or orchard to every house) – hence dense San Francisco and dispersed Los Angeles.

5 This is well borne out by Barbara Franziska Neumann's (2002) study of two London Squares: *From Space to Place*. Dissertation at Oxford Brookes University.

6 As in Foster's Reichstag and Greater London Council buildings, and Rogers' proposed Welsh Assembly building.

7 Techniques for this, I describe in detail in *Consensus Design* (2002). Architectural Press.

8 Described in fuller detail in: Day, C. (2002) *Consensus Design*. Architectural Press.

9 In addition to territoriality, surveillance, boundary definition, access control and maintenance, the focus of the physical design approach (see: Newman, O. (1973) *Defensible Space*. Collier Books, New York; and Jeffery *Crime Prevention Through Environmental Design*. CPTED),

there are management and community involvement issues. See: Schneider, R. H. and Kitchen T. (2002) *Planning for Crime Prevention: A Transatlantic Perspective.* Routledge.

10 These need a careful balance between place-enclosure needs and sight-lines for security by, for instance, pruning lower branches for clear view.

11 'Local need' is an appealing concept, but its weak definition leaves openings for racistic exploitation. This can be overcome by using multi-layer criteria: work, childhood, residency, family ties and (where appropriate) language.

12 Gehl, J. (1987) *Life Between Buildings: Using Public Spaces.* Van Nostrand Reinhold, New York.

13 2002 surveys found greater poverty in rural than urban Britain. Also, that Welsh farmers' income averaged around £55 a week – about the same as single persons' welfare, but for an 80 hour week! *On Your Farm* and *Farming Today*, BBC Radio 4, November 2002.

14 A concept I owe to Leopold Köhr, the father of small-scale socio-economics.

15 Maximizing the interest in changes of level mustn't penalize disabled users. Sloping courtyards need diagonal routes for wheelchairs or prams.

16 See: Grillo, P. J. (1975) *Form, Function and Design.* Dover Publications.

17 Baden-Würtemburg Innenministerium (1990) *Städtebauliche Klimafibel: 1.*

18 The British version of the well-proven Dutch *Woonerf:* pedestrian-dominated, traffic-calmed streets with 20 m.p.h. speed limit.

19 Electric buses, being rubber-tyred, don't need expensive tracks. They're common in Russia.

20 Carbon monoxide and particulates are heavy and hence accumulate in roadside basements. Sulphur compounds, steam, CO_2 and NO_X aren't.

21 Appleyard and Lintel (1971) *Environmental Quality of City Streets.* University of California; and Buchanan, C. (1963) *Traffic in Towns.* HMSO, cited in: Alexander, C., Ishikawa, S., Silverstein, M. et al. (1977) *A Pattern Language.* Oxford University Press.
200 cars per hour isn't acceptable in car-wed USA; there the developers' optimum peak is 800–1000, each way. At 10 000 vehicles a day or one every two seconds, not everyone would think this pedestrian friendly! Bohl, C. C. (2002) *Place Making: Developing Town Centers, Main Streets and Urban Villages.* Urban Land Institute.

22 London's congestion zone, introduced in February 2003, brought dramatic improvements which effectively silenced previously vociferous opposition.

23 Bohl, C. C. (2002) Op. cit.

24 Freiburg im Breslau, Germany.

25 Bohl, C. C. (2002) Op. cit.

26 Bohl, C. C. (2002) Ibid.

27 See, in particular: Cullen, G. (1961) *Townscape.* Architectural Press.

28 Thomas, D. (2002) *Architecture and the Urban Environment.* Architectural Press.

29 Alexander, C., Ishikawa, S., Silverstein, M. et al. (1977) *A Pattern Language.* Oxford University Press.

30 Hence British drovers' roads and American cattle trails.

31 Low-speed, vertical-axis wind generators are better, but also need caution!

32 One problem with CHP is finding uses for the heat when not needed for building or water-heating. Crop or product drying, woodworm-protecting timber or industrial pre-heating suggest themselves here.

Chapter 15
Building for tomorrow

Most of us spend most of our time in, near or influenced by built surroundings. We spend our lives in what were once the thoughts of architects. Today's thoughts make the world of tomorrow – an awesome responsibility. Especially so as in barely half a lifespan architecture has destroyed so much cityscape and landscape the world over; so many communities, so much ecology, local and global.

Freons from air-conditioning and foamed insulation are major ozone destroyers; heating and cooling energy, the single biggest CO_2 contributor. Most contemporary building materials are industrially processed, so energy, pollution or CO_2 expensive – aluminium, plastics and cement especially so.[1] There are other ways of heating and of cooling buildings, other, low-pollution materials to build them of. Which systems and products we choose are architectural decisions.

Architecture has effects on place, on life-supporting ecology, on the spirit of the world we live in – it also affects people. Before suburban box-land, urban filing cabinets and grab-for-yourself shopping, people lived differently. Some things were better, some worse. Unspoken values were also different. Nowadays buildings are widely regarded as 'investments' – commodities to make money for their owners. Indeed, some say the architect's role is to design profitable buildings. Architecture itself is more finely geared to profitability then ever before – it's a prime topic of professional journals. Whether or not we endorse this approach, it underlies the majority of the decisions which shape our world.

A common school of thought holds that encouraging profitability will improve the economy of run-down areas; 'quality of life' improvements follow in due course. For others, profit is a dirty word. Certainly, the pursuit of profit has left a trail of environmental destruction, destroyed individuals and divided society.

Yet just as sustainable happiness *results from* the fulfilment of giving to others or inner growth, *sustainable* profit is but a natural consequence of any interchange of goods and services which serve real community needs. This is starting the other way round; starting with benefit to others. In fact, commercial activities only succeed by listening to the situation. Some then serve, some just exploit. Likewise, architecture will only nourish if it listens to the spirit of places and the needs of the human spirit. Such an approach tends naturally to the ecologically and socially – hence economically – viable.

With conventional economic structures, any artistic involvement in making things costs more money. Many people can't afford more than the lovelessly utilitarian – so I am told. But the market shows otherwise: virtually all manufactured products try to *look* good, usually better than they are. As many things we consider essential are unattainable luxuries in other parts of the world, expense is a more secondary issue than we generally admit. The crucial issue is: how long can society remain civilized, even survive, if we continue to value use over beauty, what we (privately and materially) can *get* out of things over what we (communally and spiritually) can *give* through them?

In terms of spirit nourishment deeper than the glossy cosmetic, much of our daily surroundings approach bankruptcy. The poor and less successful often live in aesthetic disasters, surroundings that pressure their values, sensitivities and independence.

Partly as reaction, but mostly in searching for inner renewal from the deep well-springs of nature, some people seek solace in (relatively) wild environments. Wilderness, rough country, even more-or-less unpolluted and little-managed woodland, downland, heath and waterside are essential for the de-stressing, re-rooting and life-renewing all too rarely found in our daily surroundings. Nonetheless, we can go to attractive 'natural' places – parks, woodland,

I challenge any reader to find an ecologically healthy place which, however undramatic, is not also beautiful – and by beautiful I mean nourishing to the spirit. Similarly, ecologically one-sided places tend to offer only one-sided spiritual nutrition. While nature is shaped by self-balancing processes, townscape, not unnaturally, is shaped by material considerations. But why can't built environment offer as wide a range of spirit nourishment as do healthy landscapes?

moorland – and yet somehow not feel nourished. These are landscapes to look at and photograph but not to 'inhale' into the soul; landscapes in which we can't feel a living spiritual presence. In others, however, this life is very strong. You don't need to believe in fairies to experience this (although if you experience it strongly it may become hard to deny their existence!). Such places give us strength and renewal. Why? And what is it we experience there?

At the most material level we may perhaps observe that air is clean enough for lichens to grow or that human activities (including management) are in a harmonious balance with nature.

Inevitably in such places – whether lush, arid or semi-arctic – the ecology is rich. It has so many biological pathways and cycles that you can't make any one simple diagram. This gives it resilience and health. The elusive ambiguities of its multi-track systems make the whole place seem a living being.

These sort of places are food for our spirit. Even where photographically uneventful, we can meaningfully use the word 'beauty'. Aesthetics (a spiritual description) and ecological stability (a material one) are inseparable.

I sometimes have the experience that the weather is an outer picture of how I feel inside. At first sight this is ridiculous – it just goes to prove that I, and others who experience this, are psychologically unhinged! But living weather has within it many moods: a wind can be both fierce and cleansing, sunlight both relaxing and life-stirring at the same moment. Nor are the clouds ever fixed; the weather is always in a living state of change. Somewhere within these many, simultaneous, elusively indefinable moods are those that we need: moods that are outer pictures of our inner soul life. In nature, even developed or disturbed by man (as it is *everywhere* in the world), we can find these moods. Moods that bring cathartic, balancing and soul-healing influences. A wide choice of mood is also important in the *built* environment.

If sequential experiences are seen not as mere consequences of a diagram, but as meaningful adverbs, they can start to organize design. Here in the entry to a kindergarten it's important that small children shed the restrictive stress and disconnected visual-only experiences of their car journeys to school.

Entry arch to woodland path.

Sunlit-protected play yard (brick paving).

Welcoming asymmetrical entry gesture.

Dark, low, turning 'portal passage' (tile floor).

Bright place to stop and remove boots (tile floor).

Through a heavy, tactile-latched door.

Turn of direction to a spacious room, now at treetop level and with a wooden floor which sounds quite different from the previous brick or tile flooring.

It is after all in this that 90 per cent of us spend 90 per cent of our time.

Before even starting to think about places to nourish the soul we must be emphatic that places are for people. Obvious? Unfortunately not. Most places are, to a large extent, the accidental result of collections of buildings, each conceived as a separate object. Even the spaces within these buildings are often designed to provide for people as quantitative statistics to be packaged efficiently and lovelessly.

I was taught that planning starts with 'bubble diagrams' of relationships between different spaces, but no quality attached to the linking lines – the *adverbs*. Diagramatically, a lift is a perfect way to convey people, to link bubbles on the diagram. But if we think of the pleasure, sociability, experience progression and preparatory thresholds of the journey, we might choose a sloping, winding passage-way opening to many views, passing and coloured by many events. Reading the diagram as adverbs rather than mere relationships between nouns leads to entirely different planning.

Starting by organizing diagrams while leaving qualities to be added subsequently is like painting by colouring-in drawings. Paintings live in colour – colour whose effects are concentrated, enhanced and modified by shape and boundary. Likewise, places only come to life through their sensory qualities. We organize these to concentrate particular moods. Diagrams are important for organizing thoughts, but they're only a starting point. They clarify movement relationships, daylight reach, mood themes and suchlike. But until these diagrams have disappeared and been reborn in terms of experience sequences, they offer nothing to the soul.

291

Diagrams aren't to build. They stand for something richer, just as a written script is only the stepping-stone to that moment when suddenly great spiritual truths flow through an actor's whole being, transforming the words from repetition to something to touch every heart that hears.

I was also taught that architects solve problems; design proposals were referred to as 'solutions'. People can be offended if you refer to their home as a problem or a solution – to them it's a living being, rich in multiple functions both spiritual and practical, mostly inseparable.

Diagram thinking and problem solving tend to be categorical, easily pushing qualitative aspects into second place. This leads to 'covered way', 'corridor' and 'route' instead of cloister, passage and footpath. Diagram thinking can extend into adjectival descriptions like 'secluded study corner', but unless these key words 'secluded', 'study' and 'corner' are brought alive, design isn't

likely to rise above the level of a built diagram. I don't feel free in buildings where I know exactly how the architect intended me to act.

Lamentably few of the buildings around us transcend their allegiances to dead material – ease of industrial manufacture, speed of construction or monetary savings. Their materials, rigid unequivocalities, moods and subliminal messages are life-inimical, and their physical, biological and spiritual effect on places and on people are damaging. These sorts of buildings simplify architecture down to that which is photographable. As such they appeal to other photographic-conscious architects, establishing an incestuous cycle with enormous influence on the profession. All those other qualities that both arise from, and nurture, the realm of life suffer.

Buildings whose allegiance is to life are quite different. Rather than assert themselves, they create *places*. With

The classroom (opposite and above)
includes kitchen and fireplace alcoves and
play nooks.

Photography can focus on architecture or its occupants. Though our attention is normally on the latter, architecture sets the background mood. For everyone except architects the issue is not how noteworthy the architecture is, but what mood it sets.

materials attractive to touch, see and smell, their very substance welcomes us through the senses. Their forms are more mobile, life-compatible, and their qualities change with light, weather and season. They feed the soul and emanate messages of care and respect – key foundations of beauty. They nourish heart and spirit.

This is about underlying values manifesting in life-supporting form and qualities. If form leads message, however, the effects are completely different. When science fiction illustrators picture the future it's in an architecture of curvilinear towers and pinnacles, interwoven with fluid-formed trackways, often in shimmering materials. These astro-cities are set within harsh dead deserts, so depend totally upon mechanical life-support. Despite their architecture imitating the forms of living things, they have no meaningful root in place, time or living processes. They are cities built on illusion and fantasy.

Such environments aren't so far away. They win architectural awards. In films, computer games, toys, and even building forms, these enticing, outer-image forms are already here.

They have great appeal for they're the complete opposite of the world of faceless, organized, dead, mineral objects common around us. For decades, buildings for bureaucracies were anonymous, gridded boxes; bank headquarters rectangular, patterned towers. Now, they're usually more dramatic – competitive announcements. All, however, lifelessly dominate and sterilize the streetscape at their feet.

These sorts of buildings – the fantastic and the rigid – are pictures, with powerful soul effect, of inhuman polarities within society. One pole feeds personal, emotional and physical indulgence, the cultivation of desires in place of responsibilities. A lot of money is made catering for, and reinforcing, this tendency. At the other extreme lies all that is materialistic and so rationally organized that the ambiguous, unpredictable and spontaneous is suppressed. This lifeless realm controls a lot of money and with it a lot of people's lives.

These forces manifest in extreme form in the arms or narcotics trades – no wonder some think them diabolical. More insidiously, desire indulgence diminishes individual responsibility; oppressive control curtails inner freedom. Responsibility and freedom distinguish us from animals – they're at the core of being human. Whenever architecture influences people for gain or gives allegiance to things, not people or spirit-of-place, it is servant to these same dehumanizing masters.

To transform these forces to the health-giving, we must bring together the organizing and the life-filled, the rational and the feeling, the straight and the curved, the substantial and the transitory, matter and light, in a different way. We need to build buildings and places of life-renewing, soul-nurturing, spirit-strengthening qualities. Soul can only be given by souls – not by computer systems or industrial might. These have their place as aids to fulfilling our intentions; too often, however, their limitations have a shaping influence upon these intentions, leaving no room for living processes of design, construction, use and maturation. It is living processes that bring things to life.

The course of every human life is uniquely individual, yet together we share certain biographical patterns. From early life on, we develop not only physically but towards becoming self-directed *individuals*. From environment and society we meet both stress and stimulation, obstacle and opportunity. Inwardly we travel a path of transformation of lower egocentric and bodily-bound forces into higher forms which are more gift orientated, more spiritual. We make this journey with widely varying motivations, persistence, speed and success.

The earth itself is also on a journey of transformation. Human actions make more or less room for nature's health-giving forces to work. But committing ourselves to work for growth and freedom in place of ossification and enslavement ('for love rather than for money' – power) isn't enough. We need to know *how* to act.

Any action can be raised into an artistic deed, any experience to an artistic experience. This underlies the dilemma in contemporary fine art. When does the work of art *require* observers to change their inner state to experience what others consider banal as art? Or when is the *experience* of what is perhaps outwardly commonplace nonetheless so moving that it has the transformative effect of an artistic experience without demanding to be called art?

The former category predominates in the commercial galleries – like the emperor's clothes, such works are well suited to status purchasers. The latter brings a raising, civilizing, healing influence into society.

It's easy just to state intentions then prove we've achieved them. I also am not immune from this, which is why I ask you to consider the contents of this book dispassionately, neither supporting nor objecting to any potentially emotive material. Only by observing things in this way, without the fog of personal reaction, by attempting to penetrate to the true essence of their being, can we ever hope to reach objectively meaningful assessments. Looking at the architectural vocabulary – in its widest sense – in this dispassionate way, we can observe what, for example, hard smooth surfaces, mid-morning sunlight, acoustic absorbent materials and so on really *do*. We can get a sense of what they do to living spirits – to places, to people, to ourselves.

Just as our inner development steers and is steered by our biography, we shape and are shaped by our environment. This cyclical process is so indissolubly bound that we can't step outside it to shape or be shaped differently without conscious action. It is this step that this book is concerned with.

The issues are universal, but any applications, of course, involve individual situations and individual interpreters. I've given examples of how I go about doing things, examples which I hope make clear that there are no serious difficulties in working in this sort of way. Most categorically, however, I wish to avoid presenting a series of answers. There are no answers except those for which the seeds lie in every question; and every question is unique as it arises afresh in every new situation. Rather, my hope is to colour the whole way of going about things. This is like learning to speak, something to develop, cultivate, sharpen – but when you use it, to forget. This colour is, I hope, something to become part of our beings. For all of us it's not something fixed and final but something growing.

The approach this book sets out, and upon which my own architectural work is founded, may sound like impractical nonsense, the opposite of the way things are normally done, but I am convinced it is the only sensible way. Some say it stands the conventional world on its head, others that it's just ordinary common sense. I hope it's the latter.

What I write is not novel; I write the obvious. It is my belief that we all already know it – and the test of my ability to transcend the limitations of my personal viewpoint is whether you recognize truth in what I describe or regard it as so much nonsense. We may know it, but all too easily its significance gets submerged by 'real world' (namely soulless) pressures.

My plea is that the obvious is taken seriously. If it isn't, we will be known as the generation of destroyers – destroyers of places, of ecological stability and of the human in human beings. If it is, we can start to build an architecture of healing, to build places of the soul.

This book is only about the start.

Note and references

1 Aluminium has 126 times the
   embodied energy of timber: Harland,
   E. (1993) *Eco-Renovation*. Green
   Books, Devon. Only 0.02 per cent of
   original primary ingredients end up
   as finished plastic: König, H. (1989)
   Wege zum Gesunden Bauen. Ökobuch
   Verlag, Freiburg. After energy
   production, cement manufacture is
   the largest source of CO_2.

List of photographs and project-related drawings

Index

Figures in italics refer to illustrations.